SuperStocks

Tony Pow

Why you trust me

All of the below are provable. I did made some blunders and both are described in this book.

- My annuity (not recommended due to my higher tax bracket during retirement) grows to **5** times mostly using Fidelity's funds for sector rotation.

- I switched most (all in my annuity) of my tech funds to other sectors (should be cash if I had a time machine) in April, 2000. It was only provable if Fidelity keeps record for the year 2000.

- I achieved 80% return in my largest taxable account in 2009.

- I recommended to buy oil when it was $30 at Seeking Alpha, a web site for investors.

- I recommended 20 stocks in an article Amazing Return in Seeking Alpha. If you bought them on the published date, you would have beaten the S&P500 index by over 100% without considering dividends as demonstrated in my other article A Tale of Two Portfolios. Search these articles.

  I challenge anyone who had better one-year performance for recommending a diversified portfolio of 15 or more stocks.

Why you invest

You need to learn about investing sooner or later in your life. You need to take some calculated risks.

Compare the returns of the following assets: cash, CDs, treasury bills, bonds, real estate and stocks. We start with the risk-free investments and end with the riskiest. It turns out that the average returns are in the opposite order. Cash and CDs are not risk-free as inflation eats our profits. For example, the real return is negative for the 2% return in a CD and a 3% inflation rate. In addition you have to pay taxes for the 'returns'. Our capitalist system punishes us for not taking risk.

There are two kinds of risk: blind risk and calculated risk. If you buy a stock due to a recommendation from a commentator on TV or a tip, most likely you are taking a blind risk. It would be the same in buying a house without thoroughly evaluating the house and its neighborhood. When you buy stocks with a proven strategy (i.e. when/what stocks to buy and when/what stocks to sell), you are taking a calculated risk. In the long run, stocks with calculated and educated risks are profitable.

Be a turtle investor by investing in value stocks and holding for longer time periods (a year or more). "Buy and Monitor" is better an approach than "Buy and Hold" as some could lose all the stock values such as in the failure of Enron.

For experienced investors, shorting, short-term trading and covered calls would make you good profits. Simple market timing would reduce your losses during market down turns. If you buy a market ETF and use my simple market timing, you should have beaten the market by a wide margin from 2000 to 2019.

With so many frauds and poor management, do not trust anyone with your investing. Do not buy investing instruments that are highly marketed such as annuity and term insurance.

If you are a handy man and do not mind to satisfy the constant requests of your tenants, buy real estate in growing areas could be very profitable in the long run.

Take advantage of the tax laws such as investing in a 401K especially the part that is matched by your company and/or a Roth IRA.

Why you want to read this book

It should improve your financial health substantially. There are about a million investment books. Why we need another one?

- After finishing this book, I tried out the Super Stock metrics. As of 10/21/2015, the average return is 35% beating SPY beat by a huge margin. They are real trades and can be proven.

- I select proven ideas from more than 100 books besides my original ideas and experiences. I also include links to current articles that will bring more depth to the topic. It is not a novel or documenting the story of my life. All related chapters are grouped in a section for easy future reference. Some chapters are not easy to digest as they have a lot of pointers and some may require you to try them out yourself.

- Many popular books claiming the authors making million. However, usually their techniques are hard to follow. Many admitted they had been bankrupted many times. Hence, their chance of bankrupting again is very high. Is bankruptcy fine with you? I cannot afford bankruptcy past and present. My techniques minimize risking our money.

- There are many popular books combining technical and some fundamentals. They worked very well at one time and folks making million following the advice. However, look at their recent performances of the last five years. Most of them cannot even beat the S&P 500 index.

- Check the recent mediocre performance of gurus such as Buffett. They are the market and they cannot beat themselves. Their techniques may no longer work.

- The average performance of the hedge fund is terrible. You cannot depend on others to invest for you.

- One book describes ROE as the only theme (with the story of the life of the author to fill up the book). It is only one fundamental metric in my book. I also monitor what metrics work recently.

My motivation to write this book

I would like to share my experiences, both good and bad. I use simple-to-follow techniques using the free (or low-cost) resources available to us. I have been successful in investing for decades. I am enjoying a comfortable financial life. I do not hold back my 'secrets' as my children are not interested in investing. It is my small legacy in sharing my investing ideas.

If you are looking how to make 100% return overnight, there are many other books claiming to do so and this book is not for you.

This book describes how to be a 'turtle' investor making fortune gradually and surely. Before you begin, define your objective first. Surprisingly, if you do not have too much time for investing, SPY or any ETF that stimulates the market is your super stock provided you practice Market Timing described in this book.

Market timing

The market timing works for the last two market plunges. It will work again in the next one as it depends on the falling stock prices. However, I hope it will give us the ample time to exit as the last two.

This simple chart is the best-kept secret. I'm the one to publicize it and for doing that it makes a lot of folks angry with me. There is nothing to buy or subscribe as it is free from many web sites.

It is better but not possible to sell at the top and buy at the bottom. I summarize these conditions in this book. After we've detected the market top conditions, use stops to protect our profits. I will describe a better way than stops to avoid flash crash.

My steps to trade stocks

1. Search for valued stocks (many strategies to choose from).
2. Evaluate the screened stocks by:
    a. Fundamental Analysis.
    b. Intangible Analysis.
    c. Qualitative Analysis.
    d. Technical Analysis.
3. Sell stocks. Basically perform the same as Step #2.

As everything in life, there is no guarantee this book will make you money. However, the chance of success will be substantially improved especially when you practice on all the ideas presented in this book. Start with paper trading first. The Kindle version of this book is over **280** pages. It covers most topics in investing.

Click the link (http://seekingalpha.com/author/tony-pow/articles).

Bubbles

Bubbles have existed throughout our history. Bubbles occur due to the excessive valuation most likely driven up by the big institutional investors (fund managers, pension managers, hedge fund manager, etc.). Asset valuations are then driven even higher by the retail investors. For example in 3/2014, the market bubble was caused by the government stimulus with the injection of capital into the excessive money supply and subsidies. The first investors riding the wave made good money, and the last ones buying at the peak will lose.

From our recent history, we have the 2000 internet bubble, and then the 2007 (2008 for some) housing bubble. The chapter "Spotting Big Market Plunges" illustrates it was easy to detect the last two plunges. It could save us more than 25% of your portfolio in the next plunge.

Today most of the mentioned bubbles could be caused by pumping too much money into the economy by the government. However, the government cannot keep on injecting money into the economy, and ask our children to pay for our debts forever. When the injections stop, the market will drop fast and deep.

USD
As of mid-2020, the USD is doing quite well. It could be the other countries (EU and Japan) are doing worse than us, as Einstein said, "everything is relative". The strong USD is not good for exports and the global corporations would have less profits after converting them back to USD. However, the excessive printing and high government debts would shake the status of USD as a reserve currency. It will also be hurt if China sells the U.S. Treasury bonds she owns.

Bond

The bond bubble will burst when the interest rates rise. Also it will as the interest rates should have been bottomed by as of mid-2020. It is possible that it could go negative.

Stocks

There are several bubble stocks such as FAANGs. The market was peaking in Jan., 2020 before the virus breakout. Play defense with stop loss orders. The record of margin debt is a big concern. When the credit is tightened with higher interest rate, this bubble will burst.

When to act

Without a time machine, no one can pin point when most of these bubbles will burst. Your timing to act depends on your risk tolerance, your knowledge and your greed.

Today, we have the housing bubble (2007-2008), the gold bubble, the market bubble, the second housing bubble, the debt bubble, the bond bubble, the second market bubble, etc. It seems like we can never get out of the bubble cycle. In 2020, the world would be in a global recession if the trade war between the two largest economies continue. It would be worse if the trade war turns into a military war.

Since the world is economically connected better than before. When the U.S.A. sneezes, it affects our trading partners such as European countries along with China and Japan, and also their partners such as the resource-rich countries of S. America, Australia, Russia, Canada and Africa.

For me, it is safer not to try to make the last buck when the reward / risk ratio is too low. A good sleep would improve your health which is worth all the gold in the world.

How to beat the S&P500 index by 100%

I recommended 20 stocks in an article Amazing Return in Seeking Alpha, a web site for investors. If you bought them on the published date and then you would have beaten the S&P500 index by over 100% without considering dividends as demonstrated in my other article A Tale of Two Portfolios. One of the many techniques is my Pow P/E as illustrated in another article The Mysteries of P/E.

Let's say I made a mistake and it is only a 10% gain. How many fund managers can beat the S&P500 index by 10% regularly?

*** The main book: Super Stocks

The following are the super stocks I bought in the last three years. Most of my super stocks double and very few lose more than 50%. I usually keep the larger stocks for over a year to qualify for the long-term capital gain tax.

- Apple recommended in my book Scoring Stocks at $55.72 (split adjusted) in April 19, 2013; the book was published in May, 2013.
- CAMP, BSX...bought in 2012.
- AAL (doubled as of this writing).
- Many high tech companies bought in the last few months of 2013.
- My recent buy of CIMT up 40% in one day due to the announcement of being acquired.

They are all described in this book. Most of them are well-known stocks. Usually I sell them after they have been hold for a year especially if they are in my taxable account. I need money to look for the next super stock. We also look at stocks in their initial stages that give the best returns.

Timing matters. Apple was not favorable in April, 2013. The fundamentals were great. Buy it no matter what the news media said. Check out my article on Apple. I predict it will not rise in the same pace as in 2015 for many arguments in my article. Hence, time to sell in 2015.

Many high tech companies were valued in the last few months in 2013. I bought most of the five or six stocks I recommended in my blog. Fundamentals were good. After this book was published, I will include my super stocks from time to time. In Dec. 2014, they are DRAD (bought) and SCX (not bought due to low order price entered).

Ignore what the media say. A lot of time the 'news' is obsolete. It is the group thinking (or following the herd). Sometimes they magnify the news to sell their ads. The worst is that the smart money manipulates the news which tells you to trade while they're doing the exact opposite. Popular books are no different. One predicts Dow 40,000 and one predicts market plunge in 2009.

Buffett told you to ignore airline stocks. However, many airline stocks made over 4 times (mine 2 times) in the last few years.

Contents

Filler: A nightmare?

I got a call from Buffett asking me to lead their stock research.
I asked him why for a nobody; you may be asking the same question. No kidding.

He told me that he should have read my book Scoring Stocks to buy Apple instead of IBM in May, 2013. It would save his company millions of dollars minus $10 for my book. Not to mention the market timing technique that had worked in the last two major market plunges.

I told him, "OK, I'll beat your mediocre returns of the last 5 years."
He said, "You can do better than that and at least beat SPY. If you do so, no one will be that stupid to leave my fund and pay the hefty capital gain taxes."

I told him, "I cannot beat the market as you are the market especially after your expensive fees. In addition, I do not know how to avoid day traders from riding my wagon in trading. Also most of my big profits were made in small stocks that your fund cannot trade besides owning the company."

I woke up trembling. I'm glad it is only a nightmare.

Introduction

After market timing, we start with the basic sections Finding Stocks and Evaluate Stocks. You can select and start with one of the many styles and strategies in Investing such as swing trading and top down strategy. Many tools are described such as ETFs, technical analysis, covered calls and trade plan.

This book consists of 6 books in one. Many books start with "Why with results" to lure you to read more and are followed by "How" and then the theory behind the section.

No one including all the Federal Reserve chairmen / chairwomen and all the Nobel-Prize winners in economics can predict market plunges. Many predicted correctly market crashes by pure luck and some even received Nobel Prizes and became famous.

The market timer works for at least the last two market plunges and hopefully it will work to the next market plunge. The chart depends on the falling stock prices, so it will not detect the bottoms and peaks precisely, but it will prevent further losses and tell us when to reenter the market for larger gains. The chart is very simple to use and there is nothing to buy or subscribe.

Granted that there are no sure-win strategies to make money, I still believe my proven strategies can provide the best guidance. Making serious money takes serious devotion of not only your money, but time and due diligence. In fact, I earn more money now than when I had a steady income. The long-term success depends on hard work and discipline more than luck.

My current strategies are more conservative as my lifestyle does not depend on that extra money. However, some strategies are more profitable and riskier than others. Choose the ones that fit your risk tolerance.

I have been a stock investor for over 30 years and a full-time investor for the last seven years with exhaustive stock research and performance improvements. This book is intended for a retail investor and I am one myself, not a professional writer who may never make a buck in the market. I use the popular tools /

subscription services that are available to retail investors and many are free of charge.

I hope this book will help other investors understand the methods that I have found to provide the greatest return consistently at the least risk. Even some of the practices of Buffett, one of the greatest investors in our generation, are not applicable in today's market, as many opportunities of the past two decades are not open to the general public. The reader should be a better investor from learning about both my good and bad investment experiences.

The book also shows you how to distinguish good data from garbage covering many investment subscriptions and advice. We would have avoided or paid more attention to the bank stocks if we follow the advice not to invest in specific sectors in this book such as the bank stocks in 2007.

This book describes why retail investors do not usually beat the index despite of the advantages we have. When we understand the problems we face, and follow the suggestions from this book, we will hopefully beat the index consistently.

This book includes many strategies geared towards trading for profits. Any strategy could be over-used. We need to use the right strategy for the current market conditions. Many investors, including many fund managers, fail to do so and achieve a sub-par performance.

Market timing is discussed in detail with market cycles, as well as by calendar such as Presidential Cycle, 'Sell in May and Go Away', best and worst times to invest, etc.

This book covers most topics in investing including diversification, profit protection, trade prices, trade positions, short selling, writing covered calls and trade plans. I offer practical solutions and guidelines via my experience.

The lessons from my bad experiences could be more valuable than the good ones. I achieved 80% return in 2009 in my largest taxable account and reveal my secrets here. The bottom fishing strategy could be most profitable during the early market recovery, but we need to discover when exactly that recovery occurs.

This book represents my decades of trading experiences, at least a thousand of simulations and summaries of hundreds of investing books I read. The strategy is backed up by profitable performances of these super stocks in real trades (not after-the-fact).

I write down my findings for my own use. I re-read and test what works and what does not work. I commit to monitor how my metrics work from time to time. A good idea may not work again, and seldom does all the time.

This book is intended for someone with more knowledge than the average retail investor.

Practical experience using the investing concepts in this book

I am not a writer but a retail investor similar to most of my readers. I've been making a comfortable living via my investment ideas that I'm sharing in this book.

I have a book Series starting with "Best Stocks 2014, According to Me" to use the concepts and techniques described in this book to find stocks.

From 12/16/13 (the published date) to 3/4/14, the list of all 135 selected stocks beat SPY by 103% and the list of 9 small cap stocks beat SPY by 500%.

http://ebtonypow.blogspot.com/2013/11/reserved_5358.html?view=sidebar

How to start

Specify your objective in investing and your risk tolerance. Stick with your ideas that work and include my ideas that make sense to you. Test your new ideas on paper before you commit real money. This book has many ideas and they are categorized by sections.

Both Fidelity and AAII (both require being a client or a member) have excellent articles. Alternatively, buy a book for beginners. To include all the basic terms and concepts, I have to double the size of this book which is already lengthy and bore most readers who already have the basic knowledge.

Click here for Morningstar classroom.
http://morningstar.com/cover/classroom.html

Click here for Vanguard.
https://investor.vanguard.com/investing/investor-education

Click here for Investopedia's Tutorials.
http://www.investopedia.com/university/

Click here for Yahoo!
http://finance.yahoo.com/education/begin_investing

Click here for Fidelity basic in investing.
https://www.fidelity.com/investment-guidance/investing-basics

How this book is organized

This book has 6 books into one covering most areas in investing from my personal experience plus the Section on Examples of Super Stocks. Most sections can be viewed as a small book. Many sections actually have been made into books. The whole book can be treated as my small, personal encyclopedia for investing.

Most graphs and tables are in landscape orientation (recommended for small screens) for both paperback and e-readers. Some graphs may not be displayed adequately on a small screen of an e-reader. E-readers may be available in the current version of Windows, so you can read e-books on the larger screen of your PC. For better orientation, just flip the e-readers 90 degrees. Some reader lets you select a table or a graph to display it to fit the screen.

A link is usually included for the most screens. Copy it to your browser to display the graphs on your PC if desirable. Instructions on how to produce some graphs are provided as you should try them out. One example is how to produce a chart on detecting market crashes.

The **font size** (Ctrl Minus for browser implementation of e-readers) and line spacing of most e-book formats can be adjusted. The unknown, special character is the "smiling face" that the current Kindle does not convert correctly as of this writing.

There are clickable links to web articles. Most of them are from my own web sites and public web sites such as Wikipedia. Some public links may not be available in the future as they are not under my control and my book offerings may change.

These links extend the usefulness of this book by making available specific topics that may not be interesting to every reader. It also provides articles (most are not written by me) for more in-depth analyzes.

Fidelity Video provides video clips to explain some basic terms and it may require Fidelity customers to sign on in order to view them. Check the trial offer from Fidelity. YouTube offers similar video lessons.

The current version provides most of the links the paperback readers can enter into your browser. Get the same information by entering a search in Wikipedia such as Dogs of Dow.

Investopedia is another source beside Wikipedia.
http://www.investopedia.com/

'Afterthoughts' includes my additional comments and ideas of minor importance.

There are fillers with tips, refreshing pictures (taken by me) and jokes (most original) to fill up the empty space of the printed book. Fillers, links and afterthoughts may disrupt the flow of reading this book. However, no readers so far ask me to take them out even in the digitized version of this book. Many page breaks have been eliminated to improve the flow of the book.

For convenience, this book uses SPY, an Exchange Traded Fund (ETF) simulating the S&P 500, as the benchmark for the market.

Annualized returns (Return * 365 / (Days between)) are used where appropriate for more meaningful comparison. To illustrate, I have a 10% return in 6 months, a 10% in a year and a 10% in 2 years. It is more meaningful to use annualized returns of 20%, 10% and 5% respectively in this example.

Usually I do not include the dividend, so you can add an estimated 1.5% to the annualized return. In addition, compound interest is not used for easier calculation, so the actual return could be even better. Many of my tests are not detailed in this book but their summaries are. It reduces the size of this book that is already huge.
Many of my tests are not detailed in this book but their summaries are. It reduces the size of this book that is already huge.

About the author

I graduated from Cal. State University at San Jose in Industrial Engineering and University of Mass. in Amherst with a MS in Industrial Engineering. I have retired from a job in IT. I have been an investor for over 30 years and have written over 20 books on investing. Here is the link to some of my articles I wrote.

Dedication

To all retail investors and future retail investors including my grandchildren.

Acknowledgement

Thanks to Seeking Alpha, Wikipedia and Investopedia for the many helpful links to enrich this book and also to Yahoo!Finance and Finviz.com for the tools and charts used in this book.

Important notices

Version	Paperback	E Book
1.0	12/14	12/14
2.0	08/16	08/16
3.0	01/19	01/19
3.2	01/21	01/21

Printed version.
ISBN-13: 978-1505385502 ISBN-10:1505385504

No part of this book can be reproduced in any form without the written approval of the author.

Book store managers can order the printed books from Createspace.com.
https://tonyp4idea.blogspot.com/2020/12/book-managers.html

Book update.
https://ebmyth.blogspot.com/2020/12/updates-for-all-books.html

Disclaimer

Do not gamble with money that you cannot afford to lose. Past performance is a guideline and is not necessarily indicative of future results. All information is believed to be accurate, but there it is not a guarantee. All the strategies including charts to detect market plunges described have no guarantee that they will make money and they may lose money. Do not trade without doing due diligence and be warned that most data may be obsolete. All my articles and the associated data are for informational and illustration purposes only. I'm not a professional investment counselor or a tax professional. Seek one before you make any investment decisions. The above mentioned also applies for all other advice such as on accounting, taxes, health and any topic mentioned in this book. I am not a professional in any of these fields. Most of the time, I use annualized for a better comparison; 5% in a month is more than 4% in a year for example. For simplicity, most of my returns do not include commissions, exchange fees, order spread and dividends. Same for all the links contained in this book. Some articles may offend some one or some organization unintentionally. If I did, I'm sorry about that. I am politically and religiously neutral. I provide my best efforts to ensure the accuracy of my articles. Data also from different sources was believed to be accurate. However, there is no guarantee that they are accurate and suitable for the current market conditions and /or your individual situations. My publisher and I are not liable for any damages in using this book or its contents.

1   Recent Super Stock performance

After I wrote this book, I bought stocks based on the super stock metrics. They have wild swings. It turns out pretty good especially compared to SPY. If I kept NHTC, it would have 180%. I sold it as it surged too high and too fast; I should have used "mental trailing stop loss" to let the stock rise. I have not practiced what I preach in my own book!

As of this writing (10/21/2015), the results are:

Stocks	Return	Bought on	Sold on
DRAD	35%	12/15/2014	
FONR	57%	01/12/2015	
FONR	54%	01/09/2015	
WILD	-11%	02/10/2015	06/19/2015
NHTC	58%	03/04/2015	04/10/2015

FONR has been bought two times.

SCX was shown in my list for evaluation but I could not find it in my positions or closed positions. SCX has a loss of 28%.

The market is risky so I quit buying stocks with these metrics after 03/04/2015.

Again, past performances have no prediction power to future performances. This book serves as an education tool.

#Filler: Miss Mia

In my first job just after the Vietnam War, every one tried to date my beautiful office mate Mia except me. If we married, then her name would be Mia Pow. She would be very popular, or very unpopular without showing her beautiful face. In any case, when she becomes a mother, she will be Mamma Mia.

2   Outline on how to start

1. First determine your risk tolerance, how much time you have for investing, your knowledge in investing and your portfolio size. When the market is risky, do not buy any stock.

2. When the market is peaking, do not invest.

3. When you have lost two trades in a row, take a break and return to paper trading until you're comfortable.

4. Find stocks with one of the many strategies using finviz.com or any free screen sites. They usually have high super stock metrics such as increasing insider purchases.

   Alternatively, you can select one of the strategies described in this book.

5. Ensure the stock is trending upwards. Check the SMA-200% in finviz.com. It should be positive.

6. Ensure the screened stocks are fundamentally sound.

7. Sell the stock when it fulfills your objective or the market is plunging.
8. Paper trade your strategy.
9. When it is thoroughly tested out and the result is good, use real money slowly and gradually. Monitor your performance.

This is the best way to start for instance gratification. The rest of the book should be read later or used as reference. This book is full of useful information and it does not narrate the story of my life as most other do. Hence, it appears to be harder to read especially some chapters (such as detecting market plunges) require you to practice with real data.

While most of my predictions are materialized, some are not. Learn from the arguments for the predictions, not the predictions themselves. When the predictions are based on educated guesses, more of them will be materialized in the long run. I do not use predictions after-the-fact as many do.

Section I: Examples of Super Stocks

We use the Airlines to demonstrate the analysis process of stocks to start and then the winners in the following chapter. Also notice that AAL has been down for about two years and it is the technical pattern for a super stock.

This is followed by Amazing Returns that you can find many stocks that fit the super stock status which is double in a year plus several super stocks in more detail. The last example is my micro-cap stocks.

Filler: Tips

- Do not believe you're always right all the time and put all your eggs in a basket.

- Even with 99.99% sure, a black swan event could happen and could wipe out your entire savings.

- The average retail investor does not beat the market due to switching between stocks and cash at the wrong time.

#Filler: Your complaint department

Depending on your investing knowledge, the more complicated concepts are harder to understand. Some strategies even require you paper trading. It is even more complicated if you do not read this book sequentially, as this book outlines chapters for beginner, intermediate and expert investors.

Do not complain on the fillers as they just take up the blank space in the printed book and you should be glad to take a break on this lengthy book.

This book is used for reference and packed with a lot of information. It is not a novel describing the story of one's life. One best seller has one theme in the entire book that ROI works (may not work any more).

1   Airlines

How to become a millionaire according to Buffett: "First, become a billionaire and then invest all in airline stocks!"

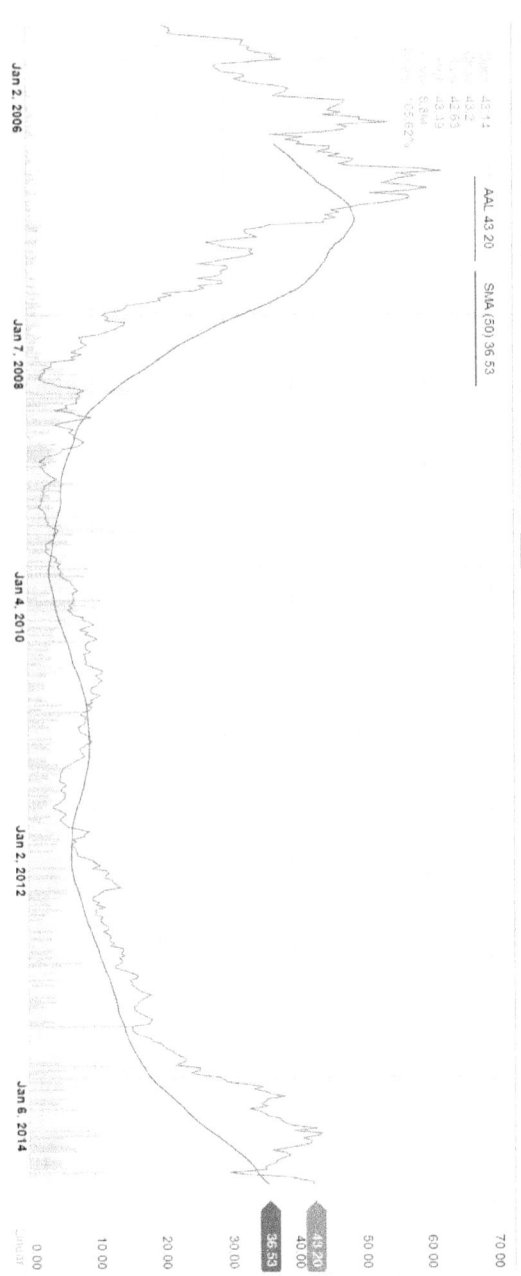

Source: Yahoo! Finance   AAL

He may be right in his time when he made the statement. But, it is not true lately as evidenced by the following chart. You can buy American Airlines (AAL) for less than $10 from 2008 to 2012 and today in 2014 it is 4 times as much. The pattern has been repeated by other airline stocks.

I cannot find a decent ETF for airlines, so I use AAL (the stock I still own). From Yahoo!Finance, it is the maximum period allowed to draw the above chart. AAL used to be AMR.

It has a peak in Nov. 2006 and it has been down until 2012.

SMA-50 is the Simple Moving Average for the last 50 sessions. It did not help you to avoid the plunge from its peak in 2006, but it reduced your loss and recommended good reentry points. Personally I prefer 200 sessions to reduce the number of trading.

Why I bought US Air (LCC)

It had appeared in my performing screens (the better performers in the previous six months) several times from 12/2012 to 4/2013. I bought them in 6/2013 two times. Due to the merger with AAL, officially they were bought on 8/12/2013 and 8/13/2013. As of 11/2014, I have a 163% gain.

The following is a summary of my evaluation.

LCC	Passing Grade	12/15/2012	4/24/2013
Score System #1	15	38	31
Score System #2	2	3	6
Price		12.78	16.30

It scored very high in the two dates I evaluated LCC.

The first score system includes grades from many investment services I subscribed. The second one has been described in my book Scoring Stocks using fundamental metrics available free.

Opportunities come and gone
If I have a time machine, I should have sold it at $45 in June, 2014 and bought it back it at $31 in Oct., 2014. As of Nov. 12, 2014, it is $43.

I used Turbo Tax to simulate how much tax I have to pay in 2014 tax return without considering any change of the tax laws. In June, 2014, I had over my limit in the long-term capital gain. That was the reason I did not sell my AAL. Taxes should not be considered in making an investment decision.

The threat of Ebola caused the stock to plunge to $32 from $45. I did not take advantage by buying more shares due to my (expensive!) vacation in October. I should have left some buy orders at 10% less than the current price. The Ebola threat was only temporary and shortly it went back to $43.

Analysis of airlines

Pros are:

1. Many airline stocks look like bargains if you look at its low expected P/E only. My Pow P/E taking consideration of cash and debt could be a better metric.

2. The outlook on the economy should be improving.

3. The falling oil price makes the airlines more profitable.

4. Air lines merger means fewer airlines and less competition.

5. Find ways to make profits such as charging for luggage. The next frontier charge could be the use of the lavatory and that is why they call themselves Frontier Airline. ☺

Cons are:

1. High debt (planes are expensive), a common and traditional problem in this industry. If AAL cannot service its debts, it will bankrupt. Its debts are more than three times its capital cap. Alarming!

2. High pension obligation, the same cause to bring down the old GM. Most especially the newer ones switch to employee-funded pensions as in most other industries.

3. High wages demanded by the unions.

4. Unable to raise the prices of the air ticket; they have not kept up with inflation over the years until recently.

5. Deregulation has its problems. The government should regulate some industries and airline is one of them. The government should do a better job on what and how much to regulate this industry. I hope to regulate the ticket prices as thy do on utilities.

6. Besides competition from other airlines, trains, high speed trains (little impact in the US), buses and cars offer a lot of competition especially for short-distance trips. Airports are usually located a long way from downtown.

   The major airlines also face competition from new, smaller with leaner operation, direct flights and newer planes with better fuel mileage, not to mention the incentives to the foreign airlines from their governments. Many attractive ones will be acquired.

7. Merger will have fewer airlines and reduce competition. However, when two losers merge together, they become a bigger loser. The Virgin Air could provide long-term synergy to the US airline, but it is too high a price to the acquirer to me. Currently, most mergers of large airlines have been done except Alaska, JetBlue and several smaller ones.

8. The hub concept is getting more impractical with rising fuel prices (now falling) and the inconveniences to their customers. The future will be less stop overs with larger and newer jets that are more fuel efficient. It could be an efficient way for some routes such as filling international flights for smaller cities.

9. High cost of terrorism.
   Most foreign airlines are subsidized by the government. Our government has bailed out other industries but not the airlines here. The only bright point is the airlines profit by jacking up the ticket prices, but you can't do it excessively in this poor economy. Besides terrorism, events such as wars and Ebola could cause the airline stocks to fall.

10. Future shortage of pilots.
    Many retire and many find new jobs in Asia. It is not an exciting profession as in the previous generation. It is also due to the military reductions in the 1990s and the raise of minimum training hours coupled with the maximum hours for pilots. However, the larger planes would reduce the number of pilots. It has not been materialized yet except in smaller airlines.

In my original article written several years ago, I recommended to evaluate the impact of a bankrupted airline. The above con conditions could be reduced for a bankrupted airline. In 2011, American Airline was under the bankruptcy protection. Following this advice, you could have bought it for $10 and make a good profit by now. Will the readers who took my advice please stand up?

China's impact

China has impact on almost all industries and airline is no exception. The growth of the airline industry depends on Asia and China in particular. The increase of Chinese travel is due to:

- The fast growth of the middle class. China becomes #1 in tourist spending. It is due to the high tariffs of foreign goods.

- China's growing business requires a lot of traveling to and from foreign countries.

Be more careful to invest in China's smaller airlines in China. Their short-distance travels are facing competition from high speed rail.

Analysis of Airline Stocks (11/12/2014)

	Passing grade	AAL	DAL	LUV
Score System #1	>=15	20	15	22
Score System #2	>=2	7	4	3
Expected Earning Yield	>5 & <35	17%	9%	6%
Debt / Equity	<1.5	3.5	.82	.31
Analyst Rating	>7	8.0	9.6	9.6
EB/EBIT	>5	3	11	13
F-Score	>7	6	5	7
ROE	>=15%	15%	83%	6%
SMA-200%	>0%	16%	20%	43%
RSI(14)	<60	71	71	75
Price		43.43	43.40	39.37

I selected three major airlines to represent the industry. I also selected the metrics and scores that are meaningful to this industry. It seems to be a good buy even after a good gain in 2014.

All three airlines pass both my score systems.

AAL and DAL are similar except that DAL has its own refinery and AAL has a huge Debt/Equity. LUV dominates in numbers of passengers within the USA and it is expanding to foreign countries close to the US.

All three airlines are overbought. The trend (SMA-200) looks good for all of them. However, the trend could be reversed very fast as we experienced it in mid Oct.

Explanation
> Scoring systems have been explained.
> Expected EY, Debt/Equity, ROE, SMA-200% and RSI(14) are obtained from finviz.com.
> Analyst Rating is from Fidelity. If Fidelity is not your broker, use Recommendation from finviz.com.
> EB/EBIT and F-Score are from GurruFocus.com.

The above is the Fundamental Analysis. It should be followed by the following:

Intangible Analysis includes the percentage of union employees and the median age of the fleet for example.

Qualitative Analysis includes articles for the company you're interested. First, start looking for articles in Seeking Alpha.

Technical Analysis times the trend and overbought condition. Many investors do not buy a stock that is in its downward trend (i.e. he price is below its SMA-200).

Conclusion

As of 11/2014, I can see airlines are bargains judging from the high earning yields. I am cautious on the high debts (AAL in particular). I predict the stock prices will still rise at least to Feb., 2015. Now, it is the window dressing time for fund managers and they will buy winners like most of the airlines. However, their stock prices could change very fast. I recommend buying them and protect your investment using stops. It belongs to the strategy "Buy high and sell higher". In addition, follow how the institutional investors and insiders trade.

Afterthoughts

- Pam Am. 1.35 billions of Chinese can tell you that the headquarter of the former Pam Am had bad Feng Shui as the road rushes directly through the building in NYC. Today's Chinese stewardesses (young, slim and beautiful) are eye candies and look like the glamorous ladies of Pam Am in her heydays.
- Click here on the joke on how to save the airline industry. PG14 and PG21 for Chinese.

http://tonyp4idea.blogspot.com/2009/11/how-to-save-airline-industry.html

2   **Amazing returns in my recent portfolio**

Amazing Returns

To achieve a consistent 10% return above the S&P 500 over many years is every fund manager's dream. To double one's investment above the S&P500 return is amazing while tripling it is unheard of. I beat the S&P500 by 700% and I can detail the history of my transactions.

Many analysts show their average yearly returns and/or their returns of their top 10 stocks this time of the year. The market is closed early today on Christmas Eve, so I have the time to check my recent performance. As a trader with many trades, it would be far too complicated for me to do the same for the entire year. I selected all the stocks I purchased in the last 90 days. Most of them are deeply-valued stocks. Let's check how I perform so far on these stocks.

Whenever you have achieved a high return such as this one, take profit as it may have reached its peaks. To me, most profits are made in swing trades with an average holding period of 90 days.

Stocks bought and their returns as of 12/25/12

Stocks	Date Bought	Return	SPY Return
BANR	12/07/12	3%	-.13%
KTCC	12/06/12	0%	.7%
QCOR	12/07/12	15%	-.1%
KTCC	12/06/12	-1%	.7%
ACTV	12/05/12	-5%	.7%
IAG	12/05/12	-1%	.7%
ADES	12/04/12	6%	.6%
NC	12/03/12	15%	-.3%
VELT	12/03/12	64%	-.3%
ANR	11/28/12	33%	4.8%
AAPL	11/16/12	1%	4.8%
C	11/14/12	13%	3.0%
DECK	11/13/12	16%	2.7%
MSFT	11/13/12	0%	2.7%

ALU	11/13/12	38%	2.7%
DLTR	11/09/12	7%	3.4%
CAT	11/08/12	4%	1.9%
MSFT	11/07/12	-8%	.5%
BSX	10/24/12	14%	.3%
BSX	10/19/12	7%	.3%
20			
AVG:		11%	1.35%

Beat SPY (in %) = (11%-1.35%)/1.35% = 716% or 7 times

Average Return = averaging each return of 20 stocks = 11%
Average Annualized Return = 148% or 122% (= 11% *365 / avg. holding period)
Average Return = Profit / Capitalization = 10%[1]

How returns are calculated

Using BANR to illustrate how the return and SPY return are calculated.

BANR	12/07/12	3%	-.13%

BANR was bought on 12/07/12 (17 days from 12/24/12) at 27.93 and it was at 30.43 on 12/24/12.
Rate of Return = (30.43 – 27.93) / 27.93 = 3%

SPY was at 142.53 on 12/07/12 and at 142.35 on 12/24/12.
 Rate of Return = (142.35-142.53) / 142.53 = -.13%

Commissions and dividends are not included for simplicity. Commissions are negligible and dividends could add about another 2% for the annual return.

Interpreting the performance result

The quantity of each stock bought is not important as I am comparing the return of the stock. However, a few stocks have been listed twice as I bought two times usually on separate dates. If I chose them as one purchase instead of two, my return would appear even better. The purchases are real, so the amount of each stock is not identical to each other.

I'm not too excited yet. This phenomenal return could be just this one time only. 90 days is a short period. Consistency could be achieved with an improved stock picking technique, plain luck or a combination. By any measure, it is an extremely decent return. However, I do not expect beating the S&P 500 by 7 times again.

My best return is from 2009 in my largest taxable account. It is over 80% beating SPY by about 3 times. 2003 is another good year for profit. These two years are defined by me as the Early Recovery stage in a market cycle and the market provides the best profit opportunity.

The four losers are MSFT (-8%), ACTV (-5%), KTCC (-1%) and IAG (-1%). The best winners are: VELT (64%), ALU (38%), ANR (33%) and QCOR (19%). The following are in 14% to 16% range: DECK, NC and BSX (2 purchases). Click here for the entire list.

Cheating the results

I could 'cheat' for better results by doing the following, but I did not:

1. Exclude stocks only purchased in last 20 days (instead of 15).

2. If my purchases of CSCO were included, the result would be even better. CSCO has been bought three times on 7/24/12 and it has gained 31% as of 12/25/12. I still have CSCO, but it is not included as it just the 90-days requirement.

3. I could include those buy orders that had not been executed due to their fast appreciation.

Hence, there are many ways to cheat and you should read others' results carefully. For me, 7 times better is the same 2 times better, so why cheat?

What stocks were included
There are 20 purchases. I bought some stocks twice and counted as two purchases. None of the stocks have been sold as of 12/25/12.

I have excluded the stocks that I bought in the last 15 days (too early for meaningful performance results) and the stocks that I am testing a strategy by trading them every month and most are in a separate account that I do not have to pay commissions.

This strategy so far looks promising with good gains and requiring almost no effort on my part. I will include the result in my blog for this book if it proves itself to be consistently profitable. It is based on common stocks of two subscription services both seeking momentum stocks.

How the stocks were picked

The majority of the stocks were screened by my selected screens that had been proven profitable in the last 3 to 6 months or are historically profitable at this stage of the market cycle. I also analyzed most of the screened stocks and assigned a score (15 and higher is a buy) based on the metrics that had reliable predication recently. I do not stick with the scoring system 100%, but most stocks I purchased twice have high scores.

The poor performers were scored as: MSFT with a score of 13, ACTV 16, KTCC 27 and IAG 23. The scoring system is OK. MSFT should not be bought judging from its low score. However, I believe MSFT has a long-term appreciation potential. The other three are the latest purchases in this portfolio and they may perform better in longer period.

The winners were scored as: VELT 34, ALU not scored, ANR not scored and QCOR 30. The scoring system is great for this group. ALU and ANR were selected from two Seeking Alpha articles and their selections were not based on scores. I read several Wall Street Journal articles on ALU and CSCO to convince me to buy both.

The average winners were scored as: DECK 9, NC 26 and BSX not scored. DECK was selected based on an article from Seeking Alpha and it seemed DECK was experiencing the same short squeeze as CROX once did. BSX was selected from a Sunday paper article.

Observations
1. I notice that most big winners (ALU is $1) have a stock price less than $10. The myth of holding quality stocks with prices higher

than $15 is not true here as most of my big winners are below $10 including ALU.

2. I did not double bet on VELT and ALU, which both turn out to be my best performers. VELT scored high in my analysis. ALU was very convincing but it seemed to be risky. 'Nothing risk and nothing gain' applies here. I did triple bet on CSCO, which is a large company with good fundamentals that were not 'discovered' by the market.

    Both AAPL and DECK gained more than 25% and then lost most of their gains during my short holding period. I should have sold AAPL as many of my fellow investors sold the winners expecting higher capital gain taxes next year. The myth of 'buy and hold' does not work here.

3. During this period, I had several buy orders not executed due to their stock prices had been sky rocketed. Market orders could be the solution. It is another example of pennies smart and pound foolish.

4. It will be interesting to check the results again in 6 and 12 months. Except ALU, all are in my taxable accounts and I usually keep them for a year to qualify for the lower tax rates for capital gains.

5. I have not described any specific method, but concepts to build better strategies to customize to your individual situations and/or market conditions. Bet the money you can afford to lose. Past performance does not guarantee future results.

6. Reading articles such as Seeking Alpha is beneficial. However, you need to do your own analysis.

7. The market has been up by .8% in last 90 days and this portfolio increases by 11%. If my portfolio amplifies the market, I wonder whether it will be down by the same rate in a down market.

8. This portfolio is quite diversified even I have not planned that way except weighing more with high tech companies. There are not big winners and big losers that could change the average return.

9. I tried not to include emerging countries such as China as I do not trust their balance sheets.

10. I have never achieved such an amazing return. I'm emotionally detached to big wins and big losses. It could be plain luck. Even the best strategy will have its "black swan" moment eventually.

11. To achieve over 100% annualized return is not sustainable by checking the top performers of S&P 500 and their returns. However, it is possible but not likely if you churn your portfolio more than once and you time the market correctly.

12. Time to take profit as most have achieved my objectives. Use the cash to buy stocks with similar appreciation potentials. You will never go broke for taking profits.

Conclusion

My three steps of making stock purchase are: 1. Market timing, 2. Screening stocks, 3. Stock Analysis and 4. When and what to sell. They have all been discussed throughout the book. Market timing and strategy (#2 and #3) does not always work, but it will be better with using them than without.

I am the living proof *against* the Efficiency Theory and the claims that stock picking does not work. It may not work from time to time, but in the long run it works.

Footnote

[1] Profit / Capitalization could be wrong. It could be 20% but actually a little less than 20%.

3   The scents of a winner

During the beginning of Feb. 2014, I sold several winners expecting to pay zero Federal tax this year. Besides tax considerations, I expected a correction was coming.

I sold the following long-term gainers: MSFT (37%), CSCO (48%) and CAT 10%. As a group, they beat S&P 500 by a small margin.

The three sold winners are BSX, CAMP and USNA. I bought BSX (138% return) two times without looking at the fundamentals at all. So, I only have USNA (99%) and CAMP (282%) to compare and hope to find some common denominators.

Here is a table comparing the two. The metrics are around the time I bought the stocks.

	CAMP	USNA	Average
Return	282%	99%	
Bought on	12/24/12	01/28/13	
Sold on	01/08/14	02/12/14	
Days held	380	380	380
Screen	CAO	BF	
Fundamentals			
Expected E/P	39%	16%	28%
Earning growth	39%	16%	28%
ROE	40%	32%	36%
Total debt		0%	
Short %	5%	28%	
Technical			
SMA200%	13%	-10%	
RSI(14)	41%	50%	46%
Subscription			
Zacks	Average	Average	Average
IBD	Best	Average-	
Fidelity Analyst	Average-	Best	
Its Cash Grade	B	A	B+
Score			
My Score	46	26	36
P-Score	3	3	3

Explanation

The following tries to find any common denominators between the two winners. I leave out blanks in the average column where there is no common denominator. It is too small a data sample to draw a conclusion compared to my usual monitors. Some metrics are identical for the two stocks. Just coincidence!

Remember these metrics are for long-term holding of stocks (for me it is one year and one day).

- Screens.
  They are both selected from screens that have been proven winners. BF is the bottom fishing screen. CAO is the screen to search for candidates to be acquired. They are described more in detail in Myth.

- Fundamentals.
  Both have pretty sound fundamental metrics. Expected E/P (P/E in reverse), Earnings Growth and ROE are above their respective average.

  Short % is good if it is less than 10%. When it is above 30% or so, a short squeeze may be coming. The shorters of USNA made the wrong decision apparently.

- Technical.
  Technical indicators are great for spotting trend, but not in spotting bottom. When you hold the stock for a year, the short-term trend will do you no good.

- Expert advice.
  As in the table, all are not conclusive except the free Blue Chip Growth that is free at least for now. The first one is a composite grade and then second one is the Cash Flow grade.

- My Scores.

I have two scoring system. Both stocks exceeded the passing grade (15) by a wide margin. "P-Score" is described in my book Scoring Stocks. "My Score" has been enhanced with the subscriptions services I am using.

Usually the second scoring system is quite reliable. It recommended buying Apple at around $390 in June, 2013. It is NOT after-the-fact as many authors did.

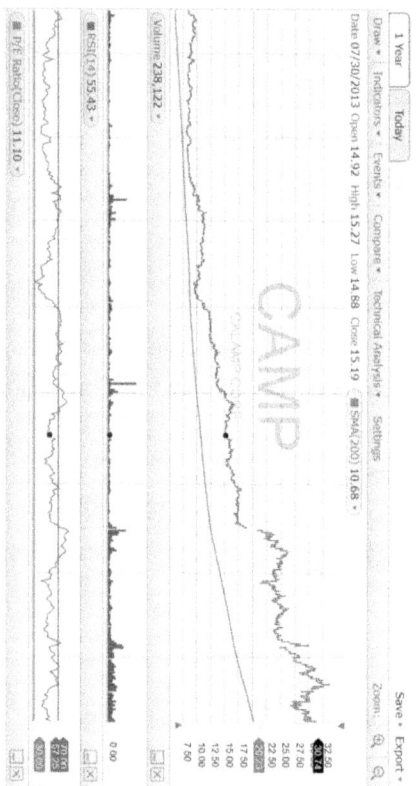

SMA-200 for CAMP. Soucre: Fidelity

Bring it up from your browser. Enter CAMP. Select Technical Indicator, then SMA, and enter 200 days.

Update

As of 4/2014, CAMP had a big plunge since I sold it. Lucky timing for me! I believe no stocks should double in a year. CAMP had returned

280% in just over a year. There are a few rare exceptions such as buying Apple and Netflix after their IPOs. I bought CAMP back after the big plunge. A fool and his money parted soon (no punch intended).

http://www.fool.com/investing/general/2014/04/25/why-calamp-corp-shares-plummeted-today.aspx

I traded LCC (U.S. Airline) making a big profit return in a month on two bets in 2013. I bought two more times in August, 2013 and as of 6/2014, it is over 163%. It scored 22 (passing grade is 15), so the scoring system works so far this time.

Common hints of a winner beside the above

o   If you are a value investor and can afford to wait for 6 months or so, find stocks with bottom prices (with low P/E preferably). If you are a momentum investor, buy a stock on price trending upwards, but do not prepare to hold it for too long.

o   Side with good management who can adopt and/or can turn around a bad situation. Remember, most of his/her staffs are usually puppets. If you do not have a visionary leader, the company will not do well. Steve Jobs had vision, but not too many in Microsoft today.

o   For huge profits, invest in small companies that do not pay dividends as they need to plow back all incomes to research and development. It is too risky for me to invest in penny stocks though. I prefer companies that have a good niche such as a new technology, a new drug, etc. The best time is about 6 months after the IPO. By that time, the vision of the management and the marketability of the products and/or service are clearer. Most likely we have missed Microsoft, Google, Apple and Wal-Mart in that stage. However, in every decade or so, we have one or two such companies.

4   Winning trade with CAMP

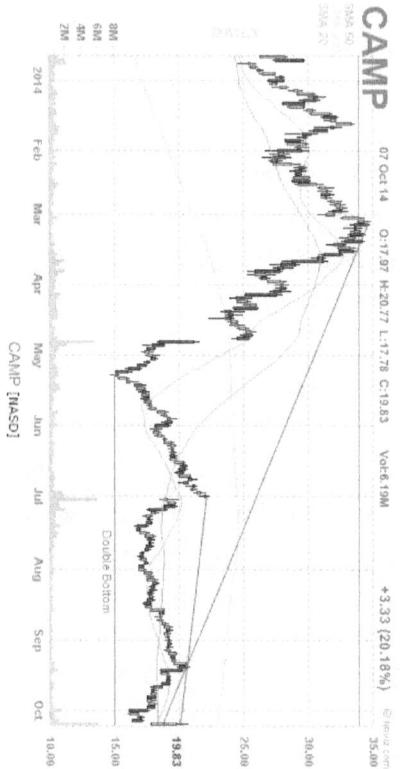

My trading on this stock involves several buys and sells so far. Here is the trade history. In 12/14/12, I have two buys. As of 10/07/14, I still own the stock.

Buy On	At	Sell On	At	Days	Return	Ann. Return
12/14/12	8.06	01/17/14	32.07	389	298%	279%
12/14/12	8.06	01/08/14	30.00	380	272%	261%
04/24/14	18.48	06/17/14	20.11	53	9%	61%
04/28/14	17.56	10/07/14	19.80	162	13%	29%

CAMP is a good stock to trade as the fundamentals were quite good most of the time. When the fundamentals are good, buy it. When they are bad, sell it.

I can tell the price and its P/E were exceedingly high in Jan, 2014 and that's the reason I sold it besides qualifying for the long-term capital gain. On 1/17/14, the stock was high valued at $32.07 with P/E = 24 and RSI = 65. It was even higher valued at $32.80 with P/E = 104 and RSI=67.

It looked like a double top to me in Jan. to March. A double top predicts a plunge. The price dropped almost half in April, 2014 and I picked the stock up two times at decent prices. From the chart, notice the double bottom, a technical indicator that predicts a surge. Use the double top and bottom as a secondary indicator.

Today, the stock was up by about 20% after the earnings announcement. The forward P/E looks very decent and so is my Pow P/E (similar to P/E with cash and debt into consideration) with almost one dollar cash per share and only 1% debt/equity.

5   Tech stocks in last 20 years

I tried to use my historical database to test out NASDAQ 100. The return is great. To illustrate, from 1/4/1999 to 6/6/2001, the annualized return is 54% vs SPY's 1.6% without considering dividends.

Do not 'wow' too early. The reason of the high performance is due to the survivor bias. Many internet companies were taken out from the index and/or the database, and hence the performance as a group is deceivingly high.

The following chart is for the popular high tech companies for the selected 10 years. For every one of the following successful high tech companies, there must be many that do not make it.

	1990-2000	2000-2010
	Annualized Return	Annualized Return
Microsoft	940%	-4%
EMC	7500%	-7%
Apple	20%	65%
Dell	8200%	-7%
Average	**4000%**	**12%**

The above figures are estimates for demonstration without considering dividends and compounding. Dell has been privatized today. Now, we can draw some conclusions.

- Tech stocks usually beat the S&P500 index. Risk usually pays.
- 1990-2000 are the golden years for tech stocks.
- 2000-2010 are not so good for tech stocks due to the crash of 2000. If it is not for Apple, the return of this portfolio would be negative.
- Except with Apple, it indicates the first ten years (or the early phase) of the tech stocks give the best returns. After they become mature companies, they seldom maintain the same growth rates. The worst of the group in the first 10 years become the best after 2000.

Buy when the market does not favor this sector

Interestingly, you should buy when the institutional investors are dumping such as buying Apple in May, 2013 as recommended in my book Scoring Stocks. Ensure they have value first by scoring them fundamentally and allow at least one year for the market to recognize the values.

I reviewed my old blog and found some bargains I described in 12/03/2012. Here is the performance summary. Again, all performance returns are annualized.

The stocks are AAPL, CSCO, INTC, MSFT, XRX, STX, WDC and ALU.

	One year later	Two years later
Ann. Return	84%	59%
SPY Ann. Return	28%	23%
Beat SPY by	200%	157%

Interestingly, AAPL is the weakest performer in both tests. It must start with a high price.

#Filler: Laughing in the grave

I asked my friend Danny why he needed a new phone. He told me it was for improving productivity – game productivity? He also told me he had been waiting for 2 days and 2 nights in the cold.

Either I was dumb in not following his logic, the productivity is HUGE, he is a blind social climber, or the work of a master salesman who is now laughing in the grave, counting his money and singing Danny Boy.

I told all my friends that I had ordered a 2020 Tesla to boost my social standing. LOL.

6   Apple

iGeneration

Almost everyone has an iPhone. Folks including myself in the lower class of the society carry imitators and/or those 'outdated' iPhones that are several months old.

My grandchild of just over one year old had a good time in playing with the iPad and it usually kept her busy for hours. Before she could say Mom, she said "I" for iPad. During my family gatherings, my cousins communicate with each other via their smart phones even when they sit next to each other. When they do not text messages, they play games with their smart phones.

Even with one pair of eyes and one pair of ears, they can play iPad, listen to iPod and text using iPhone at the same time. Thanks Apple for demonstrating what multi tasking really is. I prefer to do one task correctly than several tasks incorrectly. Chinese and Indian students are leaving us further behind by spending more time in study. Do you believe those children spending extra 2 hours every day in games would accomplish the same later in life?

Some parents have a hard time to explain to their children that their existence was due to the blackout of the iPad and iPhone caused by the hurricanes.

Why Apple is successful

Peter Lynch taught us to look for stocks in the mall. In this case, you do not even have to leave home.

I have a comparison of how the successful technology stocks performed in the first ten years and then the next ten years. If they survive in the first few years, most of them did incredibly well in the first ten years and not too good in the next ten years. Apple is the only profitable exception in the entire 20 years in my test. Apple had its bottoms many times and then miraculously came back stronger and better. Luck cannot be the only reason. To me, it is due to:

- The vision of the late Steve Jobs.
  Apple is not the first one to introduce most products we use today. Jobs had the passion to make them useful and

affordable. He was the slave master to drive his employees to the next level. These engineers and programmers are the best from our colleges and some are on H-1B visas. He knew how to play his China card described next.

- The China connection.
  - o Apple is the master of outsourcing. How can you find obedient workers to assemble Apple products at very low cost? These workers are better than robots. They can be trained to assemble new products in very short time and work long shifts without notice. Our unions, regulations and high living standard do not allow 'slave workers' here. Actually the 'slave workers' are quite educated and young. While many companies find defective products from Chinese factories, Apple so far finds few if not none.
  - o How can you find 40,000 technicians? Not from the USA at any cost.
  - o The large potential market. Chinese can buy similar products produced locally, but the selling point is the prestige of Apple to boost up their social standing. China will open up 4G LTE for iPhone line in more cities.
- Marketing.
  The long-line waiting for a new iPhone or iPad is the best ad money can buy and even better when it is free. Can the trick still work in the future? It will as long as we have silly folks wanting to be the ones in his/her block to own a new gadget.

Scoring Apple

When I was writing the book Scoring Stocks, first I used IBM but its low score would not be a good example. Then I switched to Apple (AAPL). It scored almost the highest. I recommended AAPL at $55.72 (split adjusted) in April 19, 2013, the date the book was published. It is another example that fundamentals work. However, when we're swimming against the tide, we need to be patient. At that time, the media and institutional investors ignored fundamentals. The best argument of not buying Apple was "Apple has turned from a growth stock to a value stock". They think they cannot get fired by thinking the same as the herd. Just garbage talk from the smartest folks!

Fundamental analysis as of 11/30/2014

	Passing grade	AAPL	Industry
Score System #1	>=15	18	
Score System #2	>=2	2	
Pow EY	>=5	6%	
Expected Earning Yield	>5 & <35	7%	5%
Debt / Equity	<.5	.32	.29
Analyst Rating	>7	9	
EB/EBIT	>5	13	
F-Score	>7	5	
ROE	>=15%	33%	27%
SMA-200%	>0%	30%	
RSI(14)	<60	79	
Price	11/30/14	$118.93	

Explanation

> ➤ The first scoring system incorporates many vendors' grades. The second scoring system is from my book Scoring Stocks using metrics available free from many web sites.
> ➤ Pow EY – Earning Yield (E/P) takes cash and debt into consideration.
> ➤ Expected EY, Debt/Equity, ROE, SMA-200% and RSI(14) are obtained from finviz.com.
> ➤ Analyst Rating is from Fidelity. If Fidelity is not your broker, use Recommendation from finviz.com.
> ➤ EB/EBIT and F-Score are from GuruFocus.com.

How Apple scores

It scores fine but not spectacular. The score from my book in April, 2013 is 5 and now it is 2. Fundamentally it is not as good as before.

P/B and P/S are usually not useful for high tech companies. However, Apple's P/B at 6 is exceedingly expensive as compared to Google's 3. When most analysts like the stock, usually it will rise in the short-term. RSI(14) shows it is overbought. To conclude, its fundamental score passes but not in flying colors.

The brief Fundamental Analysis should be followed by the following:

Intangible Analysis (described next).

Qualitative Analysis includes articles for Apple. First, start looking for articles in Seeking Alpha. Large companies like Apple are hard to manipulate, so most articles are not 'pump and dump'.

Technical Analysis detects the trend and overbought condition. Many investors do not buy a stock that is in its downward trend. SMA-200 is a good trend indicator. Its price should be above the SMA-200 (same as SMA-200% is positive).

Intangible Analysis

Apple has lost a visionary leader Steve Jobs. I hope he was not replaced by similar managers at Microsoft, who are responsible for Microsoft's lost decade with few innovative products. Apple has a lot of cash to finance new projects. High tech business is tough as they need to build a better mouse trap continuously. When the mouse trap becomes a commodity, it will not have a good profit margin. That's one reason that Buffett does not invest in Apple. If he read my book, he would buy Apple instead of IBM.

There are bright spots for Apple:

1. Apple Text Book. Imagine all students carry iPads instead of text books. Several educational apps have been created for iPads.
2. Apple TV.
    It is a loser so far with a lot of risk and potential competitors. However, the potential is great. It could give all cable companies a run for the money. Wider internet channels would make it more feasible. Will the cable companies provide these speeds to allow Apple TV and similar products to step into their turfs? Does Apple or Google have secret projects to by-pass cables' internet?
3. While the iPad and iPhone are peaking in the hardware, iTune, software and contents for these devices to access have no limit. We have witnessed how iPad helps the folks with autism and iPhones for the blind. I can envision many other similar applications.

4. Apple moves to Kindle's market. iPad is too big to be used to read books during commute. You need to hold an iPad with both hands. The mini iPad, even making fewer profit margins, will be Apple's answer to Kindle and a good addition to cover the lower end of its product lines.

5. All the mobile phone technology is originated by the first generation (if not counting Motorola) that Apple has a lot of patents. Its lawyers will milk money from Samsung and prevent cheap mobile phones from coming to the USA.

6. Apple Pay.
   I saw a similar ad from a credit card company a while ago and not recently. Apple has a proven history of picking up some failed products and turning them into gold. It is a big test for Tim Cook. Hong Kong had a similar application many years ago. The advantage of that application is you do not have to carry changes. To me, this product could be the next innovative and most profitable for Apple. Apple Pay may not make a splash in the bottom line initially, but it is an important product.

7. Apple iWear/Apple Watch.
   There will be cheap Chinese products flooded in our market. However, the selling point is the prestige of Apple and its integration to other Apple products. For a similar reason, my $50 Casino has no respect even it is more accurate and more functional than an Omega costing many times more. It will be successful, but will not make a big dent on Apple's total revenue / profit.

8. Apple has a lot of cash. Dividends usually boost the stock price and the option values granted to the management. However, it is important to plow back to development and acquiring technologies. They may have paid too much for Beats.

2016 and beyond

Xiaomi, a Chinese phone maker, will most likely come to the USA in 2016 after conquering several emerging markets including India. Its phone is almost as good as the latest model of iPhone at about half the price. It also has a low-end version priced at about $100 that would set up a standard for entry smart phones.

Xiaomi prices the latest phone model barely above the manufacturing price and makes money in the decreasing component prices. It gains more profit by stretching the model to a longer life.

Apple's lawyer will prevent its entry that Samsung found out the hard way. For starters, Xiaomi needs to modify the user interface to avoid some of the obvious lawsuits in the USA.

Even if Xiaomi will not enter the US market, it will steal more sales from Apple. Apple has to learn from Cisco. You do not want to make China angry. If they do, they may stop Apple from selling their phones in China. Hence, you may win the battle, but lose the war. Xiaomi could be one of the companies that would force the mobile phone to become a commodity product.

When the phone becomes a commodity, both companies have to make money in the content. Today Apple depends on iPhone for over 50% of its sales. In 2016, Apple stock may face some challenges even without Xiaomi entering the US market. Eventually the smart phones will become a commodity product and they may have to face Xiaomi or other similar companies.

It is one's opinion and I would face a lot of opposition from the Apple lovers; it is the same when I recommended Apple in May, 2013 when no one wanted to buy Apple's stock. Buy any stock depending on the potential appreciation (via individual analysis), not on the love of its products, the company or the management.

More on Apple.
http://ebmyth.blogspot.com/2013/11/more-on-apple.html

7   My micro-cap performance

The strategies described here have been used in my book Best Stocks 2014, According to Me. From 12/16/13 (the published date) to 3/4/14, the list of all 135 selected stocks beat SPY by 103% and the list of 9 small cap stocks as below beat SPY by almost 500%.

From 12/16/13 to 3/29/14 (today), the performances of the entire list of 9 small micro-cap stocks (RAS is not a micro cap by my definition) are:

Stock	Market Cap (M)[1]	Annualized Return
ARTX	52	234%
CPSS	176	6%
RAS	602	-19%
GST	329	83%
EVC	515	65%
LEE	171	293%
SGU	313	16%
HILL	166	491%
MNTG	147	12%
Average		131%
SPY		22%[2]
Beat SPY by		496%

[1] As of 12/16/13
[2] Annualized return

8   Lessons from selling GME

Game Stop (symbol GME) has been up 16 times from the low. There are several lessons to learn and review.

- Super stocks. Based on your time available for monitoring stocks, you should have a handful of stocks comprised the majority of your portfolio; I have about 10. GME and GILD were my super stocks at the time. Both were more than 3 times my average position.
- Stops. Both GME and GILD were in the downward trend when they were acquired. I was glad I did not use stops on them to give the market more time to recognize their real values. I sold GILD before the surge. Lesson: Do not put stops on value stocks, but it is fine on momentum and/or on short selling. With manual stops, you may lose up to 100% at most, but not 1,600% in the worst case for GME.
- Shorting. Do not short stocks when the short percent (from Finviz or other sources) is over 20%; usually I use 10%.
- Short squeeze. GME had experienced serious short squeeze. The trade volume for one day was 140M, while the number of floating shares was only 50M. Lesson: Watch for the short percent.
- I sold 1/3 at about $26 and the majority at about $40 just a few days later. I should follow my article on selling winners.
- Usually I keep good record of the stocks I bought. I did not this time. Hence, I cannot tell you my real returns and my annualized returns and the comparisons to S&P500. Most stock brokers do not give you the buy date. You need to include the metrics such as P/E and Debt/Equity for future evaluation of other stocks. A simple spreadsheet will do the housekeeping. From my estimate, I made about 300% in trading GME.
- I will not buy it back for several reasons: (1) It has more than its fair value (still losing money), (2) The short squeeze will be over if not already, (3) Most malls have few visitors as this writing, (4) The future of buying software is via downloading, (5) They do not have moats and advantage over their competitors such as Amazon and Target, and (6) The management is good in selling pet food, which is quite different from selling video games and consoles. Do not look back.
- From Finviz, I read 2 good articles on GME.

*** Book 2: Evaluating Stocks

This book and the next one "Technical Analysis" are the basic tools for all strategies. Fundamentals are more important for long-term investing while technical analysis is for shorter-term investing.

The simple formula to make money is to find value stocks and wait for the market to realize their values. Only buy when the market is not risky. Most successful investors are doing this.

The book value of a stock is simply the net worth of a company (= Assets – Liabilities). When the stock price is higher than the book value per share (i.e. 'Stock Price / Book Price' > 1), it is over-valued. When this ratio is more than 2 or less than 0.5, you have to be cautious. When it is way underpriced, there may be a critical reason.

Intrinsic Value includes the intangibles such as patents. However, both the Book Value and Intrinsic Value have not been convincing predictors from my tests. I briefly describe some basic but important metrics here.

- Expected Earning Yield (E/P). The future appreciation depends on future earnings and the current price of the stock (you do not want to overpay). I prefer a range from 5% to 30%.
- Growth of Earnings and growth of sales. Compare them to their numbers in the same quarter of last year. I prefer 10% or higher.
- How good is the management? Measured by ROE. I prefer 10% or higher.
- How safe is the company? Measured by 'Debt/Equity'. I prefer less than .5 (same as 50%). However, some industries are debt intensive.

These are the ratios readily available from many sites including Finviz.com except reversing P/E for earning yield. In most cases there is no need to dig into the complicated financial statements to start with. However, ensure they are up-to-date. For example, when a stock has a one-to-two split, the price is updated but may not be the Earnings per share, Book per share... to give erroneous info.

The predictability of most metrics changes according to the current market conditions. Monitor their performance and act accordingly. I prefer E/P but Earnings/Sales had better predictability in my last test.

How to start

Check out the Simplest Way to Evaluate Stocks in the Common Tools section.

First we filter stocks from about 7,000 selected stocks available; the number is variable from different web sites and/or services. To start with, skip stocks not in the three major exchanges, market caps less than 50 M or daily average volumes less than 10,000 shares.

We have a simple procedure to evaluate stocks for beginners and couch potatoes by using other folks' research in the Common Tools section. Furthermore, refer to Scoring Stocks to evaluate stocks using a scoring system. Some chapters have been duplicated here so you do not have to bounce back and forth.

1   Amazing returns

Amazing Returns

To achieve a consistent 10% return above S&P 500 over many years is every fund manager's dream. To double one's investment above the S&P500 return is amazing while tripling it is unheard of. I beat the S&P500 by 700% and I can detail the history of my transactions.

Many analysts show their average yearly returns and/or their returns of their top 10 stocks this time of year. The market has closed early today on Christmas Eve, so I have the time to check my recent performance. As a trader with many trades, it would be far too complicated for me to do the same for the entire year. I selected all the stocks I purchased in the last 90 days. Most of them are deeply-valued stocks. Let's check how I performed so far on these stocks.

Whenever you have achieved a high return such as this one, take the profit as it may have reached its peaks. To me, most profits are made in swing trades with an average holding period of just 90 days.

Stocks bought and their returns as of 12/25/12

Stocks	Date Bought	Return	SPY Return
BANR	12/07/12	3%	-.13%
KTCC	12/06/12	0%	.7%
QCOR	12/07/12	15%	-.1%
KTCC	12/06/12	-1%	.7%
ACTV	12/05/12	-5%	.7%
IAG	12/05/12	-1%	.7%
ADES	12/04/12	6%	.6%
NC	12/03/12	15%	-.3%
VELT	12/03/12	64%	-.3%
ANR	11/28/12	33%	4.8%
AAPL	11/16/12	1%	4.8%
C	11/14/12	13%	3.0%
DECK	11/13/12	16%	2.7%
MSFT	11/13/12	0%	2.7%
ALU	11/13/12	38%	2.7%
DLTR	11/09/12	7%	3.4%
CAT	11/08/12	4%	1.9%
MSFT	11/07/12	-8%	.5%
BSX	10/24/12	14%	.3%
BSX	10/19/12	7%	.3%
20			
AVG:		11%	1.35%

Beat SPY (in %) = (11%-1.35%)/1.35% = 716% or 7 times

Average Return = averaging each return of 20 stocks = 11%
Average Annualized Return = 148% or 122% (= 11% *365 / avg. holding period)
Average Return = Profit / Capitalization   = 10%[1]

How the returns are calculated

Using BANR to illustrate how the return and the SPY return are calculated.

BANR	12/07/12	3%	-.13%

BANR was bought on 12/07/12 (17 days from 12/24/12) at 27.93 and it was at 30.43 on 12/24/12.
Rate of Return = (30.43 – 27.93) / 27.93 = 3%

SPY was at 142.53 on 12/07/12 and at 142.35 on 12/24/12.
 Rate of Return = (142.35-142.53) / 142.53 = -.13%

Commissions and dividends are not included for simplicity. Commissions are negligible and dividends could add about another 2% for the annual returns.

Interpreting the performance results

The quantity of each stock bought is not important as I am comparing the return of the stock. However, a few stocks have been listed twice as I bought two times usually on separate dates. If I chose them as one purchase instead of two, my return would appear even better. The purchases are real, so the amount of each stock is not identical to each other.

I'm not too excited yet. This phenomenal return could be just this one time only. 90 days is a short period. Consistency could be achieved with an improved stock picking technique, plain luck or a combination. By any measure, it is an extremely decent return. However, I do not expect beating S&P 500 by 7 times again.

My best return is from 2009 in my largest taxable account. It was over 80% beating the SPY by about 3 times. 2003 is another good year for profit. These two years are defined by me as the Early Recovery stage in a market cycle and the market provides the best profit opportunity.

The four losers are MSFT (-8%), ACTV (-5%), KTCC (-1%) and IAG (-1%). The best winners are: VELT (64%), ALU (38%), ANR (33%) and QCOR (19%). The following are in a 14% to 16% range: DECK, NC and BSX (2 purchases). Click here for the entire list.

Cheating the results

I could 'cheat' for better results by doing the following, but I did not:

4. Exclude stocks only purchased in last 20 days (instead of 15).

5. If my purchases of CSCO were included, the result would be even better. CSCO has been bought three times on 7/24/12 and it has

gained 31% as of 12/25/12. I still have CSCO, but it is not included as it just hit the 90-days requirement.

6. I could include those buy orders that had not been executed due to their fast appreciation.

Hence, there are many ways to cheat, so you should read others' results carefully.

What stocks were included

There were 20 purchases. I bought some stocks twice and that counted as two purchases. None of the stocks have been sold as of 12/25/12. I have excluded the stocks that I am testing a strategy by trading them every month and most are in a separate account.

How the stocks were picked

The majority of the stocks were screened by my selected screens that had been proven profitable in the last 3 to 6 months, or are historically profitable at this stage of the market cycle. I also analyzed most of the screened stocks and assigned a score (15 and higher is a buy) based on the metrics that had a reliable predication recently. I do not stick with the scoring system 100% of the time, but most of them stocks that I purchased twice have high scores.

The poor performers were scored as: MSFT with a score of 13, ACTV 16, KTCC 27 and IAG 23. The scoring system is OK. MSFT should not be bought judging from its low score. However, I believe MSFT has a long-term appreciation potential. The other three are the latest purchases in this portfolio and they may perform better in a longer period of time.

The winners were scored as: VELT 34, ALU was not scored, ANR was not scored and QCOR 30. The scoring system is great for this group. ALU and ANR were selected from two Seeking Alpha articles and their selections were not based on these scores. I read several Wall Street Journal articles on ALU and CSCO to convince myself to buy both of them.

The average winners were scored as follows: DECK 9, NC 26 and BSX was not scored. DECK was selected based on an article from Seeking Alpha and it seemed DECK was experiencing the same short squeeze as CROX once did. BSX was selected from a Sunday paper article.

Observations

13. I notice that most big winners (ALU is $1) have a stock price less than $10. The myth of holding quality stocks with prices higher than $15 is not true here as most of my big winners were below $10 including ALU.

14. I did not double my normal purchases on VELT and ALU, which both turned out to be my best performers. VELT scored high in my analysis. ALU was very convincing but it seemed to be risky. 'Nothing risk and nothing gained' applies here. I did triple my purchase on CSCO, which is a large company with good fundamentals that were not yet 'discovered' by the market.

    Both AAPL and DECK gained more than 25% and then lost most of their gains during my short holding period. I should have sold AAPL as many of my fellow investors sold the winners expecting higher capital gains taxes next year. The myth of 'buy and hold' does not work here.

15. During this period, I had several buy orders that were not executed due to their rising stock prices. Market orders could be the solution. It is another example of pennies smart and a pound foolish.

16. It will be interesting to check the results again in 6 and 12 months. Except ALU, all are in my taxable accounts and I usually keep them for a year to qualify for the lower tax rates due to capital gains.

17. I have not described any specific method, but these concepts help you to build better strategies to customize to your individual situations and/or market conditions. Invest the money you can afford to lose. Past performance does not guarantee future results.

18. Reading articles such as Seeking Alpha can be beneficial providing they are not 'bump-and-switch' scheme. However, you should do your own analysis. It is your money after all.

19. The market has been up by .8% in the last 90 days and this portfolio increased by 11%. If my portfolio amplifies the market, I wonder whether it will be down by the same rate in a down market.

20. This portfolio is quite diversified even that I have not planned that way except weighing more with high tech companies. There are no big winners and no big losers that could change the average returns.

21. I tried not to include emerging countries such as China as I do not trust their balance sheets.

22. I have never achieved such an amazing return. I'm emotionally detached to big wins and big losses. It could be plain luck. Even the best strategy will have its "black swan" moment eventually.

23. To achieve over 100% annualized return is not sustainable by checking the top performers of the S&P 500 index and their returns. However, it is possible but not likely if you churn your portfolio more than once and you time the market correctly.

24. Time to take profits as most stocks here have achieved my objectives. Use the cash to buy stocks with a similar appreciation potential. You will never go broke taking profits.

Conclusion

My three steps of making a stock purchase are: 1. Market timing, 2. Screening stocks, 3. Stock Analysis and 4. When and what to sell. They have all been discussed throughout the book. Market timing and strategy (#2 and #3) does not always work, but it will go better with using them. I am the living proof *against* the Efficiency Theory and the claims that stock picking does not work. It may not work from time to time, but in the long run it works.

Footnote

[1] Profit / Capitalization should be a little less than 20%. The original 10% is correct when you invest all the 20 stocks at the start of the beginning of the investment period. I bought these stocks on different dates. If I assume the average time of all the stock purchases is at a mid-point, then my average capitalization is only half and hence giving a 20% return.

It is slightly less than 20% as I did not include the stocks that I bought in the last 15 days. Use the number for a comparison and that's why we have to be concerned with the performance from most investment subscriptions.

2   A scoring system

This scoring system helps you to select whether you should buy a stock or not. In this system, when a stock scores higher than 2, it is a buy. As a group, the highly-scored stocks usually perform better than the lowly-scored stocks in a year.   The basic concepts are described here.

An Example

For illustration purposes, we use two metrics: Forward P/E and ROI.

First we convert Forward P/E into Forward E/P by flipping the two values. Assuming Forward E/P should have a higher weight than ROI, multiply E/P by 5. The average ROI is 10% (simplified for illustration), so minus it by .1.

 Score = Forward E/P * 5 + (ROI -.1)

For example, a stock has a P/E of 10 (E/P = 1/10= .1) and ROI is expressed as 25%.

 Score = .1 * 5 + (.25 - .1) = .5 + .15= .65

Some parameters by some sites are expressed in grade such as A, B, C and D. For simplicity, if it is A, then the value is 2 otherwise it is zero.

 Score = if (Grade = "A", 2, 0) + ...

Test your system on paper with at least 3 months of data. Check whether your scoring system works. It works when the higher the score corresponds to the better the return. Adjust the weight on each metric and see whether your scoring system improves its predictability.

Again, it is simplified for educational and illustration purpose. Try even more different metrics and check whether the metrics still work in the current market. The next metrics to include could be Equity Summary Score from Fidelity, Debt/Equity and Quarter-to-Quarter Earnings / Sales.

Monitor your scoring system

I am sure that many have tried to use most of the metrics and they still cannot find the Holy Grail. I believe the predictability power of each metric is influenced by the current market conditions. For example, the fundamental metrics such as P/E predict better than the growth metrics such as PEG during the market bottom. You should test the performance of each metric every 6 months or so.

You may have two scores: one for short term and one for long term. The stocks you want to keep in the short term may not be the same kind of stocks you want to keep in the longer term. Short term is 3 months (one month for me) and long term is 12 months for me. My definitions could be different than yours. Value metrics are more important for the long term while growth metrics are more important for the short term.

However, 12 months is too long a period of time and during this period the market may change, so it is better to change it from 12 to 6. To illustrate, energy stocks were great in 2007, but they plunged in 2008. If your scoring system for long-term holding was constructed based on 12 months' data in 2007, the system would have been misleading in 2008 for energy stocks in this example.

I find the short-term scores have a better prediction power than the long-term scores. However, I keep profitable stocks more than 12 months to qualify for the better tax treatments in taxable accounts, and sell the losers less than 12 months. Evaluate the purchased stocks every 6 months to decide whether you want to keep them for another 6 months. Use stops and trialing stops (for winners) to protect your portfolio.

Besides monitoring the metrics in your scoring system, monitor the scores.

The market is not always rational

Sometimes the scoring system fails: When the poorly-scored stocks perform better than the highly-scored stocks. The market is not always rational. Most scoring systems depend on fundamental metrics. When the market switches its favor from value to growth, adjust the score system accordingly. I have found that more than one time that the stocks scored in the top 5% did not perform, so be careful or skip the top 5% (sometimes 10%). The events such as a pending lawsuit or an expiring drug do not show up in metrics, and that is why we need to do other analysis such as Intangible Analysis.

Some metrics almost always work such as the positive predictions of excessive insider's purchases. The insiders know the company typically better than others. When they buy their own company's stock at market prices, they must know it has good appreciation potential. They have many reasons to sell their company's stocks. However, when they sell a large percent of their holdings, be cautious.

When the stock loses more than 30% in a month and you cannot find valid reasons, it may be a good indicator for potential appreciation ahead. Some suggestions are:

- Do not modify your scoring system during market plunges.
- The best strategy is to use the screens (same as searches) that have worked well for the last 90 days.
- Find out why your fundamental metrics that used to work do not work now. You may want to add more weight on growth metrics, and vice versa on value metrics.

An example of monitoring the metrics

This is what I found in monitoring the performances of the metrics as of 3/2013. It is based on a limited database of about 300 stocks with holding periods varying from 1 to 15 months. It has an average of 8% (16% for shorter term). The following is for educational purpose only.

1. The foreign stocks are not doing well: South America (average return is -21% for 7 stocks), Israel (-18% for 2), China (-10% for 7). Europe (0% for 17) and Canada (5% for 16, and most are in natural resources). If I ignore the foreign companies, the return of the portfolio would be increased substantially.

2. The following metrics work fine for the long term only: Forward (same as Expected) Earnings Yield (E/P) and Fidelity's Equity Summary Score.

3. P/B. The stocks with P/B less than 1 perform better than the stocks with P/B greater than 2 (10% vs. 4%).

4. There are no definitive conclusions on Cash / Market Cap, PEG and Return of Equity (a surprise to me) in this monitor.

5. The stocks that were cheaper by 50% to their average 5-year P/E (available from Fidelity) have performed better than those stocks that were cheaper by less than 2%.

6. The ratio of Short / Market Cap between 25% and 30% has better performance than other percentages. It is a contradictory ratio and it could be a short squeeze (a condition that the stock is running out of shares to sell short).

7. There are many composite scores from different vendors that I subscribe to and they are not disclosed here.

8. Based on the above, I will modify my scoring system. I will still have two scores, one for short term and one for longer term.

Short-term scoring system

The scoring system should work better in the shorter term. For testing this system, I used the above data base, but deleted stocks that have been over 8 months old. It is still a small data base of about 190 stocks.

The result is different from the above as the time frame has been reduced. Here is the summary.

1. The predictability of screens (same as searches) performs about the same as the last monitor. A few screens are better than others. I will not use the under-performing screens with real money.

2. The stock grades from several vendors are not a good indicator this time.

3. Expected (same as Forward) Earnings Yield (E/P) has been a good indicator.

4. Cash Flow is a good indicator (different from the last monitor).

5. Fidelity's Equity Summary Score is a good indicator. Finviz has a similar score, but I prefer to use Fidelity's. Fidelity places higher weight on opinions from analysts that have a better prediction on this stock than others. It eliminates some of the conflict of interest between the analysts and the investing banks s/he works for.

6. The Short Percentage between 25 and 30 is a good contrary indicator (could be a good chance for a short squeeze).

   Its value of less than 10 % is a good indicator. The rest of the range is not conclusive.

7. Cash / Market Cap, Insider Purchase, P/B, ROE and Dividend stocks (>3%) are not conclusive in this monitor.

8. P/S with values less than 0.8 are a good indicator.

9. For some reason I do not know why and how to explain: the top 10% of the top-scored stocks did not perform better than the other stocks that pass.

   It happens in both my two scoring systems. Be suspicious of them and it has happened for more than once. However, the stocks that scored in the bottom 10% are consistently poor performers and that's a good indicator.

There are many other parameters that may be of interest to you. Include them in the performance monitor.

3   Simplest way to evaluate stocks

Beginners should trade ETFs only. This chapter is for the readers who are ready or getting ready to trade stocks. In general, ETFs are diversified, less volatile than trading stocks. However, stocks offer higher profit but higher risk.

Many stock researches have already been done recently and some are available free of charge. I have no affiliation with Fidelity except I retired from it. You can open an account with them with no balance. Their Equity Summary Score is one of the best indicators; I check out **value** stocks with score higher than 8. Concentrate on fundamental metrics such as P/E for long-term holds, and momentum metrics for short-term holds. Add criteria to limit the number of screened stocks. Finviz.com is a free screener.

Several sources

The popular ones are Morningstar, Value Line, The Street and Zacks (currently free for rankings of individual stocks). If they are not free, check out whether they are available from your local library. I have 3 simple ways to evaluate stocks starting with the simplest. In addition, read the articles on the selected stocks from Fidelity, Finviz, Seeking Alpha and many other sources for further evaluation.

Fidelity

Select only stocks that have Fidelity's Equity Summary Score 8 or higher. There are tons of information about a stock. Once a while I did not agree with the score such as SHOP and ZM that scored high in August, 2020. Include the following for your analysis.

A modified stock selection based on a magazine article

Most metrics are available from Finviz except EV/EBITDA.

1. Forward P/E (expected earnings and not based on the last twelve months). It should range from 5 to 15 (10 to 25 for high tech stocks). EV/EBITDA (from Yahoo!Finance) is a better choice as it includes the debts and cash than P/E; it would be more effective if it uses forward earnings. If you do not use EV/EBITDA,

ensure Debt/Equity is less than 0.5 except for the debt-intensive industries.

2. ROE (Return of Equity) measures how well the company uses the capital. I prefer stocks with ROE greater than 5%.

3. Volatility. Conservative investors should select stocks with a beta of less than one (i.e. less volatile).

4. Insider Transactions for sales (i.e. negative) from should be less than 5%. If it is -5%, most likely the insiders are dumping it.

5. Compare the metrics such as P/E and Debt/Equity to its five-year average and its competitors (available in Fidelity).

6. Momentum. Check out the SMA-50 (actually SMA-50%) and SMA-200. Ideally they should be positive. SMA-50% is especially important for stocks you do not want to keep for a long time.

7. Check out articles on the stock as some recent events (for example a new lawsuit) have not been included in the metrics.

8. Compare the trend of the sector this stock is in. Under Finviz, enter the related sector ETF.

Summary
The sources are Fidelity (Equity Summary Score and various comparisons), Finviz and Yahoo!Finance (for EV/EBITDA). Value stocks should be held longer.

Category	Score / Metric	Value /Momentum
Score	Fidelity's Equity Summary Score	Both
Value	EV/EBITDA	Value
	P/E cheaper compared to 5-year avg.	Value
	P/E cheaper compared to its sector.	Value
	Insider Purchases	Both
Safety	Debt/Equity	Value

		Compare it to its sector.	Value
Momentum		50-SMA%	Momentum
		200-SMA% (for long term holds).	Value
Articles		Check out latest events	Both
Market		No purchase if market is risky.	Momentum

A simple scoring system using Finviz

Bring up Finviz.com and then enter the stock symbol.

No.	Metric	Good	Bad	Score
1	Forward P/E[1]	Between 2.5 and 12.5, Score = 2	> 50 or < 0, Score = -1	
2	P/ FCF[1]	< 12, Score = 1	>30 or < 0, Score = -1	
3	P/S[1]	< 0.8, Score = 1	< 0, Score = -1	
4	P/ B[1]	< 1, Score = 1	< 0, Score = -1	
	Compare quarter to quarter of last year			
5	Sales Q/Q	> 15%, Score = 1	< 0, Score = -1	
6	EPS Q/Q	> 20% , Score = 1	< 0, Score = -1	
			Grand Score	
	Stock Symbol Date[2]	Current Price	SPY	

Footnote

[1] Negative values for Sales (due to accounting adjustments), Equity and Book are possible but not likely.

[2] The last row is for your information only. SPY is used to measure whether it will beat the market by comparing the return of this stock to the return of SPY.

The Score

Score each metric and sum up all the scores giving the Grand Score. If the Grand Score is 3, the stock passes this scoring system. Even if it is a 2, it still deserves further analysis if you have time. You may want to add scores from other vendors. To illustrate on using Fidelity, add 1 to the score if Fidelity's Equity Summary score is 8 or higher. Monitor the performance after every 6 months or so to see whether this scoring system beats the market.

Very basic advice for beginners

Beginners should stick with U.S. stocks with Market Cap greater than 800 M (million), Debt/Equity less than .25 (25%) except for debt-intensive industries such as utilities and airlines and Forward P/E between 5 to 20 (25 for high-tech companies). These metrics are all available from Finviz.com, which is free.

Do not have more than 20% of your portfolio in one stock (unless it is an ETF or mutual fund) and do not have more than 30% of your portfolio in one sector.

For more conservative investors, buy non-volatile stocks whose beta (available from Yahoo!Finance) is less than 1. Beta of 1 represents the market (the S&P 500 index). For example, a stock with beta 1.5 statistically fluctuates more than 50% of the market and hence it is very volatile.

Try paper trading to check out your strategy and your skill in trading stocks. If your broker does not provide one, use a spreadsheet to record your trades or check the availability of simulator.investopedia.com.

#Filler: Silence is golden

I am glad I did not give advice to a friend who had to decide whether to take a lump sum payment or an annuity. The correction in March, 2020 would wipe out a lot of his portfolio if he took the lump sum payment. No one would share his profits when the predictions are correct, but the blame if it does not materialize.

It is same in investing that nothing is certain. With educated guesses, we should have more rights than wrongs especially in the long run.

Section I: Fundamental metrics

1   Mysteries of P/E

If you believe you can make good money by selecting stocks with low P/Es solely, dream on. If it were that easy, there will be no poor folks. However, buying fundamentally sound companies would reduce the risk and improve the chance of its appreciation.

P/E is the most misunderstood indicator. To me, it is the most useful one among all metrics if it is properly used. Earnings are the key to stock appreciation and P/E measures its value. To illustrate on P/E, you pay a million for a hot-dog cart in NYC. Even if its earnings increase year after year, you will never recoup your investment as you have paid too much even for a good business.

"Buy stocks with P/E below 15 and earnings positive" is not true in many cases. P/E growth (PEG) should be considered at least as a prospect of the company. Many retailers were destroyed by Amazon and many newspapers were destroyed by Facebook and Google. Which sector do you want to buy: the sector in up trending or the dying sector even with a better P/E?

Most old books on value are based on old industries that are no longer applicable in today's market. Read these books but ask the above question.

Better definition

P/E should be inverted as E/P, which is termed as Earnings Yield. Earnings Yield is easy to be compared and understood. It takes care of negative earnings for screening stocks and ranking (comparing stocks with the better P/E first). If you sort P/E in ascending order, your order will be wrong with the negative earnings but right with E/P.

It is usually compared to a 10-year Treasury bill yield (or 30 years) or a CD rate. If the stock has 5% earnings yield and your one-year CD is 1%, then it beats the CD by 4% in absolute numbers and four times better. However, the CD is virtually risk free (with deposit amount limits in most banks). Earning yield is an estimated guess and it may not materialize.

Many ways to predict E/P

- Based on the last 12 months. Project it to the Forward E/P. It is also called the last twelve month E/P.

- Based on analysts' educated guesses. Guesses may not materialize. Based on my experience, the expected usually predicts better than the one based on the last 12 months. This is the one I use most and many investing subscriptions provide this Forward P/E (same as the Expected P/E) or expected E/P.

Usually I do not trust the analyst's opinions due to their conflict of interest. However, the earnings estimate is my exception.

- Based on the last month or the last quarter. Latest information could be better for predictions. However, they are not good for seasonal businesses such as the retail where most sales are done during the Christmas season.
- Besides the Pow PE described later, I take the average of the earnings yield EY as:

The Avg. EY = (EY from the last twelve month + Expected EY + EY from the current month of prior year) / 3

It averages out using figures from the past, the present and the future. If no one has used it, I claim shamelessly it is my original idea.

Best E/P could not be the best

Very high E/P could be signs of troubles ahead such as a lawsuit pending, fraud, etc. If you find companies E/P over 50%, it means two years' profits could be equal to the entire cost of the company! I can tell you right away that they probably smell fishy unless you believe that there is a free lunch in life.

However, from time to time, some bargains do exist due to certain conditions, or the Wall Street is just wrong about the company. You need to find out whether they are bargains or traps. When the E/P is low (sometimes even negative) but is improving fast, it could mean big profits for you. Fundamentalists may miss this opportunity in the early stages, which is also the most profitable time to buy. This could be a turnaround.

During a recession, a good company will have a hard time in promoting a new product as the consumers are thrifty. At the same time, it usually is the best time to develop products if the company has enough cash to finance it. In this case, there will be no alarm even with negative earnings. The only alarm is when the company cannot meet the debt obligations.

Some companies can manipulate earnings via dirty tricks in accounting. It could make this year look really good, but it is harder but not impossible to continue the same trick for many years. Check out the footnotes in the financial statement.

E/P and PEG

For value investing, E/P is usually used and the higher the better. Watch out when it is extraordinarily high.

PEG (P/E growth) measures the rate of improving P/E.

PEG = (P/E) / Earnings Growth Rate

As described, E can be based on the last 12 months, expected or the average. I prefer expected earnings and they call it Forward PEG.

They have similar problem with P/E: You want a low PEG but not a negative PEG. I propose "Earnings Yield Growth" far easier to understand and the problems with negative earnings.

Which of the following two stocks do you want to buy based on their historical earning yields and earnings growth?

1. A stock that has a 10% earnings yield with no earnings growth.
2. A stock that has an 8% earnings yield with 50% earnings growth.

If the earnings growth continues, in next year the second stock should pay 12%, substantially better than the first stock. This is another reason we should use forward earnings rather than historical earnings.

PEG may give a low value for companies that pay high dividends. To correct it,

PEG = (P/E)/ (Earning Growth Rate + Dividend Yield)

When the general market favors growth stocks, weigh more on growth metrics including PEG. I claim no credit on the adjusted PEG.

Fundamental metrics

E/P is one of the metrics you should use but not exclusively. If the earning yield is high but the % of debt is high too, then a good bargain may not be as good as it appears to be. Pow P/E considers this effect.

Some other metrics may not be easily found in the financial statements such as the intangibles, insider buying, pension obligations, trade secrets, losing market share, brand name, customers' loyalty, etc. It is interesting that most metrics change its ability to predict from time to time.

Most likely I can make most fundamental metrics including attractive P/E at the expense of increased money borrowed. The stock would look rosy in the short term, but not in the long term. Hence, pay attention to Debt/Equity.

P/E variations

There are other P/E variations like Shiller P/E (same as CAPE and PE10). Shiller P/E can also be used to track the current market valuation. It is controversial and its value is easily misinterpreted. Hence, use it as a reference only unless you understand all its issues. I prefer to use two year average of the P/E instead of 10 as I believe the market changes too much over a ten year span. Currently Shill P/E does not work that well as before. It is due to the excessive printing of money.

Personally I prefer to compare a company's current P/E to its average P/E in the last 5 years. Also compare it to the average value of the companies in the same industry. The average P/E for high-tech companies is different from supermarkets for example.

P/E is more reliable for a group of stocks (SPY for example) instead of individual stocks which have too many other metrics and intangibles to deal with.

When you compare the total return of an ETF to a corresponding index, you need to add the respective dividends to the index to ensure a fair comparison of total returns. As of this writing, the S&P500 is paying about a 2% dividend.

EV/EBITDA is another way to measure the value of a company. This metric has its advantages and disadvantages over P/E. Click the above links for more information which is beyond the scope of this article.

Garbage in, garbage out

I do not trust most financial statements from emerging countries especially the smaller companies. Watch out for fraudulent data. Most metrics can be manipulated. Recently I have a US stock that lost 18% in one day due to the SEC's investigation of its financial data.

The announced earnings may not be reflected in the financial statements that you use from the web. Ensure your data is up-to-date by checking the date of the financial statements. Seeking Alpha has transcripts for the earnings announcements that would save you a trip to attend the companies' quarterly meetings.

Sector and entire market
You can find the value of a sector using the P/E of an ETF for that sector. It is similar for the market. For example, use SPY (an ETF simulating the S&P 500 index). If it is lower than the average (15 to me), then most likely the market is good value and a buy signal. It is one of the many hints for market timing.

Where to use P/E
Each highlight of the following corresponds to one of my books. Click it for the description of the strategy.

My book on top-down approach starts with a safe market, then sector analysis, fundamental analysis, intangible analysis and optionally technical analysis. P/E is one of the many metrics in fundamental analysis.

There are many styles of investing. In general, fundamental analysis is important when you hold the stock longer.

- P/E is important in Long-Term Swing, Dividend Investing, Retirees and Conservative Strategies.

- My max value is 20 and 25 for tech companies. I ignore it if they have high potential for appreciation that could be indicated by insider purchases.
- P/E is moderately important in Short-Term Swing and Sector Rotation.
- P/E is the least important in Momentum Strategy and Day Trading.

Summary

Again, one metric should not dictate the reason to trade a stock. Compare the company P/E to its industry average and its own five-year average. In addition, many industries have cycles. If you buy it at the peak of the industry, the P/E may mislead you. Besides fundamental analysis, you need to consider intangible analysis and time the entry / exit point by using technical analysis. Intangible analysis evaluates information that cannot be summarized into numeric metrics such as a lawsuit pending.

True P/E

"EV/EBITDA" is available from Yahoo!Finance and other sources. The true EY is "1/Ture PE". I call it "True" for the lack of a better term as it represents the financial situation of the company better. This could be the most important metric for many.

Earnings can be manipulated. For example, the company management can lower the P/E ratio by buying back its stocks. In this case the earnings per share is boosted but in reality there is no change in the company's financial fundamentals. The true P/E takes into consideration of the reduced cash. EBITBA stands for "Earnings Before Interest, Taxes, Depreciation, and Amortization".

Be careful when EV or "EBITDA" is negative. Most likely you should avoid the stocks with a negative EV.

Pow P/E

You should use the described "EV/EBITDA" and hence "Pow P/E" can be ignored. There are some cases that Pow P/E is better: 1. "EV/EBITDA" may not be available for reasons such as negative asset and 2. Use of Forward Earnings instead of Earnings based on the last twelve months. The following is an exercise on how I simulate it from Finviz.com with metrics that are readily available.

I modified P/E to take care of cash and debts. I use my last name due to being easier to distinguish from P/E and it has nothing to do with my ego.

Pow P/E = (P - Cash per Share + Debt per Share) / (Earning - Interest gained per share - Interest paid per share)

To illustrate this, the stock price is $10 and it has $2 in cash (actually cash and securities). The real price of the stock is $8. When we ignore the cash and debt, we have to ignore the interests gained and paid.

Many companies park the cash in bank accounts that do not generate much interest today. Some cash-rich companies such as MSFT and CSCO have better P/Es after excluding the cash per share.

My official definition:

The above is for simple illustration. I need to expand it here.

Pow P/E = (P - net short-term asset per share + liability per share) / (Earning - Gain from short-term asset per share - interest paid per share)

You can get the short-term asset and liability from the financial statement and divide it by the number of shares. In addition, pension liability should be included in the liability. As before, I prefer the expected earnings.

In this calculation, P could be negative and so is E. It is misleading when both are negative to generate a positive Pow P/E. Interpret the number accordingly.

When either one is negative, most likely the fundamental is not correct. There are many examples of bankruptcy when both of them are negative. Avoid companies with negative earnings and high debt unless there is a good reason such as a turnaround. The previous GM was one of the examples in this situation.

Stock buyback could reduce the outstanding shares. It would improve most metrics that use earnings per share such as P/E. However, if the company borrows money to buy stocks, it would deteriorate the debt metrics or its cash position. Pow P/E handles this situation well if the financial statement is up-to-date.

It is similar to the concept "Earnings before taxes and interests". If you can find the P/E based on this, use it. Mine is easy to calculate from Cash/Share provided by Finviz.com. Ignore my ignorance if someone already uses this simple concept.

Using IBM as an example to calculate Pow P/E based on 12/31/2013 financial statements.

Pow P/E = (187.57 - 10.62 + 98.00) / 15.06 = 18.26

Take out the gain from short-term assets and the interest paid for simplicity.

P/E is not always important

The following is my test from 1/2/2020 to 10/14/2020. RSP is similar to SPY except that the stocks in the S&P 500 index are equally weighed. EY (= E/P) is Expected Earnings Yield and there is no stocks with EY less than 0. DY is Dividend Yield. GPE is the growth of P/E. As in my book, I use annualized returns and dividends are not included. This test does not mean a lot, but it tells us what these metrics behave during this period, or it indicates **Value is not a good metric in this period**, and it may indicate momentum is better in this period.

It is very rough testing and there are many limitations in the database. However, the conclusion is quite convincing to me and some are opposite to the contrary beliefs. For example, I expected the higher EY the better, but not in this test.

	Annualized Return	Indicator	Comment
RSP 500 All	-2%		
EY (top 10)	-54%	Bad	Contrary
GPE (top 10)	-20%	Bad	Contrary
Select All or top 100.			
DY = 0	16%	Good	
DY (top 100)	-19%	Bad	
DY / 1 and 2	2%		

EY 3 to 4		15%	Good	Second best
EY 2 to 3		6%	Good	Third best
EY 1 to 2		31%	Good	Best
EY 0 to 1		-39%	Bad`	

I use some metrics from a service I subscribe that are not included here. Two major metrics of this subscription have a return of around 20%. Most subscriptions including the free Fidelity (to some extent) give you three composite scores: Total, Fundamental and Timing. I wish to check out the recent predictability of Fidelity's Equity Summary Score if they have a historical database. Most of them take out the delisted and /or bankrupt companies in their databases.

#Filler

Do not complain on the examples are old. If I updated them, I have to continue to update them every 3 years. I have a life too.

Do not complain on my unpolished English unless your native tongue is not Chinese and write books in Chinese. LOL.

#Filler

People with power + People with money = Corruption

2   *Fundamental metrics*

ROE

Return of equity (ROE = Net Income / Equity) could be the most important financial indicator to determine how well the management is doing their job. However, in recent years, this metric has been over-used and loses its prediction reliability.

The company's return on equity for at least the last five years would indicate how the stock price endures major financial downturns as well as upturns.

Comparing the ROE to the average ROE for the sector is a good indicator on how well the company is managed compared to its peers. Some sectors including utilities have low average ROEs.

Market Cap (Capitalization)

Market Cap = Total no. of outstanding shares * share price

I recommend the beginners buy U.S. stocks with a market cap greater than 800 M (million). Here are the current conventions (everyone's convention is different) and they should be adjusted to inflation.

Class	Market Cap (million)
Nano Cap	< $50M
Micro Cap	$50M to $250M
Small Cap	$250M to $1B (billion)
Mid Cap	$1B to $10B
Large Cap (Blue Chip)	$10B to $50B
Mega Cap	>50B

The higher the cap is, usually the less risky the stock would be. Nano Cap and Micro Cap are reserved for speculators or owners of the companies. Small Cap and Mid Cap are for knowledgeable investors as most institutional investors would skip these stocks in these caps especially Small Cap. Large Cap, Mega Cap and some Mid Cap are the stocks traded by institutional investors. They are thoroughly researched continuously.

My metrics

My current favorites are Forward P/E, PEG, Fidelity's Equity Summary Score, Short % of outstanding shares, Free Cash Flow, ROE and Debt Load / Equity.

In addition, I use many summarized metrics from different sources. For example, one of my subscription services gives me a composite rank for fundamentals and another one for momentum.   To illustrate, click here for Blue Chip Growth which is no longer free for stock analysis. Enter IBM as the stock symbol. As of 2/2013, it gives C for a Total Grade, D for Quantity Grade and B for Fundamental Grade. The Total Grade is usually a composite grade of other grades.

Use the metrics to screen through the stocks to reduce the number of stocks for further consideration.

Mid, high and low values of common metrics

Metric	Mid Range	Low Range	High Range
P/E (last 12 months)	< 10	>40	< 4
Price / Cash Flow	< 12	>30	< 4
Price / Sales	< 2.5	>3	< .2
Price / Book	< 2.0	>4	< .2
PEG	< 1.5	>2	< .2

High Range means good values (although in this table it means low numbers), but sometimes it is too good to be true. Low Range means bad values. To illustrate, many internet stocks in 2000 had P/E over 40 (bad) while a neglected bargain stock has a P/E of 3 (supposed to be good). A bargain could also mean they could have some hidden problems. In reality, I prefer the Mid Range. Using P/E to illustrate, it should be between 4 and 10. Adjust the range according to your personal tolerance and the current market conditions. If the market trend is up, you may want to relax the range to 5 to 12 for example otherwise you cannot find too many stocks for further evaluation.

These values are my selections based on data for about 10 years. They are used for predicting the performance of a stock in a year; review the ranges every 6 months in the current market.

The metrics with the high-range and mid-range values offer better predictions for the stock price appreciation. From the above table, the stocks with the low-range values have a better chance than other stocks to lose money in a year or so. Some favorable numbers could be high values instead of low values such as ROE.

However, the range values could change. When the market favors momentum or you do not keep stocks for less than a month or so, the momentum metrics including PEG and price growth could be better predictors. We need to check to see whether the current market favors which metrics: Value or Growth – some web sites and subscription services identify the current favorite. In addition, the performance of each metric should be evaluated every 3 to 6 months. In addition, new range values need to be adjusted with the above table.

Fundamental metrics take a longer time (about 6-12 months vs. 1 month for momentum metrics) for the performance to materialize. The metrics in the above table besides PEG are all fundamental metrics. Except for financial stocks, P/B is always worthless.

Examples of searching with high range values

Stocks with low-range values for most metrics (such as 40 in P/E in the above table) could be risky. Hence, select the stocks with the mid-range value (e.g. 10 for P/E). Avoid the low-range values indicated by the metrics.

Here is one example of selecting stocks with high range values of P/E and P/B. Most likely, you will not find too many stocks with these criteria.

$E > 0$ and
$P/E < 4$ and
$P/B < .2$

E is earning per share and we need the company to be profitable.

High range values could indicate something is wrong with the company, e.g. a lawsuit pending. I would consider a P/E of less than 4 is suspicious. However, very small companies are often neglected by the market, so they could be solid companies. Don't forget to do your due diligence and spend more time in thoroughly evaluating the stock and its industry.

The stocks with the low-range values have a greater chance of losing money in the next year or so. That is proven statistically as a group despite some exceptions. AMZN[2] is not a valued stock by its high P/E or its high P/B. However, if the company is investing for the future by building infrastructure and capturing the market share, you may ignore these unfavorable metrics. Personally I prefer fundamentally sound companies today.

Note. P/B is not a good metric for established companies and / or companies with a lot of research such as IBM. Many metric formulae are outdated due to ignoring intellectual properties, patents and market appeals such as brand names.

Example of a search for mid-range values

E > 0 and
P/E < 10 and
P/E > 4

In this case, you only include companies with positive earnings and P/Es within the range from 4 to 10 exclusively. You should find many companies with the mid-range values of P/Es.

Add other filters such as minimum price, market cap and average volume. If you do not find too many stocks, relax your criteria (start with mid-range values in the table), and vice versa to limit the number of stocks. If you usually find stocks with a screen but not today, it usually means that the market is over-valued and that you cannot find many bargain stocks.

Again, it is the first step to narrow down the number of stocks to be analyzed. Your metrics will not cover stocks with special situations. For example, IBM always has had a high Price/Book value for as long as I can remember and therefore it does not mean it should be excluded.

The searches based on fundamental metrics help us to narrow stocks for further evaluation. Occasionally I abandon the scoring system for some stocks under special conditions.

Compare company's metrics to its sector averages
This could be the most powerful comparison: Compare Apples to Apples.

You may want to compare the metrics of a company to the averages of that sector. The average of supermarket's P/S is extremely low and hence it has no meaning to compare a supermarket's P/S to most other sectors. Some sectors like utilities need high debt to run a utility company.

However, when the average P/E or other metric of a sector is suddenly lower than its historical average, it could mean that sector is out-of-favor and/or the sector is having a better value.

This following table compares Apple to its sector and a retail sector on a specific date for illustration. All the metrics will change.

Metric	Apple	Computer	Retail
P/E	11	19	24
(5 year average)	16	17	15
PEG	.6	N/A	1.4
Price /Cash Flow	9.4	8.1	9.2
Price /Book	3.3	3.0	3.6
EPS Growth	-6%	-42%	2.6%
(last 5 years)	62%	45%	11%
Operating Margin	20%	15%	8%
ROE	30%	14%	19%
Debt / Equity	2%	7%	88%
Inventory Turnover	76%	53%	4.55x

From the above table, some metrics only make sense for an industrial sector (Computer for Apple). In this case, you may want to compare AAPL to Computer, and not to Retail.

"Debt / Equity" indicates that the retail sector needs to borrow more than the computer sector for example. Of course retail stores has high Inventory Turnover.

Top down approach

First, compare whether the market is risky. Second, select the best sector; there are many sites including Finviz.com to select the best sector. Then compare the fundamental metrics of the major stocks within that sector.

Some metrics do not apply

Using financial institutions as an example, usually P/B is more useful than P/CF. However, the quality of a loan (not a metric here) is more important than all metrics as we found out in 2007. P/S is more important for retails. However, the expected P/E is most important for most other sectors.

When you believe a sector is the currently best (a criterion available in many screeners), select the best stocks in this sector.

Compare metrics to its five-year average

If the company's five-year average of P/E (available in Fidelity and many other sites) is 20 and today it is 10. It is 100% under-valued by this standard. Also, you may want to try other metrics such as debt/equity and compare it to the five-year average.

Growth Metrics

The growth metrics are growth rates of the stock price, sales, earnings, etc. They are useful for growth investors.

Even for value investors, the earnings growth rate is very important, as most stocks with substantial gains have increased their earnings growth first. If the earnings has grown but the price remains the same (i.e. PEG), then the potential for price appreciation will be higher and most likely it will return to the historical average P/E.

Momentum Metrics

Momentum metrics is part of growth. The rates of increase of the stock price, the volume... are the major metrics. Earnings revision is another one especially in earnings announcement seasons (usually 4 times a year).

Fidelity and many subscription services provide a composite rank with name Timely or similar name. The following could be part of this Timely score: SMA-50, Q-Q sales increase and recent price appreciation. In my momentum portfolio, I use these metrics and ignore all the other metrics as my average holding period is less than 30 days for momentum strategies.

Insiders' buying

Insiders sell their stocks for many reasons. When insiders buy a lot of their companies' stocks at market prices, take notice. Insiders know better than anyone about the health of their companies and their industries.

Select Insiders' purchases from one of the available sites such as Finviz.com. Ignore the option exercises. I prefer the high ratios of Net Total Purchase Value / Market Cap and the purchases by more than one insider. Be careful that the insiders purchase the stocks after selling a similar amount of stock in a brief time span.

OpenInsider is a good site for this info.
InsiderSights is a good one too with more capable tools that would take more time to learn.

Where to get the metrics
You can get this information from the web site with no or low cost such as Finviz.com, your broker's site, AAII (very low cost) and Fidelity.

The following subscriptions are at a little higher cost but they are still less than $1,000 per year: Value Line, IBD, Zacks, Vector Vest and Stock Screen 123. Many data from different vendors are duplicated such as P/E. You will save time by concentrating on one or two sources.

Many vendors provide a composite metric such as a value metric to cover P/E, debt... and a timing metric to cover Technical Analysis indicators, PEG, price appreciation rate...

Short % is a useful metric available in Finviz.com. For Fidelity customers, you can click on Research and then Stock. Enter the stock name, and then click on Detailed. I find Fidelity's Analysts' Opinions quite useful.

Finviz.com provides a lot of useful information free of charge. It also provides a screen function. The 'Help' button describes Finviz's functions and all the metrics monitored.

Other sources are: Insider Cow, NASDAQ Guru Analysis ...

Monitor the recent performance of the metrics
The predictability of most metrics has proven not to perform consistently as many investors and fund managers found out. My theory is that the specific metric works better in some market conditions than others. To test which ones work better currently, check their performance in the last three months and use those that perform well. This is what my scoring system in the book Scoring Stocks is based on.

Why some metrics fail sometimes
Most investors are using metrics to screen stocks, but few are successful consistently. Some investment companies have top analysts dedicated to projects looking for the right strategy. My guesses why they fail are:

1. Metrics need to be monitored to see its effectiveness on current market conditions.

2. Besides fundamental metrics, there are many intangibles.

3. When they have too many followers on the same metrics, they will not work such as ROE in the last several years.

4. Fundamentals need time (at least 6 months) to reflect the value of the stock. You're swimming against the tide as a fundamentalist. Trading momentum stocks using basic fundamentals will not work.

5. Watch out 'Garbage in and garbage out'. Some emerging countries do not have an organization similar to SEC to ensure the integrity of the financial statements of a company and some audit firms are being paid to cover their eyes. Even though there are frauds in some U.S. companies and with their auditors.

6. The metrics may be derived from obsolete financial statements. Check out the date. The most updated one could be available from the company's website.

7. Some companies borrow a lot of money to dress up the metrics such as P/E and ROE. They will look good short-term but not long-term. Ensure the debt/equity has not been increased recently for this purpose. I recall one utility spin-off had incredible fundamentals except the debt load. It is so high that all these fundamentals will deteriorate in the future due to servicing its high debts.

Footnote

[1] The stocks are classified into sector and then sectors are divided into industries (same as sub sectors). For example, oil is a sector and oil exploration and oil services are industries under the oil sector. For simplicity, I intermix the terms here as many sectors do not need further sub classifications for this discussion.

[2] AMZN is not a value stock by any standard. As of 1/1/2013, its P/E (from last 12 months) is 157 and P/B is 15. Both fall far into my low-range values. Its price rises from 256 from 1/1/13 to 270 today (1/22/13). Today its P/E is ridiculously over 3,000. The investors are betting AMZN's internet sales will take over the concrete stores and its investors do not care about profit but rather for market share. Does it sound familiar in the internet era? Its price momentum is indicated positively by any chart. It may be a good stock for traders, but it is too risky for a swing trader and a long-term investor like me (yes, I wear two hats). I do not short stocks in a rising market, but this could be an exception.

Afterthoughts

*   The only recommendation from a very popular investment book I read is to select stocks by the return of equity (ROE). I will save you the time and money to read that book. I read the entire book in an hour at Barnes and Noble's and it saved me some money / time, not to mention cutting down trees for that book. Basically it does not work today.

- DAL has an interesting Debt / Equity of over -1000% due to the negative equity. For a comparison, you may want to use Debt / ABS(Equity).

- Once in a while, I found the financial data was not consistent from different sources. Try to check out any discrepancy in the dates of the financial data of your sources. The financial statements from the company websites usually have the most updated data.

- Current Ratio = Current Asset / Current Liability. If it is below 1, then the company is having a tough time in meeting its current cash obligations.

- Dividend Yield is a valid metric for matured companies. I do not use it to evaluate growth companies or companies that need to plow back cash for research and development.

- If you use Finviz.com, you find three margins: profit, gross and operating. I prefer to use profit margin that is more useful for most companies. The other two may be relevant in some sectors.

  http://www.investopedia.com/terms/p/profitmargin.asp
  http://www.investopedia.com/terms/g/grossmargin.asp
  http://www.investopedia.com/terms/o/operatingmargin.asp

  Use Wikipedia for more description.

- Enron had millions in profits but negative cash flows. Earnings can be manipulated but not the cash flows.

  Insiders' selling usually does not cause any alarm unless excessively. Most insiders sell most of the stocks they have before these companies go bankrupt. Just common sense!

- Why fundamentals are important. (http://seekingalpha.com/article/1612442-its-shorting-season)

  On the same day when this article was published, RVLT was up 10% due to increasing sales in the earnings conference. However, the company is still not profitable. It shows how tough shorting is even with good arguments. That's why do not expect every purchase is profitable. However, with the educated guesses, you should beat the market in the long run.

- Due to my ignorance, limited time or my short period of holding stocks, I have not used intrinsic value that often.

  Book value is different from intrinsic value. Book value is calculated by summing up the values of all pieces of a company such as a building and all equipment.

  Intrinsic value is the real value of a company. When two companies have the same book value and market cap, the company that generates more profit than the other one usually has a higher intrinsic value. When the intrinsic value is higher than the stock price, it is underpriced in theory.

  The following link provides more info on intrinsic value.
  http://en.wikipedia.org/wiki/Intrinsic_value_%28finance%29

Filler: Happy Mother's Day Poem

The following is my translation from poet Yu's work in Chinese. I changed some words as some could not be translated effectively. I added the title "Two Cries".

-------- Two Cries -----------

I cried at two unforgettable times in my life.

The first time when I came to this world.
The second time when you left this world.

The first time I did not know but from your mouth.
The second time you did not know but from my heart.

Between these two crises, we had endless laughs.
For the last 30 years, we had joyful laughs that had been repeated, repeated...

You treasured every laugh.
I cherish every laugh for the rest of my life.

3   Finviz parameters

Most metrics are described in Finviz (via Help), Investopedia and/or Wikipedia and my chapter on P/E. The following are my personal comments and why I feel some metrics are more important than others. Compare the ratios to the companies in the same sector and also its averages from the last 5 years.

From your browser, enter Finviz.com. Enter a symbol (I used ABEO for discussion). A chart is displayed with the prices and volumes for the last nine months. SMAs (Single Moving Average) are displayed sometimes with other technical indicators. Intraday, Daily and Weekly options are available.

Besides the metrics described next and the chart, it describes what the company does, analysts' recommendations (I prefer Fidelity's Equity Summary), insiders' trading and articles that are good for qualitative analysis. "Financial Highlights and Statements" are materials for more in-depth analysis and they were more important decades ago when most financial ratios had not been calculated for you.

The following metrics are roughly based on the flow of Finviz from top to bottom and left to right. I skip those metrics that I believe are not too important. You can also place your cursor on the metric to have the description from Finviz. Some metrics are left blank when they are zero or negative. For example, the Debt/Equity of YRCW in 1/2019 is blank (same as null) due to Equity being negative. From Yahoo!Finance, it has a total debt of 888M.

- **Index**. Most of us trade stocks in the three major exchanges in the USA. Stocks listed over-the-counter are too risky for most of us. Skip the stocks in local exchanges and foreign exchanges if you are not an expert on these stocks. I screen the stocks and then ignore the stocks that are not in the Dow, NASDAC and Amex.

- **Market Cap** (MC). To me, stocks below 50M are risky even they could be very profitable. Ensure the Avg. Volume is at least 10,000 shares and / or your order is less than 1% of the average volume. Some small stocks are controlled by the owners and have small volumes. In this case you cannot sell your stock easily.

Float = Outstanding shares – Insider shares.

Usually it does not matter as they are typically the same. However, it does for small companies with large insider shares. Most of these owners do not want to sell their family businesses and hence they reduce the chance of being acquired entirely or partly for good prices.

- If **Forward P/E** (a.k.a. Expected P/E) is not provided, use the P/E which is based on the last 12 months. Alternatively, calculate the E by using the E from P/E and multiplying it by its growth rate. It may not be seasonally adjusted. I prefer Expected P/E (or called Forward P/E) as it provides a better predictability power from my limited research.

  Finviz.com leaves the P/E and some other metrics blank if the earnings are negative.

  Compare the P/E or Forward P/E with the average P/E for the sector and its average P/E for the last 5 years that are available from Fidelity.com. Some sectors have high P/Es. If the sector is cyclical, the earnings could be affected.

- **Cash / share**. It is used to calculate Pow P/E and Pow EY. To illustrate, if the stock is $10 and it has $10 cash / share without debt (i.e. Debt/Equity = 0), most likely it is underpriced as you can get the whole company for nothing. You should find out why the price is so low.

- **Dividend %** is useful for income investors. The payout ratio should not be more than 30% except for matured companies.

- **Recs**. Select stocks with 1 or 2. Do not base your stock selection on this recommendation alone. There have been many bad recommendations that could cost you a fortune in losses.

- **PEG** is a measure of the growth of P/E and hence a growth metric. The lower is better if earnings are positive. If earnings are negative, then the reverse is true. It is a defect in using P/E and PEG and that's why I recommend EY (Earnings Yield), earnings yield, and EYG, earnings yield growth.

If there are two companies with the same P/E, the one with a better PEG ratio is better. If two companies have the same E/P, the company with higher Earnings Growth (EPS Q/Q) would be favorable.

- **P/B**. Book value (= Total Assets − Total Liabilities) may not include intangible asset such as patents. Do not trust it 100%, so is ROE which is based on book value. Negative equity is possible when Total Liabilities is more than Total Assets.

- **P/S**. If two companies are unprofitable, this ratio can be used. I prefer profitable companies.

- **P/FCF**. I prefer it to be greater than 0 and less than 50 for value investors. Most metrics can be manipulated easily, but not this one.

- **Sales Q/Q** reduces the seasonal deviation. To illustrate, retail sales for the Christmas season should be compared it to the same season in prior year.

- **EPS Q/Q**. Same as above. I prefer the growth of EPS over Sales. The Q/Q ratios are growth metrics. When a company terminates its unprofitable product(s), its Sales Q/Q could be down but its EPS Q/Q could be up. In 2000, many internet companies had great Sales Q/Qs but negative EPS Q/Qs.

  Q/Q comparison (quarter to quarter) takes out the seasonal variations.

  When the company buys its own shares, EPS could be misleading as E is fixed and the number of shares is reduced.

- Positive **Insider** Transactions are favorable. So is Institutional Transactions as institutional investors move the market.

- Insider Own, Shares Outstanding and Shares **Float** determine the number of shares that are available for trading. A small Float with a high Insider Own limits trading and the stock should be avoided in most cases. Compare your trade position for the stock to the Avg. Volume.

- **Profit Margin**. I prefer it over Gross Margin and Oper. Margin which does not include interest expenses and taxes. When you sell software, the Gross Margin is high as it does not include development, support and marketing, etc. A retail store has low Gross Margin.

- **Short Float**. I prefer it to be less than 10%. If it is greater than 10%, the shorters could find something wrong with the company. If it is over 25%, I would check the fundamentals. If they are good, I would buy expecting a short squeeze potential. It has been risky but proven to be profitable for me.

- Technical metrics: **SMA-20**, SMA-50 and SMA-200. If they are all positive, it means the trend is good. SMA-20 is short-term trend and SMA-200 is a long-term trend. If you are short-term swing investor, stick with short-term trend and vice versa. The first two are momentum grades.

- **RSI(14)**. If it greater than 60% (some use 65%), it is overbought. If it is under 30% (some use 25%), it is under bought. Use it as a reference. Most stocks making new heights are always overbought.

- **Beta**. A volatile stock fluctuates a lot. It is good for short-term traders. A beta of 1 means the stock would fluctuate with the market and more volatile if it is higher than 1.

- Management performance is measured by **ROA.** It is also judged by **Analysts' Rec.** and Institutional Ownership (except for small companies). The confidence of their own ability, the company and its sector is measured by Insider Ownership and Insider Purchases.

- Avoid all bankrupting companies at all cost. Debt/Equity, P/FCF, Cash/Sh., P/B, Profit Margin, Forward P/E, Short Float, RSI(14), SMA20% and SMA50 would give us hints. Need to summarize all the info and study many other factors such as obsoleting products (including drugs).

- Unless you have concrete information, do not buy stocks a week or so before the Earnings Date.

More useful information:

- The price chart. It has a lot of features such as the resistance line. Some charts include technical indicators such as double top (a bearish warning) and double bottom (a bullish sign).
- Description under the symbol. It briefly describes what the company (sector and industry) does and its country of registration. You want to buy a stock within a sector that is trending up. For example according to Finviz, Apple is in the Consumer Goods sector and the Electronic Equipment industry.

  If you do not want to buy foreign stocks, skip it if it is not listed in the US exchange.
- Articles on the company for qualitative analysis.
- Insider trading. Pay more attention to the insider purchases at market prices. Use common sense.
- The last line lets you open Yahoo!Finance and other sites.

Your broker's web site

Your broker web site should have plenty of tools to analyze stocks. As of Dec., 2018, Fidelity lets you use their extensive research free by opening an account with no position restriction. I describe some of their metrics that should be beneficial to your research.

- Equity Summary Score. Potentially good buy when it is 7 (8 for conservative investors) or higher. With some exceptions, you should avoid or short stocks if the rank is 0 to 3. The stocks ranking from 4 to 6 could be turnaround candidates if they are supported by good Q/Q Earnings and/or good news.

- The 5-year averages are good yardsticks. For example, in Dec., 2018, C's P/E is about 9 and the average is 14. Hence it is a value buy.

Other sources

If you have other sources (most require a subscription or being a customer), skip the stocks that have one of the failing grades. Ignore them if there is a new positive development such as increased insider purchases.

Vendor	Grade	Fail
Fidelity	Equity Summary Score	< 4
IBD	Composite	< 50
Value Line	Proj. 3-5 yr. return. Also its composite rating	< 3%
Zacks	Rank	5
Vector Vest	VST	< 0.7

You may be able to find Value Line and IBD at the library. Try out the free stock reports from your broker first. Finviz and Seeking Alpha should have articles (now fewer free articles) on stocks and earnings conferences, which could have important information after separating from the "welcome" and garbage talks.

Compare the P/E to the average P/E for last five years in Fidelity.

Yahoo!Finance has several good info and it is free. When negative values such as Equity in Finviz.com, you need to use this site for the total debt. "EV/EBITDA" is better than "P/E" as it considers debt.

MarketWatch.com has many articles on the market in general and personal investing.

If the stock is closed to the Earnings Date (found in Finviz.com), you should avoid trading the stock and/or consult Zacks' ranking which is currently free for individual stocks.

Section II: Beyond fundamentals

Buy stocks based on appreciation potential, not based on when and what you traded the stock for.

1   Qualitative analysis

This is the last analysis to evaluate a stock fundamentally. Then the next is technical analysis which is used to find an entry point (also the exit point) for the stock.

Where quantitative analysis fails and why

I find that some stocks with high scores fail and some stocks with low scores succeed as indicated by my performance monitor. The scoring system still works statistically for the majority of my stocks.

- Reasons why stocks with low scores perform in addition to the described in the last discussion:

    o Over-sold. The institutional investors (fund managers and pension managers) dump them first, and then followed by the retail investors. These big boys will buy these stocks back when they reach a certain price range. RSI(14), a technical indicator described in the Technical Analysis article, is useful to detect these over-sold stocks. This metric is readily available from many sites including Finviz.

    o The falling price (P) improves all fundamental metrics that have the stock price such as P/E and P/Sales. However, the trend of the price is down.

    o The company has turned around after fixing its problems and/or the market has changed for the better.

    o The current problems have been resolved but not known to the public. It includes resolving a lawsuit, a new product, a new drug, or a new big order, etc.

    o Heavy purchases by insiders. The company's outlook is not shown in its financial statements. Sometimes the insiders hide them so they can buy more of their companies' stocks for themselves.

- Reasons why stocks with high scores plunge in addition to the described in the previous discussion:

- The company's fundamentals and its prices have reached or closed to the maximum heights. They have no way to go but down. It is particularly true when the stock's timing rating is at or close to the highest point. TTWO that I gifted to my grandchildren had been 5-baggers in the last few years before it plunged in 2018.

- It has reached its potential value (or a target price) and it is time for many investors to take profits.

- Sector (or stock) rotation, particularly by institutional investors who drive the market.

- The outlook of the company, its sector and/or the market is deteriorating.

- The stock price may be manipulated. There are many reasons to pump and dump the stock. Shorting is not recommended for most investors. However, some experienced shorters make money consistently when they find valid reasons to short stocks.

- It could be due to a new serious lawsuit, a new competing product or drug, canceling a major order, etc.

- Downgrade by analysts. They could spot some bad events such as product defects, violations of regulations or accounting errors / frauds. The downgrades are more important than the upgrades that could have conflict of interest.

- The financial statement had been manipulated. The SEC may ask for an investigation.

- Does not meet the consensus in earnings announcements, which have been over-acted by many investors.

Qualitative Analysis

We need to do further analysis after the quantitative analysis and the intangible analysis. Check out the company's prospects. Check out the date of the article and any potential hidden agenda items from the author. Older articles may not have much value.

Be careful on 'pump-and-dump' manipulation written by authors with a hidden agenda. It has happened especially on small companies before even SeekingAlpha.com has its share. Here was an article that tells you to sell NHTC. There was another article to tell you to buy ARTX. They fit into this category.

The sources are:

1. Seeking Alpha.
    Type the symbol of the company to read as many articles on the company as you have time for. Today this site and many other similar sites require you to be a paid member. If you cannot find too many good articles, check out the articles from Finviz.com.

    Recently, I read an article on AMD and it said it may have good profits in the next two years with the game consoles. The outlook of a company is not shown by any fundamental metric which are far from favorable.

    Following a well-known writer, I bought IBM without doing my due diligence (my fault). It went down more than 15% quickly. You can learn from my mistakes.

2. Research reports from your broker. If you do not find many, open an account with one that provides such reports. Some subscription services such as Value Line provide such reports.

3. Yahoo!Finance board. Most comments are garbage. However, once in a while you find some great insights. Usually you cannot find any info from other sources on tiny companies.

4. The most recent company's financial statements. They are usually available in the company's web site.

5. 10-Ks from Edgar database (www.sec.gov/edgar). Check out new products and its potential competition, key customers, order backlog, research and development and pending lawsuits.

6. Check out the outlook of the sector the company is in and the company itself.

7. Check out its competitors.

8. Some companies are run by stupid people. I received information via my email saying that my mutual fund account could be treated as an abandoned property. I have been cashing dividend checks every year and why it would be considered as an abandoned property. I called them right away to close my account.

   The tall and handsome guy presented articulately how he would turn around JC Penny on TV. I could tell you right away that all his tricks had been tried by other companies such as Sears, and most did not work. The intelligent investor does not care about how handsome, how articulated, how rich his family is and how many advanced degrees from prestigious colleges he possesses. If he does not make sense, do not buy his preaching and his company's stock. [Update. As of 5/2020, J.C. Penny filed for bankruptcy protection. If you had this stock and my book, you would have saved a lot of money minus $10 for my book!]

9. Check out its business model. Some business models do not make business sense and some do. Here are some samples.

- Giving razors makes sense, as the customers have to buy the blades eventually and keep on buying blades for life.

- Supermarket M lowers prices on common merchandises such as Coke and it works. They make money by providing inferior (but profitable to them) products that you cannot compare prices easily such as meat and seafood.

  Eventually there will be a supermarket in my area to satisfy me both in price and quality or at least make a good tradeoff.

- Last week it had been brutally hot. I went to a Barns & Noble's bookstore to enjoy reading the updated books and enjoyed the air conditioning. When there are more free loaders like me than customers, this business model does not work.

2   Intangibles

I give a score for each stock I evaluate. Occasionally some stocks with poor scores have great returns and vice versa. In general, the scoring system works. It has been proven statistically and repeatedly from my limited data. I stick with high-score stocks with some exceptions.

Once in a while I change my scoring system to adept to the current market conditions. To illustrate, the market bottom phase and early recovery phase of the market cycle favor value more than momentum/growth. Here are some of my recent experiences and strategies:

- I double or even triple my stake on stocks with high scores. In the longer term, they are consistently better winners than the average with some minor exceptions. Besides the score, look at the intangibles described in this article.

- Watch out for the stocks with outrageous metrics such as P/E of 4 or less. It could be a big lawsuit pending, an expiration of some important drugs, etc. Also, be careful with scores in the top 5%. From my statistics they do worse than the average. Their problems may not show up in the current financial statements.

- The technology of a tech company cannot be ignored even though the company's P/E is high, that I set a limit of 25 instead of 20 for other stocks. The value of the company's technology and patents will not be shown in the fundamental metrics except from the insiders' purchases at market prices.

  For example, IDCC rose about 40% in 2 days. There was a rumor that Google was buying the company and/or Apple was bidding on it too for its mobile technology. Charts usually would flag this kind of event. For non-charters, use the SMA-20% from Finviz.com. They could be a little late as the charts depend on rising prices.

- There are more acquisitions during a market bottom (same as early recovery). The companies with good technologies are bargains and the larger companies especially those in the same sector understand their values better than most of us. These potentially profitable companies will not be shown by their scores explicitly. When corporations have a lot of cash or the credit is cheap, they are looking for smaller companies to acquire or invest in. The candidates are usually small, beaten up, low-priced and having valuable intangible assets such as technologies, customer base and/or market share of the industry segment. 2009-2012 was just the perfect environment and the before that was 2003. I had at least one stock in each of these periods and they appreciated a lot.

- The opposite is Netflix, Chipotle in 1/2012 and Amazon in 1/2013. They are over-priced by any measure. However, the mentioned companies are investing in the future. The shorters (not for beginners) are having a tough time in making money on them. When their P/Es are higher than 40, watch out. Some could be OK in the mentioned companies, but usually they are not. Do not follow the herd and your due diligence will verify whether they will still go up.

  Use reward/risk ratio. It is based on experiences. To illustrate, if the company has the equal chance to go up 50% and go down 25%, then it is a buy and the reverse is a sell.

- The retail investor just cannot possibly know about some events until they actually happen. For example, ATSC dropped 15% due to losing its second primary customer. Fundamentals cannot predict this kind of events. Charts can signal this event, but usually they are too late unless you watch the chart all day long.

- After a quick run up, TZOO plunged due to missing some negligible earning expectations. It seems the original climbing prices already had the perfect earnings growth built-in.

  I do not understand why a company loses 10% of its market cap when it missed by 1% of the expected earnings. It could be driven up and down by the institutional investors. Evaluate the stock before you act. Acting opposite to the institutional investors could be very profitable for the right stocks. Avoid trading before the earnings announcement dates (about 4 times a year for most stocks).

- The following are not easily found in financial statements: industry outlook, patents, good will, market share, competition, product margins, management quality, lawsuits pending, potential acquisition, pension obligations, advertising icons, etc. That is why we need to read articles on the stocks in our buy list or our purchased stocks.

- The financial data could be fraudulent or manipulated. I do not trust small companies in emerging markets. I have been burned too many times. Check the company names such as foreign names, ADR and their headquarter addresses (from the company profile in most investing sites).

  Earnings can be manipulated with many accounting tricks. A jump in earnings from last year may not be as rosy as it looks. Check the footnotes in the accounting statements. I usually skip financial statements unless I have big purchases in mind as my time in investing is limited.

- Cash flow cannot be easily manipulated. It is good information whether the company will survive or not, but to me it does not prove to be a consistent predictor in my tests, but an important red flag for companies on their way to bankruptcy. Examples abound.

- Repeated one-time, non-recurring and extraordinary charges are red flags.

- Stay away from the companies where the CEOs are over-compensated. As of 7- 2013, Activision's CEO raised his salary by more than 600%, while the stock lost its value in double digits.

- Value stocks. Need to know why they become value stocks (i.e. fewer investors want to own) even they are financially sound. For example, there are two primary reasons for the downfall of a supplier to Apple: 1. Apple is declining in sales and 2. Apple is switching suppliers to replace their product. Technology companies are continually building better mouse traps. They could turn around in a year or so with better products.

Conclusion

Buying a stock is an educated guess that its stock price will rise. Fundamentals do not always work, but they work most of the time:

1. When we buy a value stock, we're swimming against the tide. Hence, we need to wait longer (usually more than 6 months) for the market to realize its value. The exception is the Early Recovery phase (see the Market Cycle chapter) and it has faster and larger returns than most other stocks from most other stages of the market cycle.

2. Some metrics are misleading. Book value could be misleading for an established company such as IBM. The image of the cowboy in a tobacco company could be a very important asset that is not included in its financial statement.

3. The market is not always rational.

Afterthoughts

- Brand names of big companies are one of the most important intangibles. Here is a strategy to buy big companies in a down market. It has been proven that it works. However, do not just buy these companies without analysis.
  http://seekingalpha.com/article/1324041-buying-brand-names-in-a-bear-market-can-make-you-rich

- The reputation of a company takes a long time to build but a bad incidence to destroy in the case of GM such as the delay in recalling the killer switches.

Filler 12 noon is not 12 pm

The Chinese restaurant I went to says they are open at 12 am. Are they   wrong   or   is   the   world   wrong?

The next hour after 11 am is 12 am, NOT 12 pm. The one who set it up did it totally wrong and no one complains about it until now. If I were born earlier, I would have corrected it. If I were born here, I would be the president and every one would have a job by now.

3   Avoid bankrupting companies

Avoid the bankrupting companies at all costs. Here are some hints that a company is going bankrupt:

- I had several companies that had lost most of their stock values. It turns out that most were Chinese companies. I did have some losers from Mexico, Israel and Ireland. I believe most were set up to cheat investors. Most if not all had 'rosy' financial statements. Avoid them, especially small companies in emerging countries.

- Many U.S. companies failed due to fraud, poor management, and/or the management betting wrongly. When the CEO is using the company as his own AMT, or having an extravagant life style, watch out. If they promise you a return doubling the current rate of return of the market, listen to your wise mother: there is no free lunch. Despite so many real examples, still fools are born every day, because greed is a human nature.

- Do not follow the 'commentators' on TV. They have their own hidden agenda which usually is not in your interest.

- Many companies fail due to their lack of ability to pay back their loans. Except for specific industries and situations, avoid companies with high debt (Debt/Equity over 50%). Financial institutions and companies that have high debt in order to finance their products for their customers such as utilities are the exceptions.

- I have a screen named Big Losers beating the market by more than 600% in Early Recovery (a phase defined by me). However, some bankrupted companies are not included in the database which is termed as survivor bias. Hence, the actual result is far worse than the 600%. I still use this screen but skip these companies using the following yardsticks.
    - o The companies are usually safe with high Free Cash Flow / Equity and high Expected Profit / Stock Price.
    - o The following are red flags: low Free Cash Flow / Equity, high Inventory and high Receivable (esp. relative to its Payable), high P/B (over 30) and high net Debt/Equity (over 1 to 3 depending on the industry).
    - o P/PFC should be greater than 0 and less than 50. A healthy cash flow may not be able to service the debt if it is too huge. Hence, compare it to Debt/Equity.

Compare the cash flow per year to debt obligations per year.

- New government regulations could bankrupt an industry. What would happen when the U.S. takes out the rebates and subsidies of solar panels? When the U.S. banned solar panels from China, one of my Chinese stocks went bankrupt. Also government bailed out bankrupting companies such as Chrysler (that I made a good profit) and AIG Fannie Mae in 2008.
- Serious lawsuits- Most U.S. companies are required to file this information in their financial reports.
- Obsolete products. Newspapers, retail and similar products would be replaced by the internet. The opposite is new products such as virtual reality products.
- Many companies run out of money during the development phase of the major products. Many are too optimistic in their business plans.
- If you expect the market will recover in 2 years, ensure the company's cash and net income can support their burn rate for at least two more years.
- Many investing sites (most require subscriptions) have safety scores.
- If the Beneish M-Score is greater than -2.22, the company is likely an accounting manipulator.
- Choose companies with Z-Score higher than 3; it does not applicable to financial companies. Both M-Score and Z-Score are available from GuruFocus, a paid subscription. Z-Score does not work for financial institutions.
- Z-Score metrics are: "Working Capital / Total Assets" (A), "Retained Earnings / Total Assets" (B), "Earnings Before Interest & Taxes / Total Assets" (C), "Market Cap / Total Liabilities" (D) and "Sales / Total Assets" (E).
  Z-Score = 1.2 A + 1.4 B + 3.3 C + .6 D + E
- Market timing- It does not always work, but it is far better to follow a proven technique than not. It is far safer to take money out of the market when the market is too risky or is plunging. The big losers are companies that provide non-essential products in a down turn.
- Small companies could be risky but very profitable. Typically they have a low stock price (less than $5), small market cap (less than 50 M), low sales (less than $25 M) and low institutional ownership (less than 5%).

- Avoid companies when their own bond ratings are not equal to AAA or AA (www.moodys.com).
- The fall of a sector such as oil in 2015 could drive the related companies, or even a country to the brink of bankruptcy.

Investing is risky to start with. However, investing especially in stocks has been proven to be the best vehicle to beat inflation.

Section III: Selling stocks

We sell stocks when the reasons to own no longer apply by a good margin. In most cases, the sell decision should be based on data more than one quarter.

I sold ALU when it gained 40% in a few weeks' time. It gained more than 300% later when it was acquired. For rising stocks, we should adjust the stop orders. Do a mental stop order instead of just a stop order to avoid flash crashes. When the price of a purchased below a specified order, you place a market order to sell it. Use trailing stops for appreciated stocks.

1   *When to sell a stock*

There are many reasons to sell a stock as follows.

Personal

1. Has met my targets/objectives.
    It could be a 10% gain in a very short-term swing, x% return in 4 months for a short-term swing or y% gain after a year for long-term trades. Define x and y depending on your risk tolerance and how often you trade.

    I bought 4 stocks in one day during the August, 2015 correction and placed sell orders with 10% more than my purchase prices. I sold one in a day and another one within a month. This is my strategy for correction – sometimes it works and sometimes it does not.

    Never look back. Do not blame yourself when the prices are better than your trade prices. When the market is volatile, use a higher percent of the current prices. Be disciplined. Stay on the same strategy and detach yourself from emotions.

2. Realize that we have made a mistake. Do not let your ego block your eyes. It could be due to bad analysis, bad, data, unexpected fraud, lawsuits, and/or unforeseeable events that you have no control of. It is better to get out with a small loss. I prefer a 25% loss as a threshold for long-term strategies and a 10% (or less for some strategies) loss for short-term strategies.

    We have to ensure whether it is a mistake or not. If the 'mistake' is just bad luck or due to conditions we cannot possibly predict or control, then it is not a mistake. If it is a mistake, learn from it. When we diversify, one bad loss should not cause a big dent in our portfolios. The stop loss is a good tool most of the time except when there is a flash crash.

    If the criteria have been faithfully followed and it does not work well, check out whether your criteria are wrong, or it does not work on the current market conditions.

3. When we have too many stocks in the same sector, we will want to replace some stocks to better diversify our portfolios.

   When the sector is rising, we want to weigh more on that sector at the expense of diversification, and vice versa. Set a limit of how many sectors you should hold.

4. Need cash for living expenses.

5. To reduce a tax burden by selling some losers. Tax consideration should not be the primary reason for selling. Take advantage of the favorable tax treatment for long-term capital gains. In short, sell losers within the short term limit (currently a year), and sell winners after 365 days; check the current tax laws.

   Harvest tax losses. Sell losers and buy back similar stocks (or same stock after 31 days to avoid wash sale). It is not too clear in which you can buy back the same loser in your children's account under the current tax law.

6. To take advantage of a lower tax. In 2013, we can pay virtually zero (except the increase of tax on social security payment) Federal income taxes on long-term capital gains when our income is below a specific tax bracket (15% as of 2015). Check out the current tax laws. Evaluate the sold winners for a possible buy back.

Market Timing

7. When the market or the sector plunges, sell stocks or stocks within the sector.

   For temporary peaks, evaluate which stocks in your portfolio to sell based on fundamentals. The objective is to raise cash for buying opportunities.

Deteriorating appreciation potential

8. There may be some stocks that have a better appreciation potential than the ones you currently own. Churning the portfolio by replacing better stocks may cost some brokerage commissions (some are free today) and taxes for taxable

accounts, but it improves the quality and the appreciation potential for the entire portfolio.

9. The company's fundamentals have changed for the worse. If you use a scoring system, compare the current score with the score you actually bought the stock for. Apple is a good example from 2013 to 2015. Buy when the fundamentals are good and sell when they are not.

   The basic fundamentals are expected P/E, the quarter-to-quarter earnings growth rate / the sales growth rate, and Debt /Equity.

   When your stocks have passed the peak and started to decline, sell them. When they are heading to bankruptcy, sell them fast.

Hints that the fundamentals are degrading

Evaluate the stocks you own at least every 6 months and check their daily news at least once a week that can be easily done using Seeking Alpha's portfolio function.

- The cash flow is decreasing fast. Cash flow is not a particularly good predicative indicator for appreciation, but a good indicator on whether the company will survive. This metric is very hard to manipulate.

- A new or pending lawsuit. Check out how serious the lawsuit is and be aware that a minor lawsuit can be ignored. Companies always sue against each other.

- A big drop in sales. Do not be alarmed when a new product, or a new drug is going to replace a major product. Compare sales to the same quarter of prior year to avoid seasonal fluctuations (Q-to-Q info I available from Finviz.com).

- Management deteriorates- One hint is the deteriorating ROE from the last quarter.

- The extravagant life style of the CEO and the many easy loans to officers.

- Poor operations. They include recalls of products such as the GM recall on ignition switches, product secrets being stolen and customers' credit card info being stolen. Boeing's 747-Max is a warning call.

- A successful product from the competitor, or the current product is losing its market share, or becoming a low-profit commodity.

- Insiders and/or institutional investors are dumping the companies' stocks far more than the averages (2% for me) especially in heavy volumes and by more than one insider.

  o Have more than one insider dumping a lot of the stock within a month and no insider purchase in that month.

  o Have more than one insider decrease their holdings by more than 10%.

- When the SEC or any government agency pays attention to a company, it usually means bad news.

- Deceptive accounting practices have been discovered.

- Increasing receivable and/or inventory at an alarming rate.

- Earnings have been restated too many times.

- Short percentage is increasing fast – someone found something wrong with the company.

- The invalidity of 'one-time charges'.

- Abnormal return rate of the company's pension fund comparing to the average of the companies in the same sector.

- Too many and too costly reconstructing charges.

- The entire stock market is plunging as indicated by our chart in detecting market crashes.

- The stock price does not move up with good news. It shows the price has peaked.

- The accumulation amount is far less than the sold amount. When the stock price is up, the accumulation is less than the sold stocks when the stock price was down the last time. It indicates that no more accumulation is ahead and hence the stock will be down most likely.

Afterthoughts

- Another article on this topic.
  http://buzz.money.cnn.com/2013/04/05/stocks-sell/
  An article from Investopedia. Nothing new but it is worth having the same second opinion.
  http://www.investopedia.com/financial-edge/0412/5-tips-on-when-to-sell-your-stock.aspx

- It also depends on your strategies. I sell most of my stocks in my momentum portfolio within a month. At least one strategy I know of does not keep any stock during the peak stage of the market cycle – the easiest time to make money but also the riskiest time.

  If you use charts for trading, sell the stocks that are below your moving averages or other technical analysis indicators. Personally I do not use charts for making sell decisions due to my limited time.

- Sell when the company is heading into bankruptcy as described before. The red flags are: 1. Negative cash flow. 2. Heavy insiders dumping the stocks. 3. Pending major lawsuit. 4. Fraud from the management.

- Risky periods for a stock.
  Earnings announcement (4 times a year), settling a major lawsuit and/or during a FDA event in approving a drug are risky periods for a stock. A fluctuation more than 5% in either direction is normal. Some use options to buy insurance. Most ignore it. For the majority of the time, heavy insider purchase is a good indicator.

2   Selling a winner

Let the profit rise and at the same time protect your profit. Tesla quadrupled its value in 6 months. Examples abound such as Amazon and Yelp.

You do not want to sell these rocket stocks even if their fundamentals do not make sense. Buffett does not touch these stocks and he usually misses these big gains. However, many of these rocket stocks such as BRRY (Blackberry) will eventually fall losing most of their value. I bet the institutional investors move the market in either direction and usually they read the same analysts' reports. You profit as a contrarian if you have a good reason to act against the herd.

The following example uses a 10% trailing stop. Set the stop at 10% of the current price (i.e. 10% less than the current price), not the purchase price. You need to change the stop when the price rises but do not change it when the price falls. Review your stops every month or more frequently if time allows.

To illustrate, when the stock price rises to 100, set the stop at 90. When the stock price falls to 90, sell the stock at the market price. When the stock price rises to 200, change the stop at 180.

The stop should also be set according to how volatile the stock is. Some stocks are more volatile than others. Most charts show the resistance line. This line assumes the stock price should not fall below this line in normal fluctuations. Set the stop at 2% below this line so your stock will not be stopped out in theory.

To avoid flash crashes, do not place stop orders. Instead, do it mentally (mental stop is my term). When you see that the stock falls below your stop with no sign of a flash crash, sell the stock using a market order.

Of course, there is no bullet-proof scheme. This one should work in the long run. This is my suggestion only, so examine whether it works for you. Small cap and/or stocks with small average volumes fluctuate more.

Examples

I have too many bad examples of selling the stocks too early and sometimes holding them too long.

I made over 40% in a few weeks on ALU, but it went up more than 300% in the next two years. It was acquired in early 2016 by Nokia paying a good premium. I was right that ALU had a lot of valuable patents and I was wrong to dump it when I found out Cisco did not have any intention to acquire it – a big mistake by Cisco and the U.S.

FOSL is another example to teach us to use mental stop loss. FOSL was priced at $33.70 on 1/4/2010. Its fundamentals were just fine with an expected E/P (expected earnings yield) at 6% but decreasing earnings. It gained 115% later in 2010 - not expected.

On 1/3/2011, the expected E/P was still at around 6% and improving earnings. It gained 9% for the year – a little disappointing.

On 1/3/2012, the expected E/P was 7% and a huge earnings growth. Now, we expected a better performance for the year and it did by gaining 20%.

On 1/3/2013, the expected E/P was about 6% and the earnings gain was respectable. It gained 28% to $121. So far, so good.

On 1/2/2014, the E/P and the earnings growth were about the same as in 1/3/2013. However, it lost 7% for the year while SPY (an ETF simulating the market) gained 12%. There was no warning. Did the institutional investors lose the interest of this stock?

On 1/2/2015, the E/P was 7% and the earnings growth was about the same as the previous year. It lost 69% (vs. SPY's 0% return with dividends)!

From 1/4/2010 to 1/3/2016, the annualized return of FOSL is 0% (vs. SPY's 13%). Actually, after dividends, SPY should have an annualized return of about 15%. The lessons gained here are:

- Fundamentals (using EP and earnings growth in this example) may not always work. Otherwise, 2015 should have the same gain as 2014.
- The rosy outlook of the stock may be priced in already. When the outlook fails to materialize, the stock tanks.

3   Examples of over-priced stocks

In 2011, there were discussions on the high valuation of Netflix in several articles in Seeking Alpha, an investment website. LinkedIn and Facebook shares were believed to be overvalued even before their IPOs.

Here are some of my thoughts on Netflix and the same concept can be applied to other stocks.

- Reward / Risk ratio.
  If the stock has the same probability to move up by 30% and move down by 50%, it is overvalued by 20% (50% - 30%). As of 2011, Netflix shares may rise, but it is too risky for me.
- Compare the P/E to its five-year average.
  The current P/E is 60 and the average for the last 5 years is 30. From this metric it is overvalued by 100%.

  The 'E' in P/E can be either expected (same as forward) earnings or based on the last 12 months (same as trailing or historical). It has been proven that the 'expected' is a better indicator than the 'historical'. AAII demonstrated this by comparing the performances of the expected PEG screen and the historical PEG screens over a long period of time.
- Fools who invested in the high P/E stocks and did not do their due diligence in 2000 had parted with their money fast. I could not convince my friends to take money off their internet stocks. It is similar to asking the lottery winners not to buy lottery tickets.
- Buying an expensive stock is like over paying for a hot dog cart in NYC for $100,000. The buyer will sell many hot dogs, but the rate of return of the investment will be minimal, and it will never recover the initial investment. "Buy high and sell higher" is a momentum play. It works if it is played with stops, but I prefer to "Buy low and sell high".
- Following a decent and proven investing strategy consistently should lead to success through persistence and adjustments. In the long term, a bad strategy always loses money.
- When the market favors growth / momentum (vs. value), it is OK to buy stocks with prices higher than the intrinsic values by a small percentage. The tide is on your side. However, be attentive to any indication that the market is changing direction.

4 Should you hold stocks forever?

There are many examples that you should hold onto some stocks forever such as Apple, Netflix, Amazon and Google. Interestingly there are more opposite examples such as AIG and Lehman Brothers. Hence, there is no right or wrong answer. Always continually monitor your stock holdings and the sectors they are in.

Even IBM could suffer its dips when it does not react to its market and / or make the wrong strategic decision. The Washington Post has to react to the free articles from the internet.

I have set up guidelines on when to sell. One selling indicator is when those shares lose over 25%. We have to admit that we have made a mistake, or the fundamentals of the stock have changed. Evaluate the fundamentals of the purchased stocks periodically.

Boston Chicken is one of my many big losers. I could use the money I lost to have chicken dinner every night for the rest of my life! This kind of thinking is not healthy. I decided not to buy any restaurant stock again and that is not rational either. It is an art to sell a loser, or wait for its potential recovery. From my experiences, it is better to sell the loser.

If you have a historical database, you can test out your strategy on when to sell and adjust the sell criteria accordingly. Do not try to data fit to your strategy.

Never fall in love in a stock and never be afraid to buy back a sold stock. Use fundamental metrics for making a buy/sell decision.

Taxes and diversification

Tax should not be a major consideration in selling a stock. However, you may postpone selling losers in December if your tax rate (so your tax loss value) will be better next year. If you need to offset short-term capital gains, sell some losers eligible for short-term capital losses. Postpone selling a winner to a month or so, if it can be eligible for long-term capital gain.

When your stock appreciates many, many times and you're close to your life expectant age, hold it and the cost basis will step up to the day you pass away. Instruct your heirs to buy a newspaper to get the prices of your stocks you hold or instruct your heirs to inform your broker on the unavoidable day. Today's tax law provides a range of days around the date of death; check the current tax laws.

Instead of selling a stock with huge gain, consider options: 1. give it to your children who have lower tax brackets, 2. give it to charity, and 3. save it for your estate.

When the market is plunging as detected by market timing techniques, sell most of your holdings. Be warned that market timing does not always work.

No stock is sacred

That's why we need to churn the portfolio replacing the bad stocks with better ones. More examples of failing companies that had been very promising at one time:

- The bankrupt companies due to competition: Circuit City (due to BestBuy) and Block Buster (due to Netflix).
- The failing internet companies in 2000 and the financial institutions in 2008.
- HP when PCs, servers and printers are no longer kings.
- BestBuy killed Circuit City and then it is being eaten alive by Amazon, Walmart, Costco and BJ. However, it recovered in 2014.
- Many retailers went bankrupt. I lost count of so many of the retailers in the Boston area alone.

Filler: Dream high

I heard this. The girl wanted to be a president when she grew up. She went to a circus and she said she wanted to be a clown. Her wise father said, "You can be a president and a clown at the same time".

Section IV: Experiences

1   Trade experience in 2014

Several lessons from my transactions in early 2014:

- Tax is part of the total return as defined as:

Total Return = Appreciation + Dividends + Covered Calls – Taxes – Inflation

From the current tax laws, I should be eligible for zero Federal tax on long-term capital gains as long as my tax bracket is 15% or less. I acted accordingly. However, my contribution to Medicare boosted up. Check out the current tax laws.

This year I have sold several big winners so far including BSX, CAMP and CSCO. The first two have returned over 100%. I did not sell them last year as my income bracket was higher after I converted some 401K to Roth IRA.

- Sell half of the stocks that you do not like.

I did sell half of LF and half of LCC in 2013. Both were profitable then. They were going in the opposite direction so far this year. LF is now losing about 30% while LCC (after merging with AAL) is over 150% return. Anyway it cut down my exposure to these two stocks to half. However, I bought back LCC when the prospect looked better.

- Overbought.

AAL was overbought for sure. From Finviz.com, its RSI(14) is about 65%. It may be peaking too with SMA-50% = 20% and SMA-200% = 61%. However, I have to wait for August in order to qualify it for the Federal's long-term capital gain, which is virtually zero for me this year. It would be a mistake for me if the institutional investors dumped it before August.

I still liked the forward P/E of LF at 13. It seemed their new product could not compete with iPad.

AAL's forward P/E was at about 7 but the debt was high.

- Over compensating its officers.

FBRC had granted too many shares to its officers as revealed by Finviz.com. I unloaded some quickly.

- Correction happened.

Bought several stocks during this correction. Need to wait for another month to see how they perform.

- From my book "Best Stocks: 2014, According to Me":

The stock list of over 130 stocks beat S&P 500 by 142% between 12/16/13 to 02/19/14. The Small Cap list of 9 stocks beat S&P 500 by 675% (not a typo) for the same period. They may not be sustainable.

I did buy some stocks from the list.

- I did buy ARTX from the Small Cap list of the book.

It went down 12% very fast. However, on 3/3/2014, it went up to 24%. A swing of 36% in a month or so! A guru asked us to have a 10% stop loss and I would not see the 24% gain if I followed his advice.

As of today (3/7/14), it went up by 74% since I bought it on 1/24/14.

I looked at the fundamentals and did not find anything special (so it must have been my good luck). TheStreet.com did an article and found some positives and some negatives.

There were several sell orders from insiders. However, their amounts were negligible compared to the number of shares they hold except the sell order of about $400,000 by the CEO last Dec. at

2.44 (today's price is 5.45). It seems the CEO did not expect the stock price that high.

I normally do not buy stocks with a market cap of less than 150 M and ARTX was 50 M. It appeared in two of my short lists (Best-All-Around and Small Cap) in my book Best stocks 2014, According to Me. I looked for a small cap again in March 3, 2014 and could not find similar stocks. It could mean that there were fewer bargains in small cap stocks in March, 2014.

ARTX was bought in the wrong, taxable accounts. In today's rising market (as of 3/14), I did not have enough short-term losses to offset the short-term gains of ARTX.

FUEL in the battery industry similar to ARTX has a better run. Most high tech companies are building better mouse traps. A better technology is being developed at MIT and it will replace all the current batteries in about 8 or so years.

On 3/25/14, it was up 50% in one day due to an article from Seeking Alpha and then next day it lost about 15%. It turned out to be a 'pump-and-dump' article.

- My orders on some stocks were not executed and they skyrocketed. The only way to buy them is using market orders. My new policy is to place two orders, one market order and one .5% less than the current price if I really like the stock.

2 The scents of a winner

During the beginning of Feb. 2014, I sold several winners expecting to pay zero in Federal tax this year. Besides tax considerations, I expected a correction was coming.

I sold the following long-term gainers: MSFT (37%), CSCO (48%) and CAT 10%. As a group, they beat the S&P 500 index by a small margin.

The three sold winners are BSX, CAMP and USNA. I bought BSX (138% return) two times without looking at the fundamentals at all. I only have USNA (99%) and CAMP (282%) to compare and hope to find some common denominators.

Here is a table comparing the two. The metrics are around the time I bought the stocks.

	CAMP	USNA	Average
Return	282%	99%	
Bought on	12/24/12	01/28/13	
Sold on	01/08/14	02/12/14	
Days held	380	380	380
Screen	CAO	BF	
Fundamentals			
Expected E/P	39%	16%	28%
Earning growth	39%	16%	28%
ROE	40%	32%	36%
Total debt		0%	
Short %	5%	28%	
Technical			
SMA200%	13%	-10%	
RSI(14)	41%	50%	46%
Subscription			
Zacks	Average	Average	Average
IBD	Best	Average-	
Fidelity Analyst	Average-	Best	
Blue Chip Grow	B	A	B+
Score			
My Score	46	26	36
P-Score	3	3	3

Explanation

The following tries to find any common denominators between the two winners. I leave out blanks in the average column where there is no common denominator. It is too small a data sample to draw a conclusion compared to my usual monitors.

Remember these metrics are for a long-term holding of stocks (for me it is one year and one day).

- Screens.
  They are both selected from screens that have been proven winners. BF is the bottom fishing screen. CAO is the screen to search for candidates to be acquired.

- Fundamentals.
  Both have pretty sound fundamental metrics. Expected E/P (P/E in reverse), Earnings Growth and ROE are above their respective average.
  Short % is good if it is less than 10%. When it is above 25%, a short squeeze may be possible. The shorters of USNA made the wrong decision apparently.

- Technical.
  Technical indicators are great for spotting trends, but not in spotting the bottom. When you hold the stock for a year, the short-term trend will do you no good.

- Expert advice.
  As in the table, all are not conclusive except the Blue Chip Growth's Cash Flow grade, which is no longer free.
- My Scores.
  I have two scoring system. Both stocks exceeded the passing grade (15) by a wide margin. "P-Score" is described in my book

Scoring Stocks (passing grade is 2). "My Score" has been enhanced with the subscriptions services I am using.

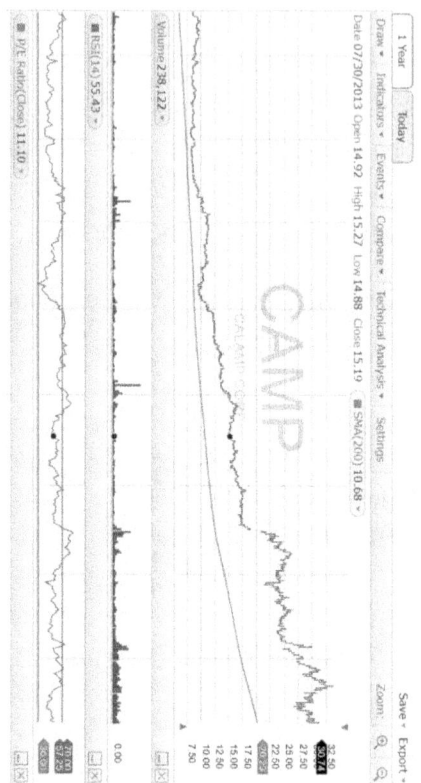

SMA-200 for CAMP. Soucre: Fidelity

Bring it up from your browser. Enter CAMP. Select Technical Indicator, then SMA, and enter 200 days.

Update

As of 4/2014, CAMP has had a big plunge since I sold it. Lucky timing for me! I believe no stocks should double in a year; I did have TTWO that had been increased the stock price 4 times for a few years. CAMP had returned 280% in just over a year. There are a few rare exceptions such as buying Apple and Netflix after their IPOs.

3 The power of correlation

If your friend says your baby is beautiful, it could be the act of political courtesy. However, if many strangers say the same, most likely it is true. It is the same for stocks.

If several subscriptions say the same thing, then most likely the stock would be a winner.

To illustrate, one service publishes their top 50 stocks. I entered the 50 stocks to a watch list in another reputable subscription service. Sort them with the ranks. Pick the top 5 stocks and do my own evaluation.

The following is my result doing this correlation of two subscription services. It is from 1/15/2014 for about 35 days. All returns were annualized. It is for illustration purposes only.

	All 50 stocks	Select top 5 stocks	SPY
Return	39%	124%	-3.87%
Beat SPY by	1,108%	3,304%	

Stocks	Return
URI	63%
GMCR	572%
MTW	186%
PII	-74%
TSCO	-127%
Avg.	124%

There is a very good chance that it is a winner if the market is not risky and it passed my evaluation.

If I selected the top 3 instead of the top 5, the return is even far, far better and there would be no losers. Why do most strategies always work after the fact or they only work on paper?

4   A tale of two portfolios

The first portfolio (20 stocks) was described in my SA article Amazing Returns more than a year ago and the second portfolio (15 stocks) was described in my book, Best Stocks 2014, According to Me, and was also mentioned in one of my comments in the article.

The first portfolio consists of Banner (NASDAQ:BANR), Key Tronic (NASDAQ:KTCC) (2 times), Questcor Pharmaceuticals (NASDAQ:QCOR), The Active Network (NYSE:ACTV) (acquired), Iamgold (NYSE:IAG), Advanced Emissions Solutions (NASDAQ:ADES), Nacco Industries (NYSE:NC), Velti (VELT, delisted), Alpha Natural Resources (NYSE:ANR), Apple (NASDAQ:AAPL), Citigroup (NYSE:C), Deckers Outdoor (NYSE:DECK), Microsoft (NASDAQ:MSFT) (2 purchases), Alcatel-Lucent, S.A. (NYSE:ALU), Dollar Tree (NASDAQ:DLTR), Caterpillar (NYSE:CAT) and Boston Scientific (NYSE:BSX) (2 purchases).

The second portfolio consists of Universal Insurance Holdings (NYSE:UVE), Gray Television (NYSE:GTN), Esterline Technologies (NYSE:ESL), Johnson Controls (NYSE:JCI), Nexstar Broadcasting Group (NASDAQ:NXST), Pozen (NASDAQ:POZN), China Lodging Group (NASDAQ:HTHT), CVS Caremark (NYSE:CVS), Home Inns & Hotels Management Inc. (NASDAQ:HMIN), Arotech Corporation (NASDAQ:ARTX), Canadian Solar (NASDAQ:CSIQ), Jazz Pharmaceuticals Public (NASDAQ:JAZZ), Motorcar Parts of America (NASDAQ:MPAA), Micron Technology (NASDAQ:MU) and Och-Ziff Capital Management Group (NYSE:OZM).

The first one has an average return of 53% beating SPY's (an ETF simulating the S&P500 index) 25% by 112% from 1-4-2013 (the published date of the article) to 1-4-2014, a year later.

The annualized return of the second portfolio is 31% beating SPY's 16% by 94% from 12/16/13 (the published date for the book) to 2/15/14 (2 months later). The choice of the end date will be explained later. Dividends are not considered in all calculations.

The second portfolio is one of several short lists from the 135 stocks recommended in the book. The best short list is from Small Cap which has an annualized return of 98% beating SPY by 512% for the same period. It consists of the following nine stocks: Arotech, Consumer Portfolio Services (NASDAQ:CPSS), Entravision Communications (NYSE:EVC), Gastar Exploration (NYSEMKT:GST), Dot Hill Systems (NASDAQ:HILL), Lee Enterprises (NYSE:LEE), MTR Gaming Group (NASDAQ:MNTG), RAIT Financial Trust (NYSE:RAS) and Star Gas Partners (NYSE:SGU). Recently, small stocks are not doing as good as before.

The returns are pretty good, but they are not in the discussion here. I would like to see what we can learn in investing.

You cannot learn from someone you do not respect

There was a lot of criticism and doubt in my original article. I welcome all of them as I can learn from the comments and in how I should be more defensive in writing. However, some do not make a lot of sense.

- The short duration would boost my annualized returns. Yes, the annualized return of a week is not meaningful, but a month is, at least for 20 stocks. The annualized return is a two-edged sword and it can amplify the losses too.
- Sometimes I do not have a choice such as comparing the performance of my momentum portfolio. It has an average holding period of one month. Now, I compare the performance of the 20 stocks for one full year.
- I could have skipped my losers. They were all real trades within the specified period in my largest taxable account. Actually, I skipped some huge winners that missed my criteria by days. Now, I use the published date of the article as the start date.
- Today's low commission should not be a concern even for 20 stocks. My commission is $5 per trade and it represents a negligible percent of the trade.

- I did have a loss at one time on my second portfolio. There was nothing to be concerned with. If you believe you never want a loss, do not invest and let inflation eat up your investment. The yardstick is whether you can beat an index such as the S&P500.

Survivor Bias

VELT was delisted and ACTV was acquired. I used my sold price for VELT and the proceeds I received from ACTV to calculate my return. Hence, the return is not precise for simplicity sake.

When you test a strategy, your return could appear better than the reality. In this case, VELT and ACTV are not selected in your test as they've been taken out of your historical database; few handle this bias.

Usually, the delisted stocks lose a lot of value and the stocks being acquired gain a lot of value, so they would balance out the effect. In reality it is not. There are more stocks delisted and/or bankrupted than the stocks being acquired. In addition, usually their average loss is more than the average gain of the stocks being acquired.

Countries and sectors

Usually, I do not trust the foreign countries that do not have a regulator similar to our SEC, especially on small stocks. VELT, a loser here, could be one.

I outlined in my books several sectors to be cautious of, including miners and ANR and IAG belong to this sector.

Size of purchase

I had double a buy on BSX and a low position on VELT. I did not place a large buy on ALU, a winner but risky at the time of evaluation. I gained some and lost some. In general, you want to double or increase the purchase when the appreciation potential is good with an acceptable risk.

Fundamental analysis works

Most of the 20 stocks scored high in my two scoring systems (one using simple metrics available to all). Value stocks need time for the market to realize their values as they're swimming against the tide. The short-term return usually does not mean anything, though it does this time.

The second portfolio is intended for short-term swings (3 months for me).

Fundamental analysis does not work

It is not contradictory. It depends on what the stocks are intended for. The second portfolio is for short-term swing trading. I used fundamental analysis to the minimum. There were about 135 stocks recommended in the book and I did not have time to evaluate each stock fundamentally in detail. If I did, the information would be obsolete. I provided a simple method in my book on how to do fundamental analysis.

These stocks are selected from the strategies (screens, subscriptions and screening recommended stocks from the subscriptions) that have been proven recently. They're described in my book The Art of Investing which covers most of my investing ideas. When you select the stocks based on momentum, do not hold them too long, as momentum usually does not last longer than 3 months.

Account

I have all the 20 stocks in the first portfolio in my taxable account and most of the stocks in the second portfolio in my retirement accounts.

I placed ARTX in a taxable account by mistake. I did not sell it when it gained more than 50% in one day due to the tax consideration.

Holding period
It is targeted for over one year for the first portfolio so they are eligible to the low tax treatment on long-term capital gains. For one year or two, my Federal tax on a huge capital gain was virtually zero taking advantage of a provision in the tax law.

I use two months for the second portfolio, as this is the time I start to sell the stocks for the short-swing portfolio. I compare different periods and this is the choice. In actual trading, I take advantage of their weekly fluctuations using technical indicators such as Bollinger Bands.

"Buy and hold" is not for me
Before 2000, market timing was a waste of time. Since 2000, we have had two market plunges with the average loss of about 45%. I have a simple chart to detect market plunges. It will not catch the peak and bottom as it depends on the falling/rising market. Hopefully, it will give us plenty of time to prepare as the last two.

The second reason I churn my portfolio is improving the appreciation potential. It is just my preference. When I sell a stock, it does not mean I'm not buying it back.

Risk tolerance

I am more conservative as a retiree. However, I was more than 'all in' (using my equity credit) in 2009. It depends on individual risk tolerance and situation.

Conclusion

Using these two portfolios, I have covered a lot of my ideas in investing. Implement the ideas that make sense to you and your requirements.

We need to have a trade plan to find stocks, analyze them, order them in the right account and sell them. Enhance your trade plan and stick to it. In addition to the described portfolios, I have one for momentum where I keep stocks for a month or less. I have other strategies such as Top Down and Sector Rotation. When the market is risky, I sell more stocks than I buy. Today I'm taking a break.

There will not be a book titled "Best Stocks for 2015". I find stocks almost once every month so it does not take too much effort to document my selections in a book. The window to sell the book is too short and it does not make it financially rewarding. But, never say 'never'.

I may have another article on my next 20 stocks in the future. The market is risky by any yardstick. Excessive printing of money causes the current non-correlation of the market and the economy. The government eventually has to reduce the money supply and they will then correlate again. Until then, I am investing more conservatively.

5   Lessons from my trading in 2019-2020

2020 is a miserable year with the pandemic, but reasonable well for the market. Again, I am too conservative and had not followed by own advice illustrated in my books. If you followed my SMA-350 (Simple Moving Average for the last 350 sessions), you should have done amazingly well. Technical chart (SMA in my case) worked far better than the fundamental in 2020. Tesla made about 6 times even the P/E was over 1,000 at one time in 2020.

I made many financial mistakes along with some good decisions in 2019. I have explained how to avoid some mistakes in my books and I did not follow my own preaching.

In the last two months of 2019, I started buying contra ETFs betting the market would go down while the market has been making new heights. The market is financially unsound but technically sound. Lesson #1: Follow the simplest market timing described in this book. Lesson #2: Never bet against the market on the year before election.

There are always two sides on the opposite views of the market. I studied them and believe 2020 could be a disastrous year for the market. No one is sure unless s/he has a time machine. Again follow Lesson #1.

I did well in buying GLD/SLV, and basic materials including IYW and two copper miners. I will unload some copper miners. Lesson #3: Every portfolio should have a small portion in gold (GLD/or similar ETFs, gold coins and an ETF for gold miners).

Stay away from Chinese stocks for the entire year. I may buy a contra ETF on Chinese stocks. The trade war and the explosive debts will drive China's economy down for a few years.

I had 50% profit in one month using my year-end strategy in 2018. From my memory, I made about 100% on YRCW and lost about 30% on another buy on the same stock. Lesson #4: "Year-End Strategy" works at least so far. Lesson #5: Sell the stocks bought using this strategy within 2 months, and hence I should use retirement accounts for this strategy.

I made some money in trading energy stocks that have been beaten down badly. The outlook of energy stocks is not good. Lesson #6: Buy low and sell high. Lesson #7: Buffett's "Be greedy when everyone is fearful and vice versa" is correct thinking.

There are many 'great' traders making millions and losing most. Lesson #8: Avoid big losses by using stops. Lesson #9: Do not speculate and be a turtle investor.

Sold METC and REI in early 2020 for 14% gain (172% annualized) and 35% (508%) respectively. They were screened from my year-end strategy in early Dec., 2019 and profited due to the daily news (Iran). Lesson #10: Combine different strategies.

I have saved the most important lesson for last. If you spend all day long trading, you will not enjoy life and it is bad for your physical health and mental health. Wish you a healthy and prosperous 2021!

#Fillers:

How messed up our welfare system?

It encourages our citizens to be lazy and let the government bail them out.
It encourages more children and teenage mothers.

Do you take a job when you lose all the goodies and free health care?

Many take care of their old parents and get paid handsomely.
One divorced his wife to boost the SSI, and then married a foreigner lady who gave him $30,000 plus free sex.

One of the best sellers in Taiwan is "How to retire comfortably with no work".

The middle class is being squeezed by the rich (who do not pay much taxes) and the poor.

6   Tips from Peter Lynch

He made a lot of money for his investors in Magellan's fund. I came in late to his funds, but I also left early when he retired early in 1990. Many did not want to leave due to the potential tax burdens. His successors never achieved the same performance in Peter's 9 years with the fund. Peter was smart enough to know that his fund was so big that it was the market, and no one could beat the market by that margin consistently.

The following is my summary and my comments on his tips from several YouTube videos
https://www.youtube.com/watch?v=IhnfqbliGC4.

1. Study more stocks and pick the best.
    Same as do your homework.
2. Emotionally detached. Do not sell at the bottom.
    No one can predict market. My article could limit the loss and save the cash for reentering the market. Buying at early recovery is very profitable.
3. Investing in companies whose products / services you understand.
    We all have expertise in our own field and the mall is better place to find good consumer products.

    However, today's mall is pretty much destroyed by Amazon.com. In this case, you should buy Amazon.com, and short many retail outfits and the mall owners. Also check whether Amazon.com has reached its growth potential or not. You may miss Zoom, but as of 10/2020, the stock is too expensive. With the momentum, I do not want to short this stock.
    Made big profits in McDonald's as the sales/profits had been rising for years. However, most of the profits were derived from real estate holdings.
    I do not totally agree with it. There are many companies that we do not know but we can learn and understand what their technologies that could be potentially profitable. Buffett did not invest in Apple as he did not use a mobile phone, but his research team should.

4. Easier to beat the professionals than expected.
   Fund managers have to stick with large companies and they cannot time the market.

5. Invest in profitable small companies.
   Small companies have a lot of risk, but they also have higher profit potential than matured companies.

6. Find a few good stocks particularly at their early stage.
   It is harder to do than say. When the stock moves from Russel 2000 to Russel 1000 (promoting from an index for smaller stocks), they could be candidates.
   A fast growing stock may never be too late to invest.

7. We can find these stocks earlier than the professionals and many funds cannot invest in these stocks.

8. Sell a stock when the fundamentals decline.
   That's where my score for fundamentals or Fidelity's Equity Summary Score comes in.

9. Do not sell when they have short-term problems such as not meeting the earnings prediction.

10. If you do not have time to research stock, buy ETFs that simulate the market. It is not Lynch's idea (as a fund manager) but mine and Buffett's.

11. Buy growing companies and sell the matured companies that their markets have been saturated (i.e. no place to grow). That's why P/E may not work all the time; you need to consider quarter-to-quarter sales growth and earnings growth; actually year-to-year for the past 5 or even more years is important.

12. Buy good cynical stocks at the bottom and sell at the top.
    It is hard to determine the bottom and the top. However, you need to ensure the company would not go bankrupt by ensuring the income can service its debt.

13. Consider turnaround companies.
    Check the balance sheet. They need cash for turnaround such as promoting new products/services. Skip those companies that have hints of failure of the turnaround. Disney was one at one time by using the hidden assets. Brand names are not included in the financial statements.

14. Do not sell when you double the profit or you loss 10%.
    Agree if they are good stocks. I have some 'good' stocks that went to almost zero value; one Chinese solar company was due to the U.S. policy banning it to the U.S. market.

Section V: Finding stocks

1 Where the web sites are

- **Free and simple screen sites**

  They are described in this article or type the following
  http://stocks.about.com/od/researchtools/a/071909screenlist.htm

    o Yahoo!Finance.
       Click here or type
       http://screener.finance.yahoo.com/stocks.html

    o Finviz.
       Click here or type
       http://Finviz.com/screener.ashx

       How to scan using Finviz (YouTube).
       https://www.YouTube.com/watch?v=aQ_0FTg9Cfw

       Screening using technical indicators (particularly useful
       for momentum stocks).
       https://www.YouTube.com/watch?v=RZRP2NeSX0s

    o Your broker.
       Fidelity's screens are more sophisticated than most.

    o More options: Google, CNBC.com and Moringstar.com.

  Here is a list.
  http://stocks.about.com/od/researchtools/a/071909screenlist.htm

- **Sophisticated screens (usually not free)**

  Most of them are more complicated and need time to learn.
  Both Vector Vest and Stock123 provide historical databases for
  back testing your screens. Zacks has an earnings revision
  database at extra cost. GuruFocus has an easy-to-use but
  powerful screen function.

AAII provides screened stocks from various screens in its low-priced subscription. Both AAII and Value Line take care of some specific industries, but they provide no historical database at least for regular subscriptions. AAII provides historical performance summaries of their screens included in its subscription.

Afterthoughts

Here are the links to screens provided by Marketwatch and NASDAQ.
http://www.marketwatch.com/tools/stockre...
http://www.nasdaq.com/reference/stock-sc...

How to find quality stocks.
http://seekingalpha.com/article/2381395-how-to-identify-quality-stocks-and-is-there-really-alpha-to-be-had

Filler
"Sell in May" could be a self-fulfilled prophecy. I prefer to sell on April 1 and come back on Oct. 15 to avoid the herd.

2   A screener example

The following is an example. Fine tune the selection criteria according to your personal criteria and risk tolerance.

- Bring up Finviz.com from your browser. Select Screener, the third tab. As of 3/24/2015, we have 7066 stocks.

- For illustration purposes, we would like to find stocks with double bottoms, a positive technical indicator. Select the Technical tab. Select Pattern and then Double Bottom. Now we have 257 stocks.

- Select the Fundamental tab that is next to the Technical tab. Select Forward P/E and then select "under 20". Now, we have 86 stocks.

- Select Debt/Equity less than .5. Now, we have 45 stocks. Some industries such as utilities are traditionally high in debt, so you can use 'less than 1'.

- Select EPS growth Q-to-Q over 10%. Now, we have 19 stocks.

- Select the Description tab. Select Country to USA. Now, we have 17 stocks.

- Select Price > 1. Select Avg. Volume "Over 100K". Select Float Short "Under 10%. Select Analyst Recs. "Buy or better". Now we have 9 stocks.

  Now we can evaluate them one by one using Fundamental Analysis, Intangible Analysis, Qualitative Analysis and Technical Analysis. The purpose of screening is to filter the 7000 stocks to a small number (9 stocks in this case).

Skip the stocks that have the Earnings Date within 2 weeks. If you already have too many stocks in the same industry, skip that stock. You can save the screen when you have registered with Finviz.com. It is free. Check the performance of your selections after 3 months or so.

3   An extension to the scoring system

The following metrics do not give good predictive accuracy during this monitoring period. Monitor them in the future. The surprise to me is that ROE does not work this time. I remember a very popular book that just uses ROE as its sole indicator to select stocks. It may be due to too many folks using the same metric.

The following scores are optional. If they are used, add the total to Grand Score.

No.	Metric	Good	Bad	Score
	Monitor the following			
1	Cash / Market Cap[2]			
2	Technical Analysis[3]	Bull, Score = 1	Bear, Score = -1	
3	ROE[1]	> 35%, Score = 1	< 0, Score = -1	
4	Debt / Equity[1]			
5	Dividend > 3%[4]			
6	PEG			
7	Compare P/E to its average in last 5 years			
8	Compare metrics to their industrial averages			
			Total	
			(Add Total to Grand Score)	

Footnote

1   Negative equity is possible but not likely. Price / Cash is easy to find and it is similar to Cash / Market Cap.
2   I use Fidelity's Elliot Wave.
    Finviz.com offers a good alternative. If SMA50 is more than 10%, it is bullish and if it is less than 10%, it is bearish.
3   The market favors dividend stocks as of 4/13. It could change when interest rates rises.

Current findings as of 10/2013

From my current monitoring (10/2013) I found the following good candidates for future conditions to add to the scoring system:

- The Total Grade and the Cash Flow Grade under Fundamental Grade Blue Chip Growth (not free now). http://navelliergrowth.investorplace.com/bluechip/password/index.php?plocation=%2Fbluechip%2F.
- Zacks (free for individual stocks) grade for short term.
- IBD's composite grade (required a subscription).

The following three should be included.

- Stocks with dividend yields > 3% and less than 5% (trying to skip the return of capital).
- Debt / Equity.
- Earning growth (current quarter to quarter from the prior year).

Filler: The New Norm

Have you noticed that the index performance was (still is I bet) wrong in MarketWatch on 3/1? The Arrow and Color indicated the market was down but actually it was up. It is so basic. Recently they said the market was down by 2% but actually it was up by 2%. If it happened in my old company, the programmer and his/her manager would be fired.

Before I posted in Facebook, they asked me to select all the pictures of a lion. I skipped those pictures with two lions and they told me I was wrong. They need to hire someone who have graduated from high school.

They told me they're college graduates. Another sad day for our education system! Have you watched the movie "Idiocracy"? If you have, you understand what I mean.

Mediocrity is the new norm!?

4 A scoring system for growth stocks

When the market favors growth stocks more than valued stocks, we would like to change our scoring system to place emphasis on growth.

In the early recovery phase of the market cycle (about one or two years after the market crash), value stocks are favorable. After this period, growth stocks are favorable in general.

There are some easy ways to find out from many financial sites which is the current favorite.

Alternatively, you can find the performance of an ETF on value stocks (SPYV for example) for the last three months and compare it to an ETF (SPYG for example) on growth stocks.

The other suggested metrics are the change of P/E (also referred as PEG) and change of Debt/Equity.

When you have a good size of the evaluated stocks, you can monitor them and change your scoring system accordingly. The following are the examples of suggested changes.

- Forward E/P. Decrease the number from 2 to 1.
- Earning Growth Q-Q. Increase the number from 1 to 2.
- Sales Growth Q-Q. Increase the number from 1 to 1.5.

5 A scoring system for momentum stocks

When you buy stocks and hold them for a month or so, you do not care about fundamentals but rather the momentum. The momentum metrics such as SMA-20 (Single Moving Average with 20 days average) would be appropriate. The other metrics are: price increases from last 15 and 30 days, earnings revisions and any catalyst (such as a new drug) and insider's purchases.

The rotation by institutional investors is a critical metric for momentum stocks.

6   Sectors to be cautious with

There are many reasons to be very cautious when investing in the following sectors. However, Technical Analysis (a.k.a. charting) would give you more hints than the fundamentals for stocks for these sectors. If the big guys are dumping, most likely Technical Analysis (or the simplest SMA-20) would tell you that.

Loan companies/banks

The financial statements do not show the quality of their loan portfolios. Following this advice, you may be able to skip the banks that melted down in 2007. The peak of Citigroup is $550 and several banks went bankrupt.

Many metrics are not relevant for banks such as Debt/Equity and EBIT. The rising interest rate would be good for banks' profits.

Drug (generic is ok)

Understanding the complexities of the drug pipelines, its potential profits for new drugs and the expiration of the current drugs may not worth the effort for most retail investors. In addition, a serious lawsuit and / or a serious problem with a drug could wipe out a good percentage of the stock price. When a drug shows unpromising sign(s) in any trial phase, the stock could plunge and vice versa.

Miners

It is extremely difficult to estimate how much ore (sometimes a miner owns several different types of ores and/or of different grades in the same or different mines) that a company has. It is further complicated by the complexities to extract and transport them. When the total of these costs is greater than its production price, the company will not be profitable. Understanding the market for ore futures is another discipline.

Many mining companies are in foreign countries such as Canada, Australia and countries in South America. Their financial statements of Canada and Australia are more trustworthy than most other emerging countries.

One potential problem of mining companies from many emerging countries is nationalization.

Mining rare earth ore is extremely risky when the profit depends on how China, a major producer of these ores, will price these ores. After China announced the export restrictions on rare earth elements, several non-Chinese companies announced to reopen their mines for rare earths, but few have made any profits as of 2013. Developed countries have stricter environmental regulations.

Coal and eventually oil suffer from the rising use of cleaner energy such as solar and wind.

Insurance companies

Insurance companies profit by:

1. The difference between the total premiums received and the total claims minus expenses in running the company.

2. How well they invest the premiums; you pay your premiums earlier than you may collect from any claims.

They can protect the profits in #1 by restricting claims by natural disasters such as earthquakes and by re-insuring. However, a bad disaster could wipe out a lot of their profits.

Even if the insurance company shows you its investment portfolio, most of us, the retail investors, do not have the time and expertise to analyze it.

Emerging countries (not a sector)

Their financial statements especially from small companies cannot be trusted, and many countries use different accounting standards. Emerging countries are where the economic growth is. I trade FXI, an ETF, rather than individual Chinese companies. I have lost a lot in small Chinese companies due to frauds and politics. To check out whether the stock is an ADR, try ADR.COM (https://www.adr.com/).

Stocks with low volumes (not a sector)

Most likely you pay a high spread to trade these stocks. They can be manipulated easier. I had a hard time trying to sell a stock owned by a few owners.

For simplicity, I trade stocks with the average daily trade volume over 6,000 shares (double it if the price is $2 or less). A better way could be by calculating the percent of your trade quantity / average daily trade volume; it would reduce the effect of penny stocks that have larger volumes due to the low prices.

Good business and bad business

Banking is a good business in a growing economy. My deposit in them makes virtually zero interest, and they loan the same money making 3%. If they are more cautious in loaning, they should make good profits.

Restaurant is an easy business to run, but it is very hard to make good money. With the rising of minimal wages, it will get even tougher. That could be the reason for so many coupons today. The high-end restaurants are doing better due to the rising stock market. The pandemic of 2020 would wipe out a lot of small restaurants.

Retailing is a tough business. Look at the top 10 retailers 15 years ago, I can only find two including Macy's that are still surviving. Most are either went bankrupt or being acquired. Even Macy's was not in good financial shape. Amazon is the killer.

Airlines are a tough business. You can tell by the average increase in fares in the last 10 years. It cannot even beat inflation. They have to charge you for everything. The next frontier charge is the rest room (especially for long-distance flights). Now I understand why they call themselves "Frontier Air". As of 2014, it is quite profitable due to mergers and lower fuel cost. The pandemic of 2020 may be the toughest time for airlines. As of 5/2020, Boeing has many serious troubles and they can only survive with a bailout from the government.

There are several software companies that produce software such as the virus detecting programs and tax preparation software. The customers faithfully buy new versions every year. That's great business.

7   Fidelity

Fidelity offers a strong screen function. The most unique feature is incorporating its Equity Summary Score (used to be Analyst's Opinion) and some outside researches such as Zacks and Ford.

From the main menu, select "News and Research", "Screen and Filter" and then "Start a screen".

The following example selects stocks with the following criteria: Security Price (2 to 250), Market Cap. (300 and above), Equity Summary Score (8 and above), Zacks (Strongest) and Ford (Strongest).

It displays the 10 stocks. Research each stock. Read the News about each stock. You may want to use Finviz.com, Yahoo!Finance and other sources to double check.

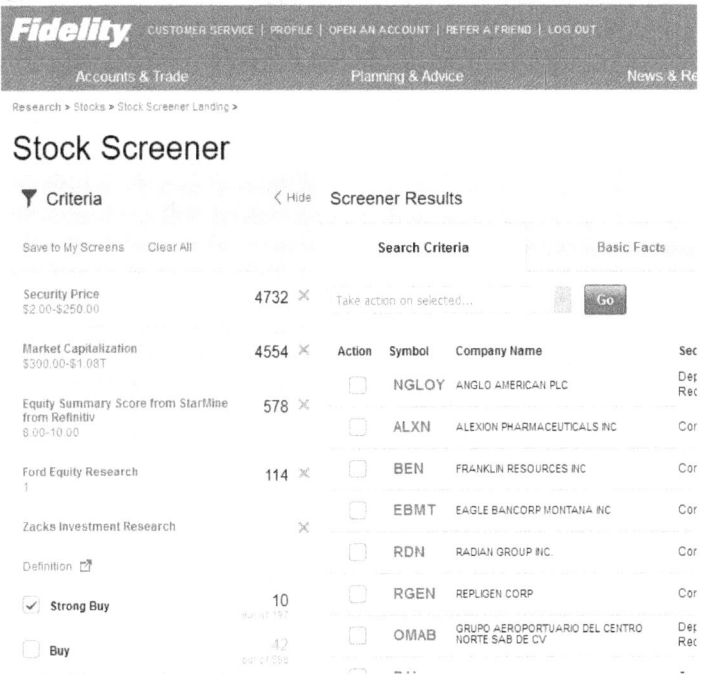

The following describes some of the features.

- Equity Summary Score. It is one of the major metrics I use in my proprietary scoring systems. They are not available to many small stocks. From my limited database in 7/2015 and for short durations, the results are:

Short Term: (7% return for the average)

Metric	Parm. 1	No. of Stocks	%		Parm. 2	No.	%	Predictability
Fidelity Analyst	Buy	150	10%		Sell	279	3%	Good

Long Term: (8% return for the average)

Metric	Parm. 1	No. of Stocks	%		Parm. 2	No.	%	Predictability
Fidelity Analyst	Buy	90	17%		Sell	208	4%	Good

It has its own limits, but they are very minor to me.

First, it does not have a historical database for verifying the screen performance such as the return after a year. However, I do not know any site that provides this function free. To work around this, I save the results in a spread sheet and update the performance.

Secondly, it does not provide many other filter criteria that can be found in other systems such as technical indicators or insider transactions found in Finviz.com. I use other sites for further evaluation.

Most investors should find that this screening is a very good tool and very easy to use.

8   Performance of my screens

I monitor the performance of my top screens every 6 months or so. Here is my September, 2013 summary. The purpose is identifying the screens that have performed well recently. It is for illustration purpose only. All returns are annualized. They are sorted by Grand Avg. in descending order.

Screen	Last Monitor 2/13	Current Test Avg.	Long-term Avg.	Short-term Avg.	Grand Avg.	Avail.
EP	39%	66%			59%	75%
BB3	35%	70%			53%	25%
LPSER	-21%	72%			49%	75%
MN	19%	53%			45%	75%
CW	64%	49%	39%	20%	38%	100%
LR	30%	37%			35%	100%
TT	30%	26%	71%	8%	35%	100%
TV2	50%	76%	14%	19%	35%	100%
BFSCB	5%	38%			31%	100%
DO	29%	24%	30%		28%	100%
AR	56%	53%	23%	6%	28%	100%
BE	81%	44%	10%	13%	25%	100%
FA	16%	27%			25%	100%
BS5BV	21%	25%			24%	100%
SE		53%	20%	-3%	23%	100%
CAO	-3%	17%	37%	12%	21%	100%
...	...	...	---	...	...	
Avg.	34%	19%	23%	5%	19%	

Screen.
They are the abbreviations. To illustrate, CAO is the screen looking for candidates for acquisition with low market caps. I have about 25 production screens. They have been selected among over 100 screens.

Last Monitor 2/2013.
Copied from the "Current Test Avg." from my last monitor in 2/2013.

Current Test Avg.

It is the average of the four tests on recent months. The four test dates are: 03/11/13 to 7/9/13, 4/9/13 to 8/7/13, 5/9/13 to 8/17/13 and 6/8/13 to 9/6/13. They are about 4 months apart. It is the most important average to reflect what worked recently.

Long-term Avg.
It is the long-term performance (about 12 months) of the actual, screened stocks. These are stocks that have been actually screened and some may have been purchased.

Short-term Avg.
It is the short-term performance (about 6 months) of the actual, screened stocks.

Grand Avg.
It is a weighted average of the above 4 return categories (Last Monitor, Current Test Avg., Long-Term Avg. and Short-Term Avg.) and they're sorted in descending order.

Run the top screens first as they have given me better returns in the past. It does not guarantee that they will perform as well as before, but they have a better chance to perform well than the screens scored below the average.

Availability.
To illustrate, if the screen found stocks in 1 out of the 4 tests, it is 25% available. These screens may not have enough data for prediction on the future results and there is a higher chance that I will not find any stocks using these screens.

Observations
The following are the personal findings on my own screens. You can do something similar to separate your top screens from the rest of your screens. Test and monitor the performances of your own screens.

- Usually the top half of the screens from the last monitor show up in this monitor though their ranks may vary.

- CAO in the last monitor should be better than it indicates. At least two companies had been acquired and they had very good returns. These two companies did not show up in the test as they're taken out from the historical database; it is termed as survivorship bias.

- CW is quite consistent to the last monitor.

- EP and BB3 have not found any stocks in actual usage. MN proves to be a good screen in these two performance monitors. I missed the opportunities to make good money from this screen – my mistake.

- LPSER is a risky screen demonstrated here and from the previous monitors. I prefer not to take unnecessary risk. Include a column of maximum drawdown as it is a good indicator to avoid risky screens.

- LR was below the average and that's why it had not been used. It is above the average in this monitor, so it will be used to some small extent.

- TT is above the average in these two monitors. The returns of screened stocks during this monitor are better in both long term and short term and hence it will be used.

- The original table (not shown here) has comparisons to SPY (an ETF simulating the market). Beating the market is my yardstick. If most of your screens beat the market, most likely they will beat the market again. However, there are exceptions such as when the market is plunging. In this case, value stocks are better than growth stocks, and cash is the king.

  The market during my last monitor is better than this period. If the return of SPY is negative in the last three months, there is a good chance that the market is trending down.

- There are some screens that just do not perform for a long while. They will not even be monitored next time. However, when the phase of the market cycle changes, the performance of these screens may respond differently.

- The test results are not always consistent. It could be due to my limited data, or the market does not behave normally.

*** Book 3: Technical Analysis (TA)

Technical analysis (TA) is the analysis of the price movements and the short-term trend and possible reversal, while fundamental analysis focuses on metrics such as price/earnings ratio and debts. TA assumes the future stock price behavior can be determined by the patterns of past price behavior – it is true more times than untrue. Traders use TA a lot and can profit by shorting stocks. Investors can use them to find the entry points and exits points and some investors only buys stocks with positive long-term trend (using SMA-200%).

Many times stock analysis based on fundamentals fail when the evaluation is solely based on fundamentals. Technical Analysis (TA) has the following characteristics:

- Most of the time, TA is profitable in the short term (less than 3 months). The weather man is more accurate in tomorrow's weather rather than a month away. TA can also signal the reversals.
- It is too many signals if you have more than three TA parameters. To start, use SMA (Simple Moving Average) and RSI(14); both are available in Finviz.com without charting.
- You can combine TA with fundamentals such as a rising SMA50 with increasing Insider Purchases. In addition, you can use more than one TA indictors.
- For market timing, TA is a huge part, but many fundamentals should be considered too. You can use similar techniques to time the market and time stocks and/or sectors such as Golden Cross / Death Cross.

Technical analysis wins for the following reasons:
- Information such as a new product or a major lawsuit pending is not reflected timely in fundamentals, but rather in technical analysis. It gives us guidance in understanding the trend of a stock or even the entire market.
- Most TAs are based on accumulated data. For example, if RSI(14) is greater than 65, most likely this stock is overbought. If there is no reason for this condition, you may consider to sell it.
- When too many investors follow TA, it would become self-prophecy.

- Do not act against the trend. The fundamentalist may buy a stock when it loses 50%, the TA investor most likely will not buy it. Many times the losing stocks will lose another 25% or so. The TA investor most likely buys it on the way up only or short it on the way down.

An example. NVRO (a stock symbol) has appreciated about 100% from mid Feb. to Oct. in 2016 despite its poor fundamentals. It has a new product that could revolutionize physical healing and eliminating pain that will not be shown in the fundamentals except by the eventual Forward P/E. Technical chart can inform us of the uptrend.

Volume is the confirmation. Institution investors drive the market. When the market (esp. the S&P 500 stocks) is down and the volume is up, there is a good chance institution investors are dumping their holdings. It is obvious when most of the indicators are up but the volume is small.

1   Technical analysis (TA)

The basics

Technical analysis (a.k.a. charting) is easier to learn than you might expect. It represents the trend of the market (a stock or a group of stocks) graphically. If more investors are in the market, the market would move upwards until it changes direction. We divide the trends into short-term, intermediate-term and long-term.

The chartists usually do not consider fundamentals as they believe they have already been priced into the stock price and some fundamentals are not available to the public. To illustrate, a new drug has been discovered, the stock price of the company jumps initially by insiders purchases and the informed. Its fundamental metrics do not demonstrate this right away, but many investors are buying to boost up the stock price as evidenced by the technical indicators such as SMA for 20 or 50 days.

The volume is a confirmation. When the stock moves up or down by 10% with a low volume, the trend is not yet confirmed.

The trend of the stock price is not a straight line in most cases. Hence a trend line is usually drawn to indicate the direction of the stock. Many investors believe the stocks fluctuate in certain ranges (i.e. channels) and the chart draws the upper value (the resistance line) and the lower value (the support line). In theory, the price of a stock fluctuates within the resistance line (ceiling for understanding) and support (floor). When it reaches its support, it becomes a buy and vice versa for a sell. Most charts including Finviz.com would display these lines.

When the price passes out of the channel, it is called a breakout. Darvas, one of the oldest and most successful chartists, profited from the breakouts of the resistance line and believed the stock was close to the support line of the new channel. Hence it would be a long way up in theory.

If it were so simple, there will be no poor folks

It works most of the time, but do not place all your money on it. For chartists, 51% is great (the same for playing Black Jack). Some trends reverse very fast such as the bio drug stocks in 2015. You need to hedge your bets such as placing stop orders. Most do not want to spend their lives in watching the trend from a big screen.

Most novices use too many technical indicators and lose in their performances to the professionals. Recently, most chartists were not doing all that great and I did not find many books on their success than a decade ago. It could be due to too many followers in similar setups. I verified it with my recent testing using Finviz.com.

Simple Moving Average

The basic technical indicator is SMA-N. It is the average of the last N trade sessions. When N is 20 (or SMA-20), we classify it as short-term. Similarly, SMA-50 is an intermediate-term and SMA-200 is long-term. I prefer 50, 100 and 250. This trend duration is important. For example, do not want to place long-term purchases using the short-term SMA-50. There are many modifications to SMA such as giving more weight to recent data, but I have not found them any better. Finviz.com includes this information without charting (SMA-20, SMA-50 and SMA-100 in percentages).

Defining the trend periods is rather arbitrary. I use SMA-350 to detect the market plunges and SMA-100 for stocks. Weighted Moving Average weighs more weight on recent price data.

It can be used to determine whether we are in bull, bear or a sideways market using SMA-50 (or SMA-200 for longer term) for the market (using SPY), the sector (using an ETF for the sector and the specific stock. The trend is up when it the price is above the SMA and the reversal of the trend.

https://www.youtube.com/watch?v=jdYNaE5GJ0k&list=WL&index=5&t=609s

The trend is your best friend
Most traders use TA for trending in a short duration. Investors can also use TA to time the entry and exit points for better potential profits. Value investors usually are patient and they do bottom fishing and they search for 'oversold' condition using RSI(14). Again high volume is a confirmation.

Many sites provide charting free of charge such as Yahoo!Finance. Finviz.com provides a lot of technical indicators without charting such as SMA% and RSI(14). It also provides screen searching for stocks that meet your technical analysis criteria.

Hands on
Bring up Finviz.com and enter any stock symbol such as AAPL. You can see the daily prices of AAPL from about nine months ago to today. Three SMAs (Simple Moving Average) are displayed as SMA-20, SMA-50 and SMA-200. The first two are for short-term trends. When the price is above the SMA, it is expected to be trending up. Again, the trade volume is used as a confirmation.

You can also see the resistance line and the support line drawn. In theory, the stock will trade within these lines. When it exceeds its resistance line, it is called a breakout, and vice versa for a breakdown. Sometimes it displays some technical patterns such as Cup and Shoulder and Double Down (both are positive patterns).

Select Weekly data. The Candle chart is better described than the Daily chart. Candles give us better descriptions of the price: open, close, high and low. The green color indicates the price is up for the period (a week in this example) and the red color indicates a down period.

In addition, Finviz.com includes some technical indicators in the metric section such as RSI. Most other chart sites are similar in the basics. Use Finviz's Help and select Technical Analysis for more description. Investopedia has enhanced descriptions on this topic.

TA patterns

There are many TA patterns such as Bollinger Bands and MACD. The patterns are based on the stock prices and many times they prove to be correct predictions especially on stocks with high volume and high market caps. Patterns have been repeating themselves many times as they are driven by investors.

Sites for TA
There are many free sites for charts with explanations of their technical indicators. Popular ones include BigCharts.com,

SmallCharts.com and Yahoo!Finance. Fidelity includes some unique features in its charts such as P/E.

Why I do not use TA as a primary tool for stock picking

My investing style is different from a day trader's. I prefer to 'Buy Low and Sell High' instead of 'Buy High and Sell Higher'. I try to find the real bottom price. TA will not find the bottom very easily but it tracks the trend better. As a bargain hunter, I do not expect the stock will rise fast as I'm usually swimming against the tide. However, value stocks could stay in the low price for a long time (i.e. value trap). I like to select stocks that turn around as evidenced by the SMA-20 and SMA-50.

With that said, my momentum portfolio has appreciated consistently and usually has the best performing stocks among all my portfolios. It is based on the timely grade from my subscriptions plus the metrics on timing.

Most chartists would also tell you to buy the stocks that have broken out (i.e. higher than the resistance line) and/or stocks at their highs. Contrary to value investing, you should exit when the trend reverses. The reversal could happen very fast and hence protect your portfolio by setting up stop loss (preferably with trailing stop) orders.

My opinion

I do not want to argue whether TA is good for you or not. You need to find that out. Most likely, the day traders and very short-term traders will profit more from TA than the investors seeking value stocks for the long-term gains.

Random remarks

Even if you do not use technical analysis, you should spend some time in learning it. It is better to marry fundamentals and TA. My random remarks are:

- The Institutional investors (insurance companies, pension funds, mutual funds, etc.) use TA and they MOVE the market. A lot of times it becomes a self-fulfilling prophecy. It is better to join them as most of us cannot beat them.

- Day traders take advantage of the institutional investors by spotting their trends.

- Most TA stocks should be good sized and have large average daily volumes. I prefer to use TA on value stocks to prevent long-term losses.

- I do know some folks making big money using TA, but I know more making good money using fundamentals. Since TA predicts the market better in the shorter term, its practitioners may have to pay higher taxes (in today's tax laws) in taxable accounts.

- Our objective should be making money with the least risk. Once you claim to belong to a certain group of either Fundamental or TA, you will be biased and forget your primary objective in investing.

- TA tracks the last two big market plunges (2000 and 2007) pretty well. The chart will not warn you right away for the upcoming plunge (as it depends on past data) to avoid the initial losses, but they will warn you to avoid bigger losses.

Afterthoughts

- Besides searching for stocks that have potential breakouts, we should check the stocks we owned for potential breakdowns. Technical Analysis tutorial.
https://www.YouTube.com/watch?v=GENBVwV8PMs

  SMA tutorial.
https://www.YouTube.com/watch?v=Na-ctpPsnks

Links

Fidelity video: Technical Analysis
https://www.fidelity.com/learning-center/technical-analysis/chart-types-video

2   Examples of using TA

I have outlined how we can spot market plunges using TA and I use it to monitor the market every three months or so (I recommend to do it every month and even more frequently when the market is risky). Here is an example of how to use it to trade individual stocks.

I have to admit I do not use TA that much on individual stocks and clearly I am not an expert in TA. If this article stirs up your interest, read more books or attend seminars / classes on TA. However, this book describes the basic and most useful technical indicators. There are many good and free articles from Investopedia on this topic. Personally I prefer to seek fundamentally sound companies at bargain prices and wait for their full appreciation. It has been proven to me many times over.

TA is very useful for momentum and day traders. With the rising volume, you can detect that the stocks are traded by managers of mutual funds, hedge funds, insurance companies and pension funds, and you profit by riding on their wagons.

Some stocks are good for TA. Usually they are larger companies with above-average volumes and are fundamentally sound. Avoid the stocks that are trending downwards unless you're bottom fishing. Let me pick CSCO (a cyclical stock) for an illustration. I bought it several times in 2012. I sold some in 2013 and 2014 making good profits. This is quite different from what short-term traders would use during the following:

The green line is a 50-day simple moving average (SMA) for the following chart using one year data.

If it does not display clearly on a small screen, type the following on the browser in your PC.

http://ebmyth.blogspot.com/2013/05/chart-for-ta-example.html

Buy the stock when it is above its SMA and sell when it is below. Following the chart would make good money based on this simple rule. Also, practice the strategy "Sell on May 1, Buy back on Nov. 1".

Not all stocks follow this profitable pattern. Fundamentalists may try to pick the bottom in late July while chartists enter positions on its upward trend. The chartists have an advantage to stay away from stocks in their downward trend.

Exponential Moving Average has better predictable power as it weighs more on recent prices. Some indicators / patterns work better in specific market conditions – all markets are different.

Volume is important as a confirmation. If the price of a stock is up with thin volume, the rise is questionable and it could be manipulated.

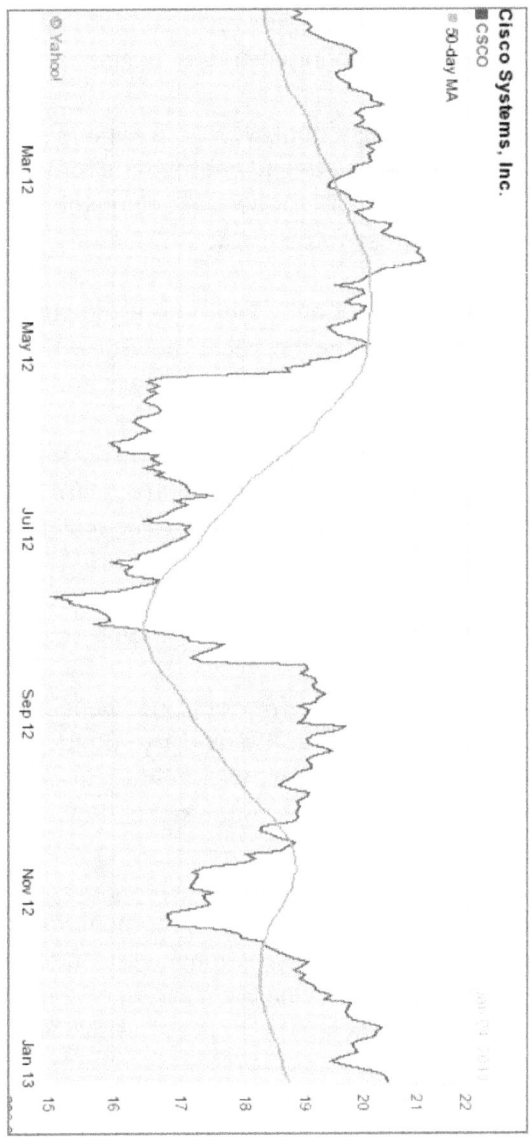

Table: CSCO   50-day SMA   Source: Yahoo!Finance

We can improve the trades by:

- Use different moving average in the number of days (50 in this example) and other indicators such as EMA (a moving average that weighs higher on more recent data). It may improve prediction accuracy and/or cut down on the number of trades. RSI(14) suggests overbought / oversold conditions.

- Instead of selling the stock for cash, consider selling the stock short. Selling short is definitely not for beginners.

- The accuracy is usually improved by a separate chart for the sector the stock belongs to and another one for the market. For CSCO, you can use an ETF for network companies and SPY (or a similar ETF) to represent the market.

  In theory and in theory only, when both the stock, the sector that the stock is in and the market all move down, the stock price has a high chance that it would move down, and vice versa.

  We use the 50 days (in SMA) for short-term holding of stocks (20 for even shorter holding period and 200 days for longer holding period). Personally I use 30 days for the sector ETF. Again, 'Days' is actually 'Trade Sessions'.

TA is not for most fundamentalists but it should be used

For a bargain hunter like me, TA would not benefit me a lot for picking stocks at their bottoms. I would try to pick up CSCO with prices ranging from 15-17 and all well below the moving average line, but TA would not show me a Buy signal. However, for short-term swing traders TA is a Godsend.

To me, TA is a good indicator for growth, momentum and for short-term trading. Some fundamentalists may use TA for entry and exit point is. Some recommend buying the stock when the price is above the SMA-200 (same as when SMA-200% is positive and that can be readily obtained from Finviz.com).

It is profitable for 'Buy High and Sell Higher' if you can are able to protect your profits effectively. This is also called 'Buy at a reasonable cost'. One's opinion.

In selecting a tool, you have to understand how, and why to use it and whether it fits your investing style. I use TA for market timing for the entire market more than on individual stocks. When I have more time, I probably would use TA more frequently.

Most of us cannot spot the bottom of a stock; I have had some success but most likely they were due to luck. When a stock is moving up from the bottom, there is a good chance it will move further up. TA shows it and the volume confirms it.

Conclusion

Even a fundamentalist like me can benefit a lot by using TA. This book touches on the very basics of TA.

Besides monitoring the fundamentals of the stocks you bought once every 6 months, you should analyze their technical indicators more often (1 month to 3 months depending on your available time). When the market is risky (close to the SMA average), run the SMA chart more frequently (say once a week).

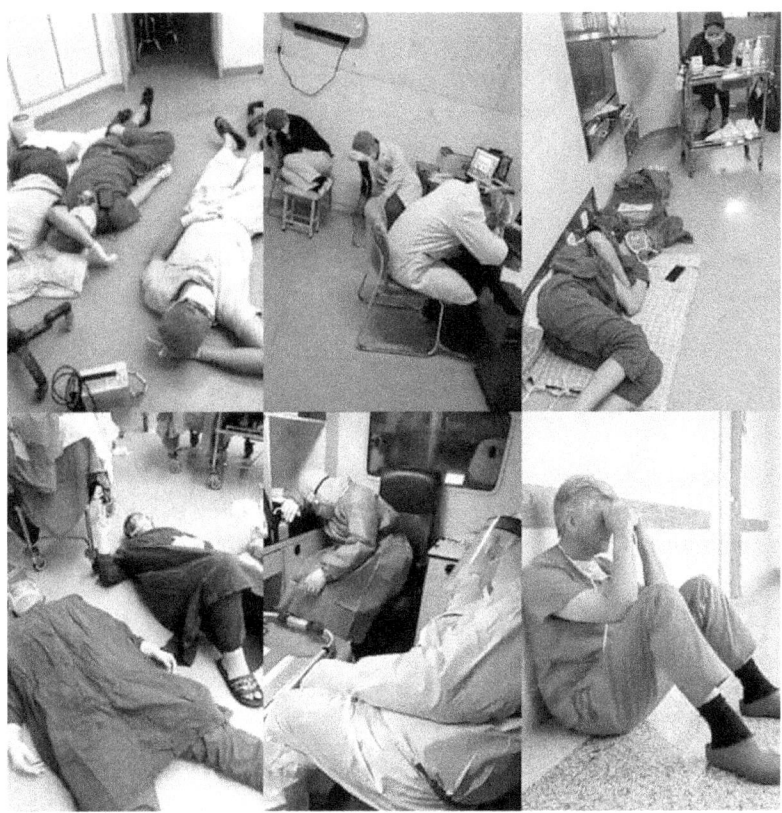

Not taken by me.
They are more important than ALL entertainers and athletes

3   Easy TA without charts

Bring up Finviz.com from your browser. Enter the stock you're evaluating. SMA-200% stands for Simple Moving Average of the last 200 trade sessions. RSI(14)% is the relative strength index for the last 14 trade sessions.

The following is just a suggestion with conservative parameters. Adjust the parameters according to your risk tolerance and requirements. Do not buy the stock with SMA-200% is < 0 (trending down), SMA-200% > 40 (peaking), or RSI(14)% > 65 (overbought).

Filler: Love is blind

The dividend lovers say that when their stocks drop by 50%, they are getting a 50% raise. There was a recent article on this STUPID logic - insulting my intelligence by just reading the title. When the company is bankrupted, they are getting a 100% raise. Should they check in the closest clinic to get their brains examined?

Love is blind and fools are fools and this cannot change the truths in our lives.

---

4   Bollinger Bands

Bollinger Bands have been proven useful for traders. In theory, the stock is traded between the upper band and the lower band forming an envelope. For more info, click the following link.

http://www.investopedia.com/terms/b/bollingerbands.asp

The following chart was drawn by Yahoo!Finance for CSCO from 8/7/2012 to 8/7/2014 selecting Bollinger Bands for the 50 days as a parameter. If you trade more often, use 20 days. If the chart is too small to display on your screen, enter the following in your PC's browser.
http://ebmyth.blogspot.com/2014/08/screen-csco-bollinger-bands-50.html

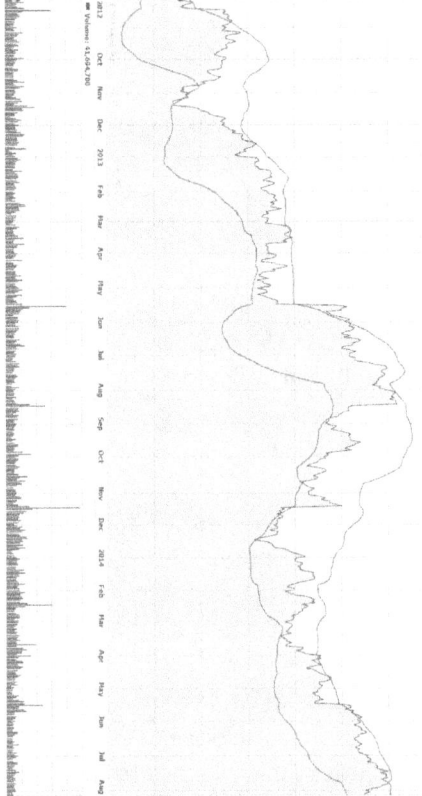

Bollinger Bands 50 Days.   Source: Yahoo!Finance

You buy the stock when the price is close to the lower band and sell the stock when it is close to the upper band.

When the stock price passes the upper band, it is called a breakout. Similar for the stock falling below the lower band.

From the above, we should make some good money.

It is advisable to use at least one more technical indicator. I recommend the RSI(14), which is also accessible from Yahoo!Finance or similar sites. When it is above 70, it is overbought, so I recommend selling the stock. When it is below 30, it is oversold, so I recommend buying the stock. However, fundamentals have not been considered. Some stocks just go to zero and some just surge.

5   MACD

MACD, Moving Average Convergence Divergence, is an effective momentum (i.e. short-term) indicator used by most traders. When the stock price is crossing above the zero line, it is a buy and vice versa. It may give false signals in sideways fluctuation.

###
Again, try to master SMA and RSI(14) first. Using too many indicators usually harms you more than helps you. You can use Finviz.com to search stocks with technical indicators.

6   Other TA indicators/patterns

They are briefly mentioned here. Click on the links or use Investopedia for more descriptions.

Double Bottom is a bullish pattern as the support line is stronger than the resistance line.
Double Top is the opposite and is a bearish pattern. I prefer the price of the second top is less than the price of the first top. It seems there are no enough investment in this stock to break out of the second top.

Resistance and Support. The stock is supposed to fluctuate between an imaginary zone of resistance and support. Short-term traders may sell when the price is close to the resistance line and close any short positions when it is close to the support line. However, breakouts from this zone are possible and many traders trade stocks on breakouts. It is a little similar to 52-week highs and lows. The trend line indicates the trend of the stock.

Cup and handle is a bullish pattern. The stock price peaks and then forms a shape of a cup and handle.

Head & Shoulder is a bearish pattern while the reversed Head & Shoulder is a bullish pattern. It signals that the peak (the head) has been reached and the second top (the shoulder) has failed to reach the previous peak.

Stochastic Oscillator. It is similar to RSI(14). Many traders use this indicator. If it is above 65, it is overbought. If it is below 30, it is oversold. In general, I would trade on an uptrend when the stock is moving from 60 to 85; it depends on how volatile the stock is. It is better to use with other indicators and as a reference.

To illustrate when to buy, one suggestion is to buy when this indicator changes to an uptrend while the price is still going down.

Many traders follow these technical indicators and SMA. They could become "self-fulfilled" prophecies.

Link

Chart patterns. https://www.youtube.com/watch?v=o6hZma0bajE

7   More on technical analysis

This chapter describes some TA indicators that can help us. Click on the following links for a better description.

- Finviz.com.
  It has SMA20%, SMA50% and SMA200% to represent the short-term, intermediate-term and the long-term indicator. SMA stands for Simple Moving Average and n for days for the duration of the average (for example, 20 days for SMA20%).

  If you are a long-term investor, use SMA-200% (or SMA-350%). Using SMA-20% would cause a lot of sells / reentries, which costs more in trading fees.

Buy when the price is above the Moving Average line and sell when the price is below it. Finviz.com provides the percent of moving above the moving average to indicate just how much the price deviates from the average.

If you hold the stock for an average of 50 days, use SMA50%, and so on. If you hold stocks for an average of 90 days, you have to create your own SMA using one of the many web sites including Yahoo!Finance and specify 90 days for the period.

Try other similar technical indicators such as EMA, which is supposed to weigh more on the more recent data. A weather man can predict tomorrow's weather better than the weather a week away.

- RSI(14) indicates whether the stock is overbought or oversold. RSI oscillates between zero and 100. Traditionally, and according to Wilder (the author of this method), RSI is considered overbought with a value above 70 and oversold with a value below 30 as described in the article.

  When it is oversold, most likely the stock will fall, and vice versa.

(http://stockcharts.com/school/doku.php?id=chart_school:technic al_indicators:relative_strength_index_rsi)

  Click here for another article.
  (http://financial-dictionary.thefreedictionary.com/Relative+Strength+Index)

- Cup and handle is a popular indicator of when the stock price would surge.
  (http://www.investopedia.com/terms/c/cupandhandle.asp)

- Double bottom indicates that the stock will move up.
  (http://stockcharts.com/school/doku.php?id=chart_school:chart_analysis:chart_patterns:double_bottom_revers)

It shows a double bottom for Apple in 2013.

8   Using Fidelity

Click "Research and News" and then "Stock". Simple charting and advanced charting are both provided.

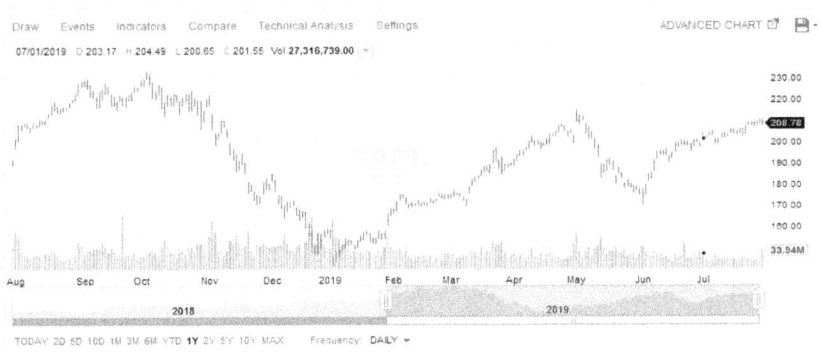

Hints:

- Fidelity provides suggested stops.
- Click on the Support and Resistance under Technical Analysis to display the Resistance Line (upper limit). Click on the Resistance Line and you can get the Support Line (lower limit).
- Click on Advanced Chart and then click on "learn how to use the chart".

Under Advanced Chart, select Draw and Trend Line. Select the upper line by touching the highest points and do the same for the lower line.

*** Book 4: Market Timing

There is no need to time the market from 1970 to 2000. From 2000 to 2014, the market crashed two times with an average loss of about 45%.

Using picking apples as an example, sometimes they may be sour but sometimes they may be tasty. The difference is picking them at the right time. It applies to market timing.

Market timing is about educated guesses. Hopefully we will have more rights than wrongs when we follow general guidelines. It would reduce risk and could benefit us financially in the long run. Recently we have more false signals than the period between 2000 and 2010. However, it is better to follow a proven system. The harm could be minimal except for tax consequences as the system would tell you return to the market briefly.

I divide the market timing in three categories by durations as follows. All time durations are estimates for discussion and all markets are different.

	Duration
Secular cycle	20 years (actually less)
Market Cycle	5 years (not the current one)
Correction: 10-20%	1 per year
5-10%	2 per year (count the above as 1)

Market plunges have losses between 30% and 55% usually. There is a gray area for the 20% to 30% losses, which does not happen often. When the market plunges, it plunges hard and fast. My techniques tell you to exit the market and when to return to equities. The techniques are based on falling prices, so they will not indicate peaks and bottoms, but they will help you to reduce further losses.

Within the secular market, there are market cycles. There is a super cycle that I ignore as I find it not too useful.

Every market is different. Today we have excessive money printing that changes all the previous logic such as the average length of a market cycle. If the USD is not the reserved currency, the market would fall. However, the correlation of the market and the economy will correlate again. We do not know when, but it will. Otherwise, we have to rewrite all the books on investing. For instant gratification, you can read <u>Simplest Way to Time the Market</u> and skip the rest of this lengthy section for now.

1   The power of market timing

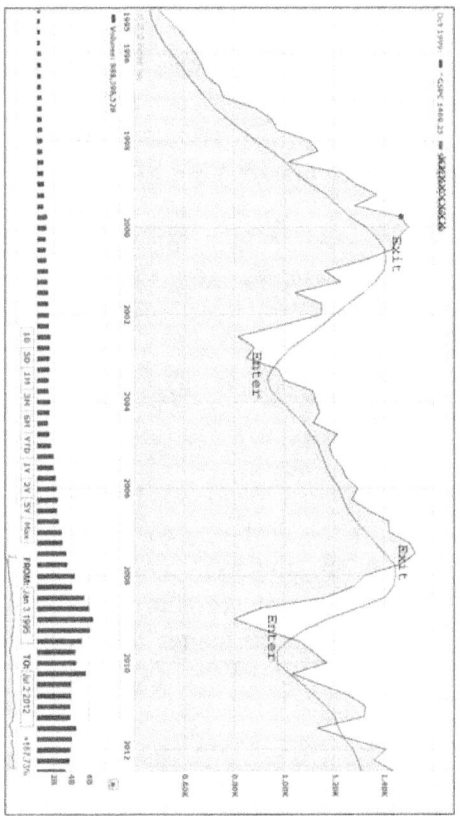

Most e-book readers allow you to select the graph to make it fit entirely on your screen. I use SPY, an ETF simulating the market. Detecting market plunges as seen in this graph indicates the exit points and reentry points also from 2000 to 9-2009 as follows.

Market Plunge	Peak	Bottom	Indicator Exit	Indicator Reenter
2000	08/28/00	09/20/02	10/01/00	06/01/03
2007	10/12/07	03/06/09	02/01/08	09/01/09
			08/01/11	11/01/11

Table: Vital Dates

For simplicity I skipped a few brief exits and reentries since 2011. You can run the simple chart once a month. When it indicates a potential market plunge is close, run the chart once a week. The last row   represents   a   false   signal.

This is based on stock prices so it may not identify the peaks and bottoms precisely, but so far it has not failed to avoid big losses and ensure big gains by reentering the market. I hope the next market plunge would give us enough time to act as these two did.

Unbelievable return with market timing

Calculate how much you made if you followed the above exit points and reenter points from 2000 to today. I bet you would have made a good fortune.

I compared the above returns with the SPY without market timing from 1-2000 to 9-2013.

There are many assumptions. Dividends and compounding are not considered. My return should be substantially better if I include buying contra ETFs during the exits and selling them during the reentries. I was shocked by the incredible return by using this simple market timing. Again, past performance does not guarantee future performances.

Summary info:

S&P 500 1-2000 to 9-2013	With Market Timing	Without Market Timing
Better	**500%**	
Gain	1,000	167
Gain %	68%	11%
Annualized gained	5%	1%
Days	4,959	4,959

Calculations:

S & P 500	With Market Timing	Without Market Timing
1-2000	1,469[1]	1,469[1]
Exit 10/01/00	1,041[2]	1,041
Enter 06/01/03	1,041	964[4]
Exit 02/01/08	1,489[3]	1,379[4]
Enter 09/01/09	1489	1,020[5]

Exit 08/01/11	1,888	1,293
Enter 11/01/11	1,888	1,251
09/03/13	2,469	1.638
Gained	2,469 – 1,469=1,000	1,638-1,469=167
Gain %	1000/1469 = 68%	167/1469 = 11%
Annualized gained	68% * 365/4959=5%	11%*365/4959=1%
Better	(1,000-167)/167 = 500%	

Portfolio with Market Timing:

[1] Both start with S&P 500 of 1,469 on 1-3-2000.
[2] 10/01/00
The market timing portfolio exits the market and remains the same value of 1,041 until 6/1/00.
[3]   02/01/08
The market timing portfolio exits the market and remains the same value of 1,489 until 9/1/09.

'1,489' is calculated as follows:
1,041 * (1 + Rate) = 1,041 * (1 + 1,379-964)/964) = 1,489
where the S&P 500 is 964 on 6/1/00 and 1,379 on 2/1/08.

The other calculations are based on the S&P 500 at 1,020 on 9/1/9, 1,293 on 8/1/11, 1,251 on 11/1/11 and 1,636 on 9/3/13.

Portfolio without Market Timing:

[1] Both starts with the S&P 500 of 1,469 on 1-3-2000. We could use the 9/3/13 the S&P 500 value, but it would not account for some compounded interest considerations.
[4] S&P 500 is 964 on 6/1/00 and 1,379 on 2/1/08.
[5] 02/01/08. The portfolio value is calculated to be 1,020 as follows:
1,379 * (1 + Rate) = 1,379 * (1 + (1020-1379)/1379) = 1,020
where S&P 500 is 1,379 on 2/1/08 and 1,020 on 9/1/09.

The other calculations are based on the S&P 500 at 1,293 on 8/1/11, 1,251 on 11/1/11 and 1,636 on 9/3/13.

I cannot believe the shocking return with market timing. I checked my calculations and there was nothing wrong that I could find.

2   Market timing example

The market is making new highs. There are always two camps of market timers. One camp predicts a crash is coming while the other predicts it will continue making new highs. This article includes both arguments and suggests how and what actions you need to take to protect your investments.

Management summary

The market is fundamentally unsound evidenced by fundamental metrics but technically sound evidenced by technical metrics that both will be described in this article. The data were obtained on 09/22/2018. The market has not changed a lot as of 01/2020.

Suggested actions

No one predicts the market correctly and consistently. Otherwise there are no poor folks. Moving the risky investments such as most stocks to cash too early would miss the potential profits. Moving it too late would risk the loss of your stocks.

Your actions depend on your risk tolerance. If you are conservative such as a retiree, you may want to have a larger portion of your investments in lower risk such as CDs and bonds. You can take one of the following three actions or combine all of the three actions.

1. When the market turns to technically unsound, it is time to move your stocks to cash. The market timing indicators may give false signals. In this case, the indicator would tell you to move back to stocks. Most likely you do not lose much except dealing with the consequences of taxes in non-retirement accounts.
2. Move a portion of your risky investments into cash, laddered CDs and/or short-term bonds. Again, the size of the portion depends on your risk tolerance.
3. Use stops. The sell orders would be changed to market orders when the stocks dip below prices specified by you. I prefer to use SPY or other ETF to determine the market direction. Some sectors and some stocks move faster than others. In one crash, my energy stocks were still profitable while the market was tanking. Eventually these energy stocks caught up and fell fast. Today's highly profitable stocks are FAANG stocks as a group.

I propose and prefer 'manual stop orders' to prevent market manipulation. However, usually large ETFs cannot be manipulated easily. Manipulators try to profit from your stop orders. Set a stop order price in your `mind. When the stock falls to that specified price, sell it via a market order.

My friend confirmed my "manual stop order":

"High-frequency trading via Algo Trading Strategy can see exactly where pre-set trailing stops are and sweep across them (play them) like strings on a violin. Pre-set a trailing stop and it is bound to be triggered because Algo hunt them down. Then watch the market rip higher."

Analysis: Fundamentals and Technical

It consists of Fundamental Analysis and Technical Analysis. The former measures how expensive the current market is and the latter measures the trend of the market.

Many metrics were obtained from Finviz.com as of 9/22/2018 while others are obtained from other websites. With the exception of Fidelity.com, all websites described here are free and readily available. It also serves as a guide on how you can do your own market timing especially after a few months.

The following chart uses SPY to represent the market of the top 500 stocks. It is market cap weighted. It means the higher the market cap the stock, the higher percent of the stock is represented in the index. It turns out most are riskier FAANG stocks.

Enter Finviz.com in your browser and enter SPY. I am not responsible for any errors.

Indicator	Pass	Current Value	Indicating
• Technical			
Death Cross[1]		SMA-50 = 2.3% & SMA-200 = 6.3%	Pass
Technical Analysis: 350 SMA%[2]	>0	Price above the SMA-350.	Pass
RSI(14)	<70	61	Pass
Duration (yr.)	<5	10	Fail
		Overall	**Pass**
• Fundamental			
Valuation			

P/E[3]	<15.7	25.4	High by 62%. Fail.
Shiller P/E[3]	<16.6	33.5	High by 102%. Fail
P/B[3]	<2.78	3.52	High by 27%. Fail.
P/S[3]	<1.50	2.33	High by 55%. Fail.
Oil price	30-100	70.71	Pass
Interest rate[6] T-Bill 1 months[7]	<5	2.05	Pass
T-Bill 3 months[7]	Yield	2.18	
T-Bill 30 years[7]	Curve	3.20	Pass
Flow to Equity[4]		-3.371M	Fail
Flow to bond[4]		7.206M	
Corporate debt/GDP[8]	<40	45%	High by 13%. Fail.
USD[5]		Strong	Fail
Gold		High	Fail
Bubble		Several	Fail
Market experts		Fear long term	Neutral
Politics		Trump	Fail
Misc.		Trade war	Fail
		Overall	**Fail**

[1] This is the market timing technique without using a chart.

[2] I tried to use SMA-400% to reduce false signals without success.

[3] Get it from http://www.multpl.com/ Same as CAPE.

[4] Get it from https://www.ici.org/research/stats. It is based on 09-12-18. "Flow to Equity" is based on domestic ETF estimate. Treat it as two phases in moving to equity. First phase of moving excessively to equity indicates the market is peaking. The second phase indicates the market is plunging when flow of equity is excessively negative.

[5] Global corporations will suffer in profits converted back to USD and hard to sell to foreign countries. [4] Get it from the above link.

[6] Rising interest is bad for corporations and high-ticket products, but good for lenders.

[7] Get it from https://www.treasury.gov/resource-center/data-chart-center/interest-rates/Pages/TextView.aspx?data=yield based on 09/21/18

[8] With the low interest rate, it may not be that critical. Corporations take advantage of the low interest rate.

Overall

Overall, technical is fine as the market is making new highs. Many aggressive investors exit the market on technical indicators only as the over-valued market could linger on for a long term such as from 2009 to 2017 so far.

Overall, fundamental is not sound. The increasing market price also is decreasing the fundamental metrics such as P/E, P/B and P/S. It is bad unless there is reason to support such as the fast earnings growth in 2009.

Many metrics are deteriorating

RSI(14) is getting closer to 65 (a passing grade specified by me).

Inverse yield curve (1.5 vs. 2.33) is about 61% apart from my interpretation and calculation. It is not a warning now but we should keep an eye on it. Most market crashes have occurred when it is 0% or negative. The theory is that in a normal case the short-term interest rates should be lower than the long-term interest rate.

Another source calculates it is 1.1% and that is very close to inversion since the last recession. From MarketWatch, the 30-year fixed interest rates is 4.66% and 1-year rate is 3.96% giving an inverse yield curve 18% apart, which is quite alarming.

Mathematically incorrect, today's full employment is at 4%. Most recessions are closely preceded by troughs in unemployment and the reverse for economy recovery.

GDP growth has been predicted from 1.8% to 3%. The 3% is from the White House for their obvious purpose. I predict it will pop up due to meeting the tariff deadlines, tax cuts and spending increases. It will then be declining to 2%. A healthy US economy should maintain 3% without special factors such as excessive immigration.

We have record debts: investors' margin, corporate debt and Federal debt. These are bubbles going to burst. Federal debt / GDP is about 95% (https://fred.stlouisfed.org/series/gfdegdq188S) today. It does not predict the market performance as this ratio was 53% and 55% before the last two market crashes. It will affect the long-term performance of the economy when we have to service the huge national debt.

We do have 10 years of stock growth at the expense of record Federal deficit. Thanks to President Obama from investors and no thanks from next generations who have to pay back our national debt. It is overdue for a correction. Hopefully it is not a crash which has an average loss of about 45%. We did have two recent corrections losing more than 10%: 2011-12 EU debt crisis and 2014-16 oil crash. The oil price has been rising from $30 per barrel to today's $70. It is still a long way from my warning of $120.

Potential triggers
Trade wars with China, Canada or EU will be the strongest trigger. Our most profitable companies are virtually all international companies. They need fair trade to prosper.

The other trigger is the possible impeachment of President Trump.

Check the validity of our charts
It seems some metrics vary. It could use after hour trading. It could be the "Days" may be "Sessions" – calendar day is different from trading session. I selected 10 years for most of the charts and StockCharts let me select only 5 years.

Here is a list of sites for charts.
https://www.stocktrader.com/2013/12/10/best-free-stock-chart-websites/
These are the three sites I use a lot: Fidelity (customers only), StockCharts and Finviz.com (missing some metrics).

As stated before, SPY may not be the best to represent the market. I prefer an ETF for 1,000 stocks and weigh the stocks evenly (i.e. not according to the market cap). Google "market timing 2020 (or current year)" for more expert info. Here is one.

Mid-year update

Basically nothing significant has changed recently: The market is fundamentally unsound and technically sound after the recent rally. The only update is our national debt is skyrocketing. Today's

"Debt/GDP" is similar to the market height in 2000 and we know what happened afterwards. That's why Buffett has accumulated a lot of cash now.

Even with the unlimited QE (i.e. printing money excessively), the high inflation and market crash predicted by many experts have not been materialized so far. This is my third prediction in "Disaster of 2020". The status of USD as a reserve currency will be shaken; I do not know when, as I do not have a time machine.

Why the market keeps going up while the economy is going down? The Fed has provided a lot of cash and the cash is chasing a fixed number of assets such as gold and stocks. It is the simple, proven theory of demand and supply. It will continue for a while as long as there is unlimited supply of money. At some point, it will pop. At that time, it could lead to a long recession, unless the economy improves as it did in 2009. The smart Fed chairman knows how it will harm the country by excessively printing money. However, he has to obey his boss who is seeking for reelection.

I expect we are in a prolonged period of low interest rates and even negative interest rates. When the rates are negative, our Treasury bonds are no longer marketable. The foreign central banks including China would dump our national debts if it has not been already started. The economy is dressed up nicely in an election year. Giving us free money is the easy way to buy votes, but the long-term effects are very harmful.

Using cheap money to buy back the company's stock would boost the stock price and hence make the management wealthier. It is a false sense of the stock value. When the company cannot pay back the debt obligations, the company would go bankrupted. If the U.S. were a company, she has gone bankrupted already.

As of 6/15/2020, QQQ (representing NASDAQ stocks) has been up 11% YTD and it is far better than DIA (representing DOW stocks) and SPY (representing the 500 large stocks in the S&P Index and losing about 5% YTD). QQQ has a lot of tech stocks while DIA has a lot of losers including Boeing. Most FAANG stocks are making record highs and QQQ is market cap weighed.

Most of the ETFs on chips have been up more than 40% in a year. I bought Amazon and two chip ETFs. I use trailing stops to protect my portfolio. Huawei is buying a lot of U.S. chips in the 120-day relaxed period. In September this year and if there is no extension, I would sell these chip ETFs fast.

I have used the strategy described in my book "Profit from the recovery of the pandemic" to take advantage of this volatile market. I used 5% as the threshold and I had too few trades; now I changed to 3%. Expecting a market crash, I weigh more on contra ETFs. As described in the same book, I bought a lot of contra ETFs, GLD and the stock of a gold miner. It is for insurance. ETFs on oil is my big mistake.

If the U.S.D. loses the status of reserve currency (not likely soon), it would bring prolonged depression and high inflation in the U.S. In this case, it is safer to invest in real estate, precious metals and profitable companies than in CDs and bonds that would lose values due to inflation.

Check out many articles on the status of the current market. Many have opposing views, so you have to make your own decision. In any case, play it safe with stops. Here is one article from MarketWatch.com.

Canary warning?

When I was working on my new book "Best stocks to buy for 2021" on Dec. 10, 2020, I found something really strange. I have never rejected so many stocks that have Fidelity's Equity Summary Score higher than 9. I rejected them as there were a lot of dumping from the insiders. Insiders know their companies better than most of us. Is it the canary telling us the market is over-valued?

Initially the following stocks have been screened by my value screens. Buy any one of the following stocks, **only** if you have good reason(s).

Symbol	Fidelity Score	Insider Purchase
BCC	9.9	-24%
GPI	10.0	-17%
HEAR	10.0	-75%

HIBB	9.4	-30%
HVT	9.5	-37%
HZO	9.5	-27%

How can HEAR score a perfect 10 while the Insiders' Transaction is -75% (I treated -2% is normal). The analysts must be wrong this time, or they believe the market will continuously make new heights. Will update the performance results later to see who is wrong.

A correction or a crash?

In Dec., 2018, the S&P500 is about 15% down and a crash is about 45% down.

If a crash is coming, there should be additional 30% down. If it is a correction (15% average), then we have it already. Should we pick up bargains now? Or, are they bargains? It is a trillion dollar question.

We need a trigger for a market crash like the financial crisis in 2008 and the internet bubble in 2000. Besides the record-high margin debt, the possibility of Trump's impeachment and a trade war, I do not see any.

Filler: CIA mistook it as a missile silo in China.

3   *Spotting big market plunges*

No one can consistently predict the correct stages of the market cycle. This chapter is intended for educational purpose only. However, if we have more rights than wrongs with our calculated and educated guesses, we should do well. As in everything in life, there is no guarantee. From 2000 to 2008, we only have one false signal for our SMA-350 out of 3 signals. Since then, we have more false signals.

Technical detection of a market plunge

The following chart is created by Yahoo!Finance. If it does not display well on a small screen, copy the following link to your browser to display it on your PC.

http://ebmyth.blogspot.com/2013/05/ta-graph-for-spotting-plunges-chapter.html

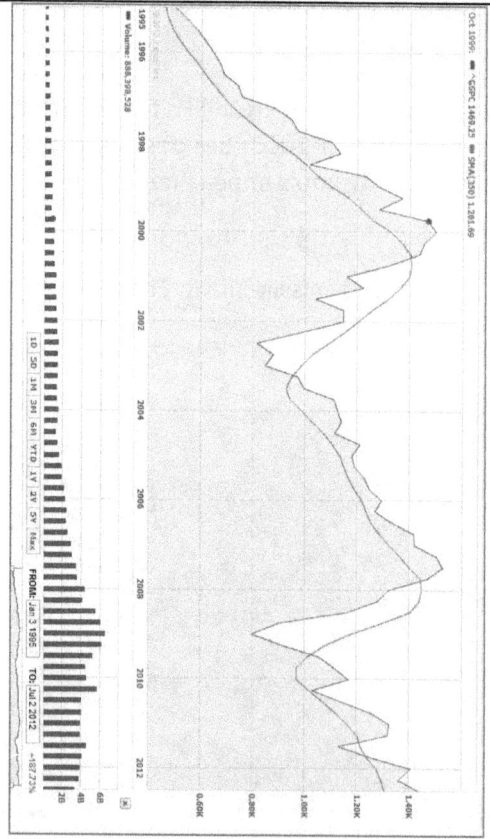

350 days simple moving average (SMA). Yahoo!Finance

The red line is the 350-day SMA, Simple Moving Average. If the stock price is below the moving average, it has detected a market plunge by this chart. Return to the market when the price is above the moving average line described as Early Recovery later. "350 days" are trading sessions. I have tried different "days" and 350 is the best fit for the last two market plunges, but it does not mean it would be the best fit the next market plunge.

We have two cycles described in the chart. From the above, we should leave the market in the first quarter of 2000 and return to the market on the first quarter of 2003.

On the second cycle, the chart tells us to get out in Dec. 2008 and come back in July 2009 approximately. Enlarge the chart by selecting 5 years instead of the maximum or use a larger monitor for a more detailed chart. The chart sometimes gives false signals to tell us to exit but tell us to reenter briefly. In most cases, we do not lose much except the tax consequences for selling. No technical indicators are perfect.

I started to come back on Feb. 2009. It was perfect timing but most likely or partly it was due to good luck. I was partially influenced by several articles I read.

Technical Analysis is based on the past data, so you cannot avoid the initial losses but it could reduce further and larger losses. From the above, the chart detected the two big plunges nicely allowing enough time to take actions. Will the next plunge be detected? It will I guess. However, it may not allow enough time as the last two.

Sometimes, we time it wrongly or prematurely and miss some gains by leaving the market too early. We need to treat it as buying insurance; it only pays big when the worst happens. When the "reward / risk" is too low, it is better to stay in cash. One's opinion.

Return to equity when the price is above the moving average (the red line). You should profit more by following the chart than 'Buy and Hold' or keeping your money under the pillow. For the last two market cycles, I returned to equities in Early Recovery (a stage of the market cycle defined by me) and profited. Can I be 100% sure for the next market plunge and come back in a timely order? Certainly not.

If most of your stocks are in tech, use QQQ instead of SPY. In addition QQQ is more volatile than SPY and the tech sector usually leads the market.

It can be created by following the steps; you need to create one yourself to detect the next plunge with current data.

- From Yahoo!Finance or any chart systems, enter SPY (or the S&P 500 index) or an ETF that represents the total market.
- Select Interactive Chart.
- Click Technical Indicators.
- Select SMA (simple moving average).
- Enter 350 days (actually it is trade sessions). Many chart systems use 'month' as unit, enter 12 or 11.67 if decimals is allowed (=350/12) instead of 350.
- Enter 1-3-2000 on "FROM:" or any "from date" that fits your screen.
- Select Draw.

Note. I switch to Fidelity for charting now as I cannot produce the same info from Yahoo!Finance. It could be my fault or a bug that should be fixed. If you cannot use Fidelity, try StockCharts.com.

Why fillers? A blank page space is too much to waste. Most if not all of the fillers are created by me.

Filler: The most powerful word
I was deeply moved by the family members of the church victims forgiving the shooter. I wrote a brief post: "Forgive" is the most powerful word in every language and in every culture. I forgot it until I received a response from Jim.

"Tony,
Without even knowing it, you made the greatest comment I have seen on here--and it had nothing to do with investing. You mentioned somewhere that "Forgive" is the most powerful word in every language. Wow."

4   Why the market fluctuates

The following chart uses SPY (simulating the market) with SMA-350 for the year of 2020 using Fidelity's charting function. It will be used to demonstrate how SMA-350 worked for 2020; the dates may be several days off. This article is written on 1/1/2021.

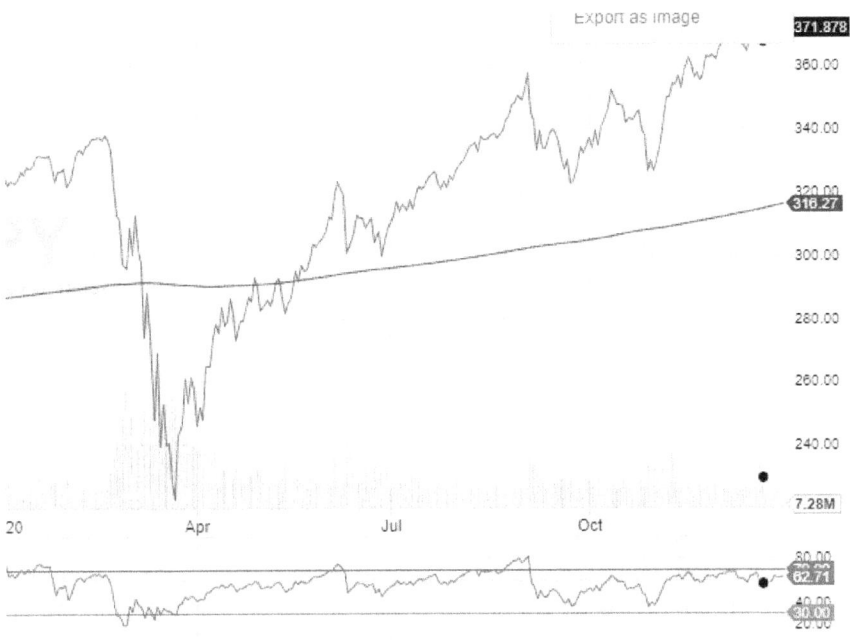

Market Timing

SMA-350 (Simple Moving Average for the last 350 sessions), described in this book, worked fine in 2020. It told us to exit the market on about 3/11/2020 and return on about the beginning of June. There were two false signals (on about 4/28 and 5/8) that told you to exit but return to the market shortly.

The other indicators are RSI(14) and P/E. Fidelity's chart uses 80 for overbought and 30 for under-bought for RSI(14). The market has been over-priced for a long while. In this case, technical analysis (SMA-350 I used in my example) works better than fundamental (P/E as one of the metrics); It has been sold for the entire 2020.

Why there is a big drop in late March and why it comes back
The trigger is the pandemic.

The market came back for many reasons:
- We understood the pandemic better.
- A lot of money in the sideline.
- The government supplies more money by printing it excessively.
- The government lowers the interest rate (almost to zero).

2021 prediction

It is quite hard to predict the market. Here are my thoughts. The market is not rational (fundamentally speaking).

For:

- The government keeps on excessively supplying money.
- With easy credit, the rising housing market leads to many profitable sectors such as furniture.
- Due to easy credit and recovering, many companies buy back their own stocks.
- Low margin interest rate usually boosts the stock market.
- If the vaccines can control this pandemic, many sectors will recover. As I demonstrated before, we have to wait one more year for some sectors such as airlines, restaurants and cruise lines.
- Trade war with China could be reduced under Biden.

Against:
- The pandemic has not been stopped.
- Unemployment is breaking previous record.
- Small businesses continue to go bankrupt.
- Complete decoupling with China.
- The government tools do not work anymore such as lowering interest rate.
- Super inflation is due to ample supply of money chasing a fixed amount of assets (stocks for example). It would also shaken the status of the USD as a reserve currency.

As in any market, there are two camps opposite to each other. Need to watch the market like a hawk and take actions accordingly (talk to your financial advisor first). I expect the plunge would cause the market to lose about 40% if it happen.

5   Market cycle

"Bull markets are born on pessimism, grow on skepticism, mature on optimism, and die on euphoria" - Sir John Templeton

The stock market has cycles as our practical interpretation of the above. It is about five years apart, but it fluctuates widely. I divide it into four stages: Bottom, Early Recovery, Up and Peak.

My defined four stages of a market cycle

We need to apply the right investing strategies to each of the four stages of the cycle.

- **Bottom**

    I would not invest for at least the first six months (or even a year) after the big plunge starts, which could lose over 25% in a few months. The exceptions are investing in contra ETFs and selling short for aggressive investors.

    I estimate it will take a year from the start of the plunge to the bottom, so I will normally sell stocks early in the plunge and do not buy stocks that are in the sector (sometimes sectors) that causes the bubble for about two years after the plunge.

    At the bottom, the high-yield corporate bonds (i.e. junk bonds) would prosper when the interest rates is decreasing to stimulate the economy.

    From mid-2007 to mid-2008, bonds suffered as the investors thought the sky was falling down - it was to those who lost the jobs and/or their houses. After that, some bonds especially the long-term bonds appreciated about 50% for the following year.

    The government lowered the interest rates and these bond prices with high interest rates surged. Correct timing in buying bonds could be very profitable.

    Long-term bonds have more impact by the interest rate: The lower the interest rate, the higher the bond prices of higher-yield bonds. The older bonds with higher interest rates are more valuable to the newer bonds with lower interest rates.

I define this period of the bottom from the start of the plunge to the start of Early Recovery.

- **Early Recovery**
It usually starts after one year from the plunge; no one can pin point the exact time consistently. By this time preferably earlier, we should have closed out all positions in contra ETFs and shorts.

Roughly speaking, October, 2007 (some use 2008) is the start of the market plunge. March, 2009 is the end of the bottom stage and the start of the early recovery stage of the 2007 cycle. However, every market cycle is different in where it starts and ends.

The one-year gain from the bottom is most profitable. It usually gains over 25% in a year from the market bottom. I, a conservative investor, had huge gains using some leverage in my largest taxable account in 2009. From my memory, I had a similar return in 2003 but I had not saved the statement as in 2009.

In this phase, value is a better parameter than growth in searching for stocks. If your investment subscription provides a composite value score and a composite timing score, the sort parameter of your screened stocks could be "Composite Value / Composite Timing" in descending order. Select the top stocks in this order. You still have to analyze the top-screened stocks.

Forward (same as Expected) P/E is a good metric. However, most companies may be losing money at this stage. Those companies that can last for more than one year with its cash reserve are potential good buys. The best appreciated stocks are beaten companies that have precious technologies and good customer bases. They could be candidates to be acquired if they are small enough.

- **Up**

Usually the growth metrics such as PEG could be better than the value metrics such as expected P/E during this phase. Most stocks are winners except contra ETFs and shorting stocks. When the growth stocks are making headlines and the defensive stocks are being dumped, this is the hint that we're well into the Up phase of the market cycle.

Locate stocks with growth metrics such as favorable PEG and high SMA-200% (from Finviz.com). Do not be scared on how much they have already appreciated. The strategy "Buy High and Sell Higher" works in this phase. Protect your profits with stops.

Ensure that they have value too. Skip the stocks with expected P/Es higher than 35 unless there are good reasons. Most stocks will gain due to the tide of the market. However, when they're overbought (RSI(14) over 65), be careful. When institutional investors sell these stocks, they will crash.

- **Peak**

  When everyone makes easy money and the interest rates is high, watch out. Stop loss and/or stop limit should be used to protect your investment. Check out whether there is any bubble that would be burst like the internet in 2000 and the finance (and housing) in 2007.

  Internet crisis is easy to spot, but not the financial crisis. In 2007 we had a cycle longer than the average which is about 5 years. The plunge is very fast and very steep – thanks to the institutional investors who drive the market down.

  Run the technical analysis chart described in the Chapter on Spotting Big Market Plunges at least monthly (weekly if you have time). Protect your investment. Do not fall in love with any stock (you can buy it back later at a deep discount). Making the last buck is a fool's game.

  Accumulate cash according to your risk tolerance. A retiree or a conservative investor would accumulate from 25% to 50% and should be ready to move to all cash when the plunge starts.

We can lower the cash percent if we use enough stop loss protection. Be psychologically prepared because the stock market may still rise for a while. There is no perfect market timing.

The 2007 Cycle

The market plunged starting in 10-2007 and ending in 3-2009 (bottom), started to recover in 3-2009 (early recover), and trended up from 2010 to 1-2013 (the up phase of the market cycle). As of 3/2016, it is the peak phase defined by me.

As of 1/2013, we have recovered all the market losses since 2007. However, as of 7/2014, the economy has not fully recovered compared to the economy before the plunge. The employment judging by the medium salary has not fully recovered and the economy is not expanding. It is uncommon that the economy does not follow the market. It is due to the excessive supply of money by the government and partly due to globalization to allow companies to hire overseas.

Although a W-shaped recession seldom happens, we have a chance today. We hope we do not have a depression and/or the similar lost decades that Japan has been experiencing. Some may conclude we are close to completing a market cycle from 2007 to 2016. As of 2016, the economy is recovering slowly and we're better than most other global economies.

Again, market timing is not an exact science as it involves irrational human beings and government interventions. The timing using market cycle described here is a guideline as it is hard to time it exactly.

The average market cycle is about 5 years, but they fluctuate. If we consider 2007 as the plunge, we have about 8 years of this cycle as of 2015.

In a typical cycle (few are typical), we have about one year in each of the 4 phases I defined (plunge, early recovery, up and peak).

Events/Triggers

There are financial events and triggers that cause the transition of one phase of the market cycle to another. They usually do not change the sequence of the phases (say not from Peak to Early Recovery), but they may change the duration of the phase. Examples are:

- The government announcing change of the interest rate,
- Change of employment, and
- Change of GNP.

Sectors in a market cycle (my suggestion)

Market Phase	Favorable	Unfavorable
Early Recovery	Financial, Technology, Industrial	Energy, Telecom, Utilities
Up	Technology, Industrial, Housing	
Peak	Mineral, Health Care, Energy, Long-Term Bond, Consumer Discretionary	
Bottom	Consumer Staples, Utilities	Consumer Discretionary, Technology, Industrial, Long-Term & high-yield Bond

The sectors that cause the recession usually take a longer time to recover. In 2000, the technology sector was not favorable in the Early Recovery phase, contrary to the above table. In 2007, the financial sector was not favorable in the Early Recovery phase. These are the "offending" sectors that cause the plunges.

In a recession, we usually cannot cut down on consumer staples and utilities, but we can cut down on buying consumer gadgets. Companies usually postpone investing in equipment and systems during a recession and expand when the economy is humming. The government usually lowers the interest rates right after the plunge to stimulate the economy.

6   Actions for different stages of a market cycle

There are different strategies for the different stages of the market cycle.

Strategies during market plunges

The market plunge is defined as the period between the market peak and the market bottom. It usually lasts for one year or two.

When you spot the potential plunge, consider the following actions. It depends on your risk tolerance and your investment style.

1. Contrary to popular belief, parking cash is a strategy too. Cash is needed later to move back to equities.

2. Be conservative: Buy stocks based on value and not based on momentum. Reduce your new purchases and take profits especially on momentum stocks. I buy one stock for every two or three stocks I sold during this stage.

3. Protect your portfolio with stop orders. It is one of the few times I recommend stop orders. If you watch the market every day, just place market orders when your stock falls to a specific price.

4. Buy contra ETFs for aggressive investors.

5. Sell cover calls. I prefer to sell the stocks I own.

6. Older folks may not want to sell the stocks with huge gains (due to tax consideration) or stocks that give them income stream of dividends. They can use options to protect potential losses for the stocks they own.

What to do after the plunge

In the first year after the start of the plunge, do not start to buy unless they are very good values. Aggressive investors should start closing their short positions/put options and selling contra ETFs.

When the market plunges, it usually takes at least one year to recover as investors believe they have to sell to protect their remaining nest eggs. Those sectors that cause the bubble will take even longer to recover.

After the plunge, watch out for the interest rate. If it is still high, it is the best time to buy high-yield bonds (i.e. junk bonds). Ensure that the corporation issuing the bonds would not bankrupt; the bonds from the old GM in 2007 lost most of their values. They will appreciate when the interest rates drops that the government would routinely do to stimulate the economy. 2008 is not a good year to invest in stocks and bonds except the contra ETFs and selling shorts, but 2009 definitely is (it is my Early Recovery phase of the market cycle).

Personally I prefer not to buy any stocks until the chart tells us to reenter the market. It is the fear that investors do not want to reenter the market. The market will always recover as in the past history.

Even before the recovery, some sectors (called consumer staple) are doing better such as health care, foodstuffs, utilities and pharmaceuticals that are always in demand. Interest-sensitive sectors such as housing and auto will suffer disproportionately. They are also called cyclical stocks. Consumer Discretionary are sectors that suffer a lot in a recession such as high tech products.

What to do in early recovery and after

When the market is starting to recovery (2003 and 2009 in the last two market cycles), the potential profit is the highest. Buy deeply-valued stocks on companies that have been beaten down. They will recover with the highest appreciation potential. I call it the bottom fishing strategy.

Larger companies are fishing too to acquire smaller companies that fit into their corporate synergy or small companies with the technology and/or the customer base they need.

Valued stocks could be defined a little differently in this phase. Many times P/E is not a good metric as most companies are losing money. 2003 is such a year. If you expect the recession will end in 2 years and the company has enough cash to survive in two years based on its annual burn rate, then it would be a buy candidate.

In both 2003 and 2009, I spotted at least one company that was acquired by a larger company. From my memory, one company in 2003 was acquired by IBM giving me more than 2 times return. In 2009, at least three companies were acquired giving me an average annualized return of over 200%.

Momentum strategy rewards us best from the end of the early recovery phase to the peak phase. The up phase started in 2004 for 2000 market cycle and 2010 in the 2007 market cycle.

Note. The parameters of SMA-200, SMA-350, SMA-90, etc. and RSI are different for market exit/reentry, correction exit and individual stocks. These are the guidelines only. Stocks are more volatile than the market and are very different among them. Hence, define the 'days' according to the historical pattern of the individual stock and how often you trade them.

Filler: My translation from my Chinese friend's poem

When you understand "everything is changing", you won't be boosting your achievements. Today's splendid life could be a mess tomorrow.

When you understand "everything is changing", you won't be sad. Today's gloom could turn into sunshine tomorrow.

When you understand "everything is changing", you know today's gain could be tomorrow's loss and vice versa.

When you understand "everything is changing", there is no need to react to today's loss, gain, happiness and sadness.

8   A non-correlation of the market and business

The Business Cycle (same as the Economic Cycle) is supposed to lag the Market Cycle[1] by about 6 months as the stock market is a leading indicator of the economy. As of May of 2013, this has not occurred. The U.S. economy does not correlate to the stock market. It seldom happens. The market has recovered most of its losses from 2007-2008 and actually is making new heights.

The economy is still in a recession considering the high unemployment / under-employment and the poor GDP growth. The global economies are more inter-connected than before, and our trade partners are also not doing well. Though there have been some recent signs of recovery in the U.S. economy, the job employment may never reach its previous peak. As of 3/2016, the non-correlation continues.

Is this non-correlation important to us, the retail investors?

For an economist, the Economic Cycle is important. For an investor, the Market Cycle is important. Economists forecast business growth, GDP growth, job growth, housing start, etc., and plan accordingly. Investors care about the potential appreciation of their portfolios.

It could be the beginning of this non-correlation for the coming decade. There is a good chance economists can no longer depend on the previous correlation to use the market to predict the economy at least for a while. As long as the market is moving up, investors are not concerned with the non-correlation.

However, most likely the market will correlate again in the future with the economy as there has always been a correlation as far as I can remember. Until the following reasons of this non-correlation change, the correlation will continue.

The reasons for this non-correlation

1. Most big companies are now global companies.
    Hiring at these multinational corporations (MNCs) depends on where the offer is for the greatest benefits including low workforce salary, educated workers, tax credits, less taxes, stable government, good infrastructure, etc. A good portion of MNCs' incomes are from foreign countries. Hence the U.S. market is getting less correlated with the U.S. economy which uses local employment as a measurement.

2. Too many government interventions.
    The government bailed out too many companies that should fail. No companies are too big to fail. It has not punished the executives/bankers to get us into this recession thru their greed.

The market may falsely expect that future failing companies will be bailed out. Hence, the stock market is expected to be protected by the government.

3. There is still a lot of easy money.
   Since the recession, banks are flooded with government money to invest. They loan out money to investors instead of loaning it to small businesses and house buyers to stimulate the economy. In addition, the demands from businesses and potential house buyers have been reduced. The cash reserves if not loaned out must be very high.

   Corporations now have the highest cash reserves for a long while. They use their cash reserves to buy back their own stocks, acquire companies and increase dividends. All these actions increase their stock values. Dividend stocks are flocked by income seekers especially with low bond yields.

   When the government borrows a lot of money (to the ceiling literally), everything including the market looks good. However, somehow and sometime the taxpayers will pay for those debts to China, Japan and whatever other treasury buyers. Today the U.S. has a benefit: It will repay the debtors with depreciated dollars (not true if 2016).

   A country loses its competitive edge if a good percentage of the GDP is used for servicing those debts. If the USA were a company that could not service its debts, it would be bankrupt. Most believe this is the primary reason.

4. Government regulations typically do not help the economy. To illustrate, the expected ObamaCare is discouraging small businesses from hiring.

5. Today's market may not be a good indicator of its value, if this were considered to be a commodity unit (a combination of natural resources including gold) instead of the USD.

6. There are too many factors that influence both the market and the economy in separate directions. Examples include the recent shale energy discovery which could improve the economy. A new war would do the opposite.

What should be done

1. The government cannot pump that much cash into the economy.

   Depreciating our currency is a short-term solution at best as it would improve our trade both ways. The status of being a reserve currency is shaken.
2. The United States government must address how to service its debt! The high debt will deteriorate the United States' competitive edge in the global markets. A high percentage of our GDP to service the debts will not help the economy.
3. We and the government need to bite the bullet with more taxes, more incentives to create jobs, less entitlements, less welfare... Ending the current two wars and avoiding future wars are almost mandatory to improve the economy.
4. The U.S. economy cannot be recovered without job recovery. The money spent in creating jobs will be better spent than on welfare and unemployment benefits. Hiring more government employees is the problem, not a solution.

Conclusion
It may be better to invest in a rising market than holding the depreciating cash. However, this non-correlation will not continue forever. The basic reason that stock appreciates is the company's ability to improve its earning. P/E is still the best yardstick on how fairly a company stock is priced. With a fixed 'E' for example and a rising 'P', the company's stock will be over-priced and will return to its average value (the average P/E for the last five years).

The correlation will be back again in a matter of time.

Footnote

[1]The market can only act as a leading indicator or proxy of economic activity if there is consensus on the direction. Sometimes what is coming in six months is fairly predictable but at other times when pundits are at odds the future course is fuzzy. So market indices are really tracking where consensus "thinks" GDP is going'.

To be clear a market index is a summary of where consensus believes the economy is headed and this sentiment is a proxy for forward earnings. For the playing stocks and not the index, it is their cumulative sentiment which acts as a guide.

Afterthoughts

- There are many other correlations. The following should correlate with the economy: construction industry, employment, commodity /commodity-related currency and oil. Once a while and for a good reason, they do not.
- QE, printing money, foreign loans (to China…), reserve currency, debt ceiling all mean the same: Live in a higher standard of living than we can afford.

  When Uncle Sam unsuccessfully uses all the tools to maintain our living standard and being the world's policeman, he runs out of tools. That will build a higher cliff for us to fall. Hopefully the shale energy will save our economy.

- The global economy still has not recovered as of July, 2013 according to this article. (http://www.telegraph.co.uk/finance/economics/10174862/Renewed-fear-of-global-recession-as-companies-rein-in-spending-plans.html)

- Here are some economic indicators. http://en.wikipedia.org/wiki/Economic_indicator

- This time is REALLY different. Your Dad's generation does not have internet, powerful PC, low-interest commission, trading at a click of the mouse… Global economies are better connected via internet, shipping… All these affect our lives and economies.
- As of 09/2020, the market is making new heights. It could be the riskiest time and many predicated the market would crash after the election. Buy defensive stocks as Buffett is doing.

7 Profitable Early Recovery

I had an 80% return in 2009 in my largest taxable account. I did not include it in my other books before as I just found the statement. Early Recovery, a phase of the market cycle defined by me, is the best time to make a profit. My chart told me to start to move to equity in September, 2009. I did in March, 2009 with other reasons. It could be luck, technique or both.

I did dip into the credit line of my equity loan (not recommended to most) due to lower interest rates than a margin interest. I paid back the loan right after I sold some stocks. The turnaround was high until I exhausted my short-term losses (tax loss harvest). The strategy is bottom fishing. Some sectors described are better in this stage of the market cycle.

I had similar success in 2003. I did not have a defined bottom fishing technique at that time. I expected the market to be fully recovered in two years. From Value Line, I selected stocks with high "Projected 3-5 year returns" and the short-term assets can last for two more years (judged by the burnt rates).

As the stocks are recovering earnings (E), the trailing P/E may not be a good indicator, but the Forward P/E may be. Most sites on evaluating stocks such as Fidelity have a value grade. Also look for candidates for acquisition. From the last recoveries, I spotted at least one such candidate. They are usually small companies (50 to 300M market cap) and have valuable assets such as customer base and patents.

An article stated that the entire company of an internet company can fit into the conference room of Exxon, and it had the same market cap as Exxon if my memory serves me right. On early April, 2000, I switched all my tech mutual funds in my annuity into traditional sectors (better to cash in hindsight) to avoid the crash.

*** Book 5: Investing strategies

The following describes different strategies or styles of investing such as Swing Trading, Sector Rotation, Insider Trading, Penny Stocks, Micro Cap, Momentum Investing and Dividend Investing. I have included many other miscellaneous strategies.

It is not possible for one individual to specialize in all the different styles described above. Typically I have read about two books on each of the strategies. I include their ideas and my ideas in this book. All these books share many common topics such as market timing and evaluating stocks. These topics have been described elsewhere in this book, so they will not be duplicated here.

You may want to paper trade each of the strategies. Select the one that is favorable to the current market (i.e. it performs best in the last three months). In addition, it has to fit your risk tolerance and your own requirements. In addition, different phases of the market cycle favor specific sectors and investing styles. For example, market bottoms favors value stocks while the Up phase (defined by me) of a market cycle favors growth stocks.

The article "Dividend better?" in Book 5 serves as a procedure to evaluate a strategy with a historical database. There are two ways to test some strategies such as "Sideways Strategy" and its opposite strategy "Momentum" without a historical database:

- Load the historical price data of SPY for example from Yahoo!Finance to a spreadsheet.
- Many charts provide many historical data right on the charts. However, typically they do not provide most fundamental metrics such as Debt/Equity.
- Update the stock prices for your strategy weekly or monthly - it will take time to collect all the data. Hence, you cannot draw your conclusions readily as the last two described.

To start, I recommend Long-Term Swing trading. Find sound fundamental stocks. Evaluate them every 6 months and sell them if their fundamentals deteriorate. Briefly I outline some of the shortcomings of the following strategies first as they all have their strengths in certain market conditions.

- Sector Rotation - Be prepared to spend more time and paper trade it. Also sectors can reverse direction.
- Insider Trading - Do not treat it as a value play (i.e. do not depend on fundamentals). Sometimes the insiders are wrong.
- Penny and Micro Cap - I prefer micro-cap stocks over the risky penny stocks. Ensure the volume is at least 10 times larger than your potential buy position.
- Momentum - Do not hold the momentum stocks too long as momentum can reverse very fast.
- Dividend - Do not buy a stock solely on the dividend yield. Today it is very popular and profitable when the bond yield is low. Watch out for the changing interest rate.

The average return of each strategy serves as a guideline only due to my limited data and the specific parameters I use in screening and evaluating stocks. When you're making money in one strategy, stick with it until the performance deteriorates. When you lose money in one strategy, find out why and return to paper trading at least until you are comfortable with the strategy.

1   Introduction

A strategy is a method or a procedure in how to find stocks (usually via screens, also known as searches), analyze the stocks, buy them and sell them. This section concentrates on screening for stocks.

I prefer value stocks (i.e. based on fundamentals). However, fundamentals are secondary for some strategies such as momentum. This book uses the same techniques in Finding Stocks and Scoring Stocks, so they will not be repeated here.

This book describes some simpler strategies and leaves the complicated ones in their own books that follow.

I read the book "What Works on Wall Street" by James O'Shaughnessy blaming many other strategies for non-performance. Later I read another book mentioning that O'Shaughnessy did not work after he published his book.

As mentioned previously, the strategy will not be effective when there are too many followers. That's the reason I provide you with many strategies and you should explore newer strategies yourself. The market favors different groups of strategies in different stages of the market cycle.

The best way to check what is the favorable strategy is to test the performances of your different strategies for the last three to six months. Several low-cost subscription services provide a historical database to make this task simple and feasible.

Traders and hedge fund managers change their strategies frequently. Retail investors should do the same.

One strategy was the poster boy for a subscription service. It worked well before. I tested it recently and it was one of the worst strategies. The lesson is: There are no evergreen strategies. Test out whether they still work in the last 90 days.

A Sample Strategy

It is an example. Adjust it to your preferences and requirements. Instead of buying stocks, just save them in a watch list and buy them when the entire market is on sale. It consists of the following three steps.

1. When to search stocks to be traded. For example, it is once a month when the market is not risky.
2. What to buy. It will be described in more detail later.
3. Sell the stock(s). When the market is plunging, your objectives have been satisfied, or the bought stock(s) does not satisfy most criteria described in #2.

Step #2. There are several steps: Fundamental Analysis, Intangible Analysis, Qualitative Analysis and Technical Analysis.

For simplicity, stick with Fundamental Analysis here. The stocks have to satisfy most of the following criteria. Try to use a screener to limit your selection. If you do not find any stock, relax the criteria or do nothing as the market may be peaking and/or expensive. Skip those criteria that you do not have a subscription to access to.

- It must be in one of the three major U.S. exchanges. No ADRs and partnerships (unless you're an expert in the countries/fields).
- Market Cap is over 100 M (or over 10B for blue chips).
- Price is over $2.
- Average daily volume must be at least 20 times more than your potential position.
- Expected P/E is less than 20 and E must be positive.
- P/Cash Flow is less than 25 and Cash Flow must be positive.
- Debt/Equity is less than 1 (preferable .5; also depending on specific industry).
- Fidelity's Equity Summary Score is 7 or higher.
- Piotroski's (from GuruFocus or other sources) F-Score is 7 or higher.

Fidelity Video:
Trading strategies
https://www.fidelity.com/learning-center/trading/types-of-trading-strategies/overview

Section I: Common strategy ideas

1 Experiences in strategies

A strategy tells you what stocks to buy, what and when to sell.

We should use one or a few of the proven strategies that match well with the current market conditions. It is not an easy job and not an exact science especially when human emotions are involved. A perfect match seldom happens. However, when it does, it can be fireworks and your pocket will be over-stuffed with money.

The following strategies are for illustration purposes only. Test them out before you use them with real money.

- We usually ignore when to sell. If the strategy such as the "Year-End Loser" shows statistically that the best holding period is 4 months, sell them before May. That's why we should have the performances at short-term, mid-term and long-term in testing strategies.

- Sideways market (such as 2015).

  Buy at dips and sell at temporary highs and vice versa. It is a correction about 5% by my definition. The market may just fluctuate in a small range.

  The hard part is to determine what these dips and bottoms are. Here are my suggestions and how we need to adjust the percentages to the volatility of the current market. To me, if it is 2% lower than the last session (or 5% lower than the highest price in the last 5 sessions), it is a temporary bottom. The definitions vary based on your personal tolerance and time for investing. To benefit in this small fluctuation, buy stocks from your watch list or any ETF that represents the market such as SPY or IWM.

  The holding period could be one day to two weeks depending on your risk tolerance. It takes advantage of the fluctuation of prices due to the good news and bad news scenario typically.

Alternatively, you determine when to sell by how much it would rise such as 2% higher than the last session (or 5% higher than the lowest price in the last 5 sessions). The disadvantage is you may never be able to sell stocks that are continuously heading down. The stop orders would prevent further losses.

In reality, the market does not behave the way we expected it to. You need to protect your loss (say sell it when it is over 15% loss). In the long run and if the market fits this sideways market, you SHOULD make money. As in life, there are no guarantees. You can load the historical price of SPY (or another ETF) to stimulate this strategy using different percentages and holding periods.

- The market is up or down steadily.

Strategies using momentum profit better than buying value stocks in a bull market. "Buy high and sell higher" is a good strategy in a rising market.

Use contra ETFs on a down ward market. The average holding period for me is 1 month (some may use 3 months). I stop using momentum when the market is too risky as I do not usually short stocks. It takes several weeks of small profits to recover from one big loss in one day that is if it recovers.

- Buy value.

The average holding period could be more than one year. You're betting against the tide, so it will take a longer time for the value to be 'discovered' by the market. When the institution retailers are selling, find out their reasons. Buy what they are selling if they are wrong (rarely but it has happened many times). It is similar to "Buy low and sell high" and "Contrary Strategy". It seems to be easier said than done, as our emotions do not allow us to act rationally. The typical retail investor usually buys at peaks and sells at bottoms.

- Turnaround and breakup of a company.

When the company fixes its major problem(s), its stock price could skyrocket.

A company may be worth more by adding up the pieces. The recent example is ALU when I bought it at $1 in 2013. At the time, the company had a market cap of around two billions but the debt is about the same. However, their patents could be worth far more than two billion.

- Follow talented investors.

  First, you need to find the talented investors who have good recent performance records. GuruFocus.com (subscription is required) shows what stocks the gurus recently traded. 2015 is not a good year for gurus.

  Check out this article.
  http://seekingalpha.com/article/2762935-a-wisdom-of-experts-portfolio

- Follow what insiders buy.
  There are many tricks to separate the gems from garbage.

- Buy at the bottoms.
  2009 is one bottom. In my definition, it is Early Recovery (usually about one year from the plunge or indicated by the chart described in this book). This bottom fishing strategy buys beaten down stocks that are fundamentally sound. The average holding time is about one year (less if there are better bargains).

  My best returns are from the last two bottoms in 2003 and 2009. At these times, there were more potential stocks for huge profits and my average holding period was about 6 months. 2009 was the only time I dipped into my credit line on my house - **not recommended to most investors**.

- Market Neutral.
  If you are a good stock picker (or believe you're one), treat the market as neutral (i.e. ignoring the market timing). For example, you pick five stocks to buy and five stocks to sell short. You make money due to your skill in picking the right stocks no matter how the market moves. In theory, you should make good money without betting on the market direction.

- Sector Neutral.
  If you specialize in a specific sector such as airlines, you may buy 2 good stocks and short 2 bad stocks in that sector. You can make good money because of your knowledge in the sector. In this strategy, compare stocks to its sector averages. You can use options to do the same if your cash position is limited.

  Trading drug stocks could bring you huge profits. To improve your odds, you need to be an expert in this field. If you're not, subscribe to a specific newsletter that specializes in this industry and has a proven track record. Weigh more on the buy side when the sector is heading up, and vice versa.

- Sector Rotation.
  Investing in a sector or shorting the entire sector could add more profit. To illustrate, the tech sector may be a laggard during a recession as most consumers will not have the spare money to buy consumer electronics, and many companies would postpone their investment in enhancing productivity and development. Every month or two, rotate to the sector that is in an uptrend. Protect your profit when the sector reverses its direction.

- Theme investing.
  When China is moving up, FXI (an ETF) would be a buy. Other examples are OIL and GLD (for gold).

- Strong USD.
  It would be bad for global companies when the profits from foreign investments would be reduced when they are converted to a strong USD. The other bet is on USD itself.

- Super stocks.
  Most are small companies with increasing sales and earnings. It is a little different from the conventional stock analysis. They are riskier but the profits could be huge. Expect one big winner for several small losers. These stocks of small companies are not followed by analysts.

- The winners are already in your portfolio.
  Do not sell your winners as they may turn into bigger winners unless you have a good reason. Do not sell them if they still pass

your recent stock analysis. During any market plunge, you may want to sell them but you should buy them back when the market recovers.

When you mismatch the strategy with the market conditions, you lose the opportunity for profit or even lose money. If the market is up or down steadily, a sideways strategy will not work for example. Matching the strategy to the current market conditions is not an easy job and sometimes it takes some luck. However, when it matches it, there could be fireworks. If you match it more times than you miss it, you should make good money.

Afterthoughts

"Buy and hold" needs no explanation. You just buy the stock and hold it forever. It is a good strategy in a secular bull market such as 1970-2000. After 2000, there are better strategies than "Buy and Hold".

A better way is "Buy and monitor" to ensure the stock you bought still has an appreciation potential.

"Buy and forget" is my term and it could be a good strategy in 2012. Buy the deeply-valued stocks (i.e. big bargains for quality stocks) and forget it until the economy comes back. I have made some profits in established companies such as MSFT, CAT and CSCO during this period.

Links
Market Neutral http://en.wikipedia.org/wiki/Market_neutral
Sector Rotation http://en.wikipedia.org/wiki/Sector_rotation

Filler: "First" as of 4/2016

This time could make some history at least for one of the following:

1. First woman president.
2. First spouse stays in the white house two times. "Buy one get one free" or give Bill another chance with the interns.
3. First non-politician president.
4. First president spending less in campaign.

2   Strategy performance

We may find some strategies performing well in testing but not in reality. Here are my possible explanations.

- Survival bias. When Lehman Brothers and other bankrupt financial institutions are taken out from your historical database, your strategy would look better. Try not to include penny stocks and stocks with micro market caps as they have a higher chance of going bankrupt. Mergers and acquisition do not offset this effect as they are fewer.
- Test windows. For example, start each test with the start of the month and end the test a year later. If the testing period is 5 years, you should have 5*12 = 60 tests. When you start with an amount and let it rise and fall for a long period, the final result would be affected greatly on how it performed in the first year. Most advertised tests are not reliable as they always cherry pick a date that is profitable in the starting years of the test.
- Test different holding periods such as 3 (1 for momentum strategies), 6 and 12 months. Some strategies are good for a short-term hold.
- The last 5 years is better than the last 10 years as it is more similar to the recent market.
- Define your tests according to the phases of the market cycle. Market Peak (a phase defined by me) should have different strategies than Early Recovery.
- Compare the performance to SPY (or an ETF that simulates the market). If most of the stocks you trade are small stocks, use an ETF for small stocks.
- Consider dividends in some cases where they are applicable. For example, for a flat market, the average 1.5% dividend makes a huge difference.
- Use annualized returns. They are better for comparison. However, the returns of less than a month should not be considered as they amplify the results too much.

- Ensure the calculations are correct. When you compare the returns to SPY, the negative values could give wrong interpretations.
- My broker calculates my performance returns and compares them to the indexes. It is handy.
  I gifted appreciated stocks to my son. My broker did it wrong in calculating performance (but correctly for tax purposes) by using the original cost basis. Hence they look far better than they actually are.
- Data fitting works sometimes but not all the time. You change the parameters to boost the best performance. Sometimes it does not work due to the market conditions that are not the same and/or your data is too small to reach a useful conclusion.

3   The best strategy

Note. Most parameters described here such as SMA-20% and Short% can be found from Finviz.com

It is Buy Low and Sell High.

It is simple but most retail investors just do the opposite: Buy High and Sell Low. The flow of money to/from money market funds turns out to be a reliable contrary indicator.

The Early Recovery in 2003 and 2009 and the later part of June, 2012 could be the best time to buy.

The above represents buying at low prices and selling at high prices. Considering P/E (positive 'E' only), buy at low P/E of a stock, a sector and the market (via an ETF) and sell them respectively at high P/E.

Here are some hints when to buy and sell with this strategy:

- Sell when everyone including your silly mother-in-law is making good money and all participants think they're financial geniuses. It could be the riskiest time. The high interest rates (my yardstick is over 5% for Fed Discount rate, the best rate the Fed lends to the banks) usually confirms this as folks falsely expect better returns even though they pay more on interest to borrow money to buy stocks.

- Do not buy the stocks that were the bubble-forming stocks such as the technology stocks in 2001-2002 and the bank stocks in 2008-2009 as some 'optimists' think it is time to return and usually they're wrong.

  Do not think the stock is a good deal when it loses half of its value. Buy them only when the root problem has been fixed. The best time to return to the market after a market plunge is usually two years after the market plunge (2003 for the market plunge in 2000 and 2009 for the market plunge in 2007/2008). Many bubble stocks never recover and many of these stocks take more than 3 years to recover. Their prices appear to be low, but no one can predict the bottom unless it goes to zero.

- Be careful in the sectors or group of stocks that have a winning streak for more than two years. Most likely they will correct. Use a stop loss to protect your profits if you want to keep them.

  You could have saved a lot if you used this strategy on tech stocks in 2000. As of 2015, dividend stocks could be the next sector to burst, but only time can tell. Do not fall in love with a stock. Yesterday's winners could be tomorrow's losers, and vice versa.

  'Buy and hold' has been dead since 2000. We have two market plunges with an average loss of about 45% from their peaks.

- Do not buy dividend stocks solely for their dividends. Most of them are matured companies; most have less growth and hence less appreciation potential. They usually lose less value in a recession after dividends. Income investors are chasing them for higher dividends than bonds.

  Except from Roth accounts, when you withdraw from your retirement accounts, your dividends will be treated as income. Check the current tax rates for income and dividend from taxable accounts.

- Buy value stocks that seem to be bottomed. It is hard to identify the bottom. When the appreciation potential outweighs the risk, it could be a buy.

- No one can predict consistently the market bottom. However, use your better judgment with educated guesses to gain an edge. Refer to the exit point using the 350-day SMA from the chapter on detecting market plunges.

- Buy the stocks that have been losing money but their burn rates can last for the entire recession. They're risky but the potential profits are great. There were many in 2003 and 2009. Even in a bad economy in 2012, a few corporations had historically low P/Es.

- Buy value stocks with a turnaround sign such as when the SMA-50% is positive.

- Buy against the experts who have unconvincing predictions. They usually exaggerate the rosy outlooks of the companies in order to sell the stocks they own. This is one of the few times you should bet against them. Use your better judgment to ensure how false their predications could be.

Using Citicorp (symbol C) as an example

Following the chapter on avoiding bank stocks, buying this stock at $550 a share could be avoided. After the big plunge in 2008, I believe it has long-term profit potential. Accumulate this stock if you believe C will be profitable in 10 years (2024) or so. Do not sell it unless there is potential for a market plunge. If so, buy it back after the plunge. One's opinion.

With our market timing (defending sector may return in two years), I checked it in mid 2009, about 2 years after the start of the market plunge. Optionally I could use the SMA-350 of the stock to determine the reentry point. However, it had no meaning due to the big plunge from $550. On 8/2009, C's P/E was negative, so I did not buy it.

Alternatively buy it for when there is a big drop in P/E regardless of the current price as follows. We started when the P/E is about 40. Normally I buy it when the P/E is at around 20. Take an exception for turnaround stocks.

Date	P/E	Price
06/2010	40	40
01/2011	13	49
08/2011	9	32

The above is for illustration purposes only, so the numbers are not precise.

As of 6/12/2014, I expected a correction, so I sold it at about $48. I only trade this kind of stocks when I see long-term appreciation potential. The other three important metrics are P/B, P/S and RSI(14). Use Forward (same as Expected) P/E if possible. The most important metric for lenders is the quality of the loans, which is hard to evaluate for retail investors. The other factor is any serious, pending lawsuits. When Lehman Brothers was gone, the governments will chase after the institutions that sold the derivatives.

Update 8/2019. C's stock price is $62.

The second best strategy

Buy high and sell higher.

When everyone is looking for stocks with the highest value, there may not be any such stocks available. It seems to contradict with my best strategy but it is not intended to. Fundamentals may not show everything about the company such as a new drug, a new product... The all-time high prices usually show that. Buy the stock when it is over the 50-day simple moving average (50 or 200 days depending on how long you usually hold a stock) via Finviz.com.

Buying fully-priced stocks is dangerous even if it may be profitable. To protect your profits:

- Be extra careful in risky market; I prefer not to buy any stock when the market is risky.

- Set stop loss orders. Recommend 10% (or 15% for volatile stocks) less than the current price. If you set a 5% stop, it would be stopped out by normal fluctuations especially for volatile stocks.

- Use Technical Analysis. When the price drops below the moving average you used, sell it. When RSI (14) is high (over 70), check out the reason as it could be overbought.

If you are not very sure, sell half of it. You will not go broke for taking profits.

As in life, there are no guarantees, but using a proven technique / discipline is far better than trading without one. Paper trading ensures the strategy fits the current market conditions, your personal tolerance and requirements.

The third best strategy

Buy very high and sell even higher.

It is the riskiest. These stocks could be bubble stocks moved by institutional investors and then moved even higher by retail investors. It may take a while before the institutional investors rotate to another sector / stocks and/or take profit.

My strategy is to follow the herd but ensure you're ready to exit.

- Find them. Usually they have break-outs. They pass the resistance, a technical term. Now, they are in the low point of the support line, so they have a long way to go to the next resistance line. It has to be confirmed with its daily volume such as 3 times or more than the average daily volume. Usually they are in the 52-week highs.

- Usually they are large caps with high trade volumes. My range is 100M to 5B. Be careful on stocks ranging from 100M to 500M. They may appreciate a lot on the positive side; they are risky and they can be manipulated easier. Stocks from 1B to 5B appreciation potential is lesser than 100M to 500M.

- Do not short them.

- Buy them ignoring the fundamentals as they are moving up with the herd sometimes for a reason and sometimes not. Alternatively, use options.

- Set mental stop losses. Adjust the stops periodically after they have been appreciated.

  Watch them every day. Bring up Finviz.com and enter the sector ETF the stock belongs to and the stocks. Pay attention to SMA200%: The higher it is, the higher chance it is peaking. When RSI(14) is over 70% (65% for sectors), most likely it is overbought. When SMA-20% is negative, there is a good chance of reversing the trend downward.

Buy and Monitor

I usually sell my stocks that have fulfilled my objectives or admitted I have made a mistake. However, some stocks keep on rising and I may miss many 3 or more baggers.

I gifted many appreciated stocks to my family members. My grandchildren will keep them for a long while. Here are the stocks I gave on 5/1/2015 (the date I gifted them) and the performances today (5/12/2018).

Stock	Total Return	Annualized return
CSCO	58%	19%
STX	88%	29%
TTWO	377%	124%
Average	174%	57%
Compare to:		
SPY	29%	10%

My point is "buy and hold" is still valid for many stocks. Buy low when they have been temporarily ignored. These stocks should have long-term potential as they will be held for a long while. My actual performance is substantially more as I bet at least double more in TTWO.

Instead of "Buy and Hold", you need buy and monitor. When they have serious problems such as Circuit City, Radio Shack, Sears…, do not hesitate to sell them.

When you time the market, ensure buy back the stocks you sold during the recovery phase of the market cycle.
My long-term grade

They are composed of the following (using metrics from Finviz.com): low Forward P/E, low Debt/Eq, Cash/sh, larger Market Cap, ROE, low RSI(14), Insider Own, Sales Q/Q, EPS Q/Q, SMA200… In addition, they have good products for the future and they invest heavily in research.

4   AAII, a source for strategies

AAII has many nice stock screens. Check out their performance summaries. You can divide the screens and their performances into groups according to the different stages of a market cycle and rank the performances. Some screens perform better in certain stage(s) of the market cycle. Most likely, the value screens should do better in market bottom (Early Recovery defined by me) and growth screens do better in a bull market (Up and Peak phases defined by me).

As a regular subscriber, the screen stock recommendations are about 15 days old (check the current policy) and the most updated screens require extra cost. Their strategy for most screens is: Sell all stocks that do not meet the criteria of the screen and buy new stocks that meet the criteria every month. This trading strategy would require a lot of trades and you need to consider their tax consequences (none for non-taxable accounts) and commissions. Trade on paper before you commit to their recommendations with real money similar to many strategies described in this book.

The basic membership with a decent magazine-publication is a good deal. If you are new to investing, there are many basic books provided on their web site.

Update 2/2016

AAII publishes its screen performance every year. Here are some pointers.

- Do not follow last year's winners. I predicted 2015 was a sideways market and 2016 is a risky market that has a good chance to turn into a bear market.
- During bear markets, the screens had lost from 10% to 83% without a single winner here. When the technical indicator SMA-350 or Death Cross tells you to exit, exit as there is no screen that would find winners.

- Every year from 2011 to 2015, the return of the market is positive after adding dividends. When the technical indicator SMA-350 or Death Cross tells you to invest, invest if you trust the charts.
- Some screens work great in one year and become big losers in another year. To conclude, there is no evergreen screen.

- It does not go earlier than 2009 in the summaries, the last Early Recovery that has the best profit potential. I recommend value stocks for this stage of the market cycle.

- For the same reason above, it does not show performances in the bear market of 2007-2008.

- I would select the screens that have a good five year average. However, the last five years is a typical bull market. Most screens do not beat the S&P500's 12% average for the last five years. You're better off buying SPY, an ETF simulating the S&P 500 index.

- AAII screens have high turnovers as they replace the stocks when they do not meet the screen criteria.

5   Adaptive strategy

What is the best metric for evaluating stocks? Most people will tell you P/E. I use estimated earnings (E) and P/E becomes Forward P/E (a.k.a. Expected P/E). Switch it over to E/P for easier to understand, and it is termed Earnings Yield (EY = P/E). However, the 'E' is not 'expected' which is better to predict future stock value. I prefer EY to be calculated with Forward Earnings and most sites do not provide it but you can calculate it easily.

When the market favors momentum stocks, fundamental stocks even with good Earnings Yields may not work. In this case, I prefer momentum stocks with EY better than average.

EV/EBITDA (obtainable from Yahoo!Finance) is better than P/E as it includes interest, debt and cash. Switch it over and it is True Earnings Yield (my term).

Some may tell you ROI and there is a successful book on ROI.

Both P/E and ROI should not be the only metric as there is no single evergreen metric. That is why most people have poor performance by following them blindly. It is the herd theory: The performance is usually decreased in the longer term when too many folks follow it.

Here is my test on the S&P 500 stocks from April 1, 2019 to July 1, 2019.
I used the top 10 stocks from each sort. Commissions, dividends and spreads are omitted for simplicity. SPY's return is annualized to 13.8%.

Value parameters

Top 10 stocks sorted by	Best SPY[1]
EY in descending order	-251%
Dividend Yield in descending order	-291%[2]

Opposite of the above

Top 10 stocks sorted by	Best SPY[1]
EY in ascending order	6%
Dividend Yield = 0	138%[3]

[1] Beat by % = (Avg. return of 10 stocks – SPY) / SPY

[2] Including dividend yields for the average 10 stocks and SPY, "Beat SPY' is reduced to -241%.

[3] Just randomly picked the 10 stocks that do not pay dividends as there are more stocks with no dividends.

6   Different investment styles

There are three major styles to evaluate stocks: Fundamental, Growth and Technical Analysis (TA).

The debate on their benefits could be endless. I believe TA is good for short term (1 month for stocks), growth for intermediate term (say 3 months) and fundamental is good for longer term (say 6 months). Here is my summary of the two (I place Fundamental and Growth into the same group for discussion here).   Market sometimes favors value (i.e. fundamentals) and sometimes growth.

TA depends mostly on the stock price and hence it predicts the trend better; it also can track oversold conditions. TA would catch the stock movement, but not by fundamental or growth metrics.

- TA.
  Most TAers do not care about fundamentals, but price and volume. They do have good arguments. A lot of data about the stock are not available or too late to be effective such as a new drug discovery, being acquired, or a serious lawsuit pending.

  The following are two illustrations on how TAers can benefit.

  When the insiders and/or analysts know about some promising new products or positive unexpected earnings, they buy and tell their families to buy. I do not judge whether it is Illegal insider trading or not. TAers notice the rise of the stock price with increasing volume and they buy. Many times the last ones to buy may end up losing money as the insiders would unload them especially when the stock prices are over-valued.

  When the institutional investors (pension fund managers and fund managers) are buying a specific stock, the stock volume and its price will both rise. TAers would notice them from the charts and jump on the wagon. To me, this is the basic reason on how good day traders make money. It usually takes a week for an institutional investor to finish trading a stock.

- Fundamentals.
  They look at the companies' metrics such as P/E, expected P/E, PEG, debt, sales growth, etc. A good company's stock price with rising profit and rising sales should appreciate in the long term. Some short the stocks of companies with bad fundamentals. In some cases, data is hidden in the financial statements that most metrics do not detect.

To conclude, the best TAers and the best fundamentalists usually make money in either market in the long run. However, fundamental analysis is easier to master and they have made more money than TAers in the long run. You find a lot of successful fundamentalists from Buffett and his followers, but not too many successful TAers. Some successful TAers even lose their accumulated fortunes. Be warned that if you do not know what you're doing in either discipline, you will lose money. Learn it and trade it on paper before committing even small amounts of real money to it.

The best way is use both disciplines in selecting stocks as described below.

- When your chart(s) displays a candidate to buy, take a look at the fundamentals. If the fundamentals are bad, be cautious. Some screens can search for the stocks with good technical patterns (Finviz.com is one).

- After you spot a bargain stock to buy via the fundamental metrics, check out its SMA-200 (Simple Moving Average for the last 200 trade sessions) or any duration that fits your purpose. If the price is above the moving average, it could be a buy.

Afterthoughts

- Try the following to see whether fundamental works better if you have a historical database.

  Fundamentals

  1. Include all stocks that are below the 200-day SMA (Simple Moving Average) - opposite of what a TAer would do.

2. The expected positive P/Es have to be between 4 and 15. In addition, both profits and sales are rising by 5%.
3. Exclude financial companies like banks and insurance, miners, bio companies and drug companies that are hard to evaluate.

TA

1. Buy stocks that cross over the 50-day, simple moving averages.
2. Never buy stocks when the market is below 200-day, simple moving average.

Check the result in 1 month intervals and 6 months intervals. My own simple test favors the fundamentals in 6 months intervals and favors TA in 1 month intervals. You may need more exhaustive testing to draw a good conclusion in different phases of a market cycle for at least 2 market cycles.

- SMA-200 (from Finviz.com without charts) and its variations are the ones most TAers use and even most experienced fundamentalists know how to use it if they want to. It is also a good indicator for the general market by using an ETF that simulates the market.
  There are many sophisticated TA indicators in Yahoo!Finance. For qualified clients, Fidelity provides a tool to back test your TA strategies.
- It may be beneficial to use fundamentals to look for stocks and use TA to find the entry and exit points. Today's screens can do it in the reverse order, or both in the same screen.
- Fundamental can be divided into Value and Growth.
  Value. I use it mostly. Especially good in early recovery phase of the market cycle.

Section II: Safer, long-term strategies

1   Super safe strategies

These strategies are for orphans and widows. The common theme is that you want to spend very little time in investing. There are better things to do than investing. You may not have the knowledge in investing or the desire to learn about investing. However, most likely the safe strategies do not beat inflation except the last strategy described in this article.

Strategy #1: CD and long-term treasury bills

They are virtually risk-free. Even if it takes almost no-effort for the strategy except in renewing the expired CDs, I still recommend some actions:

- Do not invest in a CD with a bank that you have already exceeded the government's limit on insurance. As of 2019, the standard deposit insurance coverage limit is **$250,000** per depositor, per FDIC-insured bank and per ownership category.

- Today's CDs do not beat inflation. It is our capitalist system that punishes us for not taking any risk and effort in investing.

- Some mortgage-backed bonds or similar offerings could lose all the potential value as many found out the hard way from Lehman Brother's bonds disguised as safe CDs.

- Do not buy callable CDs. They will be called to the bank's advantages.

- Buy long-term treasury bills when the interest rates is high (say 5% or higher). Buy short-term treasury bills when the interest rates is low (say less than 2%). Although you can receive your entire principle plus interest when they mature, the value of the bond fluctuates in opposite directions to the current rate. When the current interest rates is better than the one in your treasury bill, your bill will depreciate.
- Most folks buy the treasury bills via mutual funds and/or ETFs.

Strategy #2: Annuity

When you retire, it seems to be a good vehicle to buy an annuity to provide income for life. However, you have to understand the annuities' terms are defined by the sellers with their own agenda. If you believe they're in business to make you a comfortable retirement at their own expenses, think again. Very few if any are low-expense operations. Ask how much the salesman would make to sell you the annuity, and most likely you would run to the door for quick exit.

I invested in an annuity when I was working to postpone my taxes for the gains. It could be a mistake for me even I made over 4 times during several decades. My taxes after 70 ½ (the age for mandatory withdrawal of retirement accounts) will be higher than my working years. I did well in rotating sectors (offered in my annuity) partly due to luck. The total expenses (the trading fees and the management fees) are not cheap compared to most ETFs.

It is good when you have better things to do in your life than worrying about the market. It would save some taxes if your tax bracket is lowered after retirement (as most folks do). If we have a market plunge, then these two strategies would be a winner.

Strategy #3: Rotation of an ETF and cash

Rotate between SPY (or any ETF that simulates the market) and cash (or a short-term treasury bond ETF). When the market is risky, rotate your investment into cash and vice versa for SPY. This book describes market timing; it is quite simple.

For beginners, it appears more complicated than it is. You only spend several minutes every month. You will beat most mutual fund managers as most of them are not allowed to play market timing. To start, allocate a small percentage of your investing to this strategy or test the strategy on paper. There is some risk due to false signals. However, "nothing risked, nothing gained" is quite true especially for the long term.

2   Tom's conservative strategy

The following is a summary of Tom's conservative strategy as described in his profile on Seeking Alpha web site. Use it as an example and modify it to fit your investing philosophy. You need to ignore your friends telling you how much money he is making when the market is up. You also need not tell them how much money you're not losing, otherwise you will not have any friends.

Click here (for Kindle readers) for Tom's strategy.
(http://tonyp4idea.blogspot.com/2012/05/tom-armisteads-investment-strategy.html)

Ignore the date posted as this is one of the very few strategies that are evergreen. As of 12/2015, it does not perform well during 2009 (or 2010) to 2015 due to the long, unexpected rising market. However, it beats the above two strategies by good margins in the long run.

A winning strategy for couch potatoes

My friend John has a very similar strategy similar to Tom's. My friend is making money with the least risk. He only buys stocks after the market crashes and sell stocks when the market rises. Ignore all market pundits. This is recommended to anyone who does not have time to monitor his/her investment.

He bought stocks in 2008-2010 and sold them after 2010. It was very profitable for him in 2000-2008 using this simple strategy. However, he missed the gains from 2010 to 2018. It is unusual that we have such a long bull market. I beg he is still beating most mutual fund managers with this simple strategy that does not require much work.

Enhance a good strategy

Following the favorable stages to trade in the market cycle described in this book:
- Buy SPY in the Early Recovery phase (about 1 ½ year after the crash or use the entry point described in Market Timing in this book.
- Sell SPY in one or two years after the buy.

Here are some options if you have time to watch the market.

- Buy stocks (or an ETF that simulates the market) in Nov. 1 and sell them in May 1. I prefer to buy stocks on Oct. 15 and sell them on April 15 to avoid the herd.
- Buy stocks on Dec. 1 and sell them on Feb. 1 to take advantage of the best (statistically) period of the year.
- Buy stocks in the year before the election and sell them after a year.
- Add long-term bonds when the interest rates is high (say more than 5%). Switch to short-term bonds or cash when the interest rate is low (say less than 2%).
- If you have time, time the market by following my simple technique to exit and reenter the market.

Spend the rest of the time on your comfortable couch (i.e. enjoying life) or sip some fancy tropical drink served by some beautiful tropical lady on some nice tropical island. Not a bad strategy! Of course, the market is not always rational and there is always risk involved.

An alternative to Tom's strategy

Have a list of value stocks to buy and update the list periodically (say every 3 months).

When the market loses 5%, buy them at 2% less than the market prices or alternatively 5% less than the prices on your list.

Decide when to sell such as making 12% profit or losing 12%. If the market is not risky, you may want to keep them longer. It should work in a sideways market but not during market plunges.

John's Strategy

John maintains about 75% cash and only buys blue chip stocks at 52-week low. He ignores friends telling him about making good money when the market is up.

Here are my changes for better returns at the expense of taking more risk. I would maintain 50% cash and 0% in Early Recovery, a phase in the market cycle defined by me. I would also include all stocks with market cap over 1 billion and stocks close to 5% of their bottoms. In addition, I would evaluate the stocks before I buy as some stocks may go to zero.

Jill's Strategy

Jill does not have time for investing. She subscribes to an investing service. She prepares a list of stocks to buy. For illustration purposes only, the stocks should have Safety of 1 or 2 in Value Line or VST grade higher than 1.25 in Vector Vest. When the price reaches the price she is willing to pay, she does a second research with her subscription service and check the fundamental rating at Fidelity.com. If they are good, she buys it and usually keeps it until the market is risky.

3   Refined "Dogs of the Dow"

The Dogs of Dow is quite popular and even some mutual fund managers are using it exclusively. In a nutshell, you buy the ten Dow stocks that pay the highest dividend rates at year end and repeat the process every year. Ignore the stocks whose dividends are returns of capital. Click the above hyperlink or enter the following link into your browser for more info on this strategy.

(http://en.wikipedia.org/wiki/The_Dogs_of_the_Dow)

Past Performance

As of 2014, it just beat the Dow and the S&P500 by a small margin in the last decade. It worked quite well in the last four years. It could be due to the recent mild bubble on dividend growth stocks. Hence, be alert to when the dividend bubble bursts.

From Wikipedia,

"In fact, the Dogs of the Dow and Small Dogs of the Dow struggled to keep up with the Dow during latter stages of the dot-com boom (1998 and 1999) as well as during the financial crisis (2007-2009)."

My suggestion to improve the performance

1.   Avoid stocks with high expected P/Es (i.e. > 35) and P <= 0 such as most dot-com stocks in 2000.

2.   Avoid sectors such as banks in 2007.

3.   Practice market timing. Do not buy most stocks during market plunges and move back to equities in Early Recovery, a phase of the market cycle defined by me.

Improve the performance by customizing

When a strategy becomes popular, it will not perform.

Customize the strategy so we do not pick up the same stocks as everyone else does. Instead of buying the ten dogs, buy the first five dogs sorted by the forward (same as expected) P/E in ascending order ignoring stocks with zero or negative earnings.

This variation has an average annualized return of 15% (= 12% appreciation + estimated 3% dividend) from Nov. 1, 2000 to Nov. 1, 2010 from my testing. It is better than the original strategy already. The testing is for educational purposes only.

Another variation is: Buy the top five candidates on Nov. 1 and sell them on May 1 next year to take advantage of the statistically favorable period.

Further Refining Dogs of Dow

The following are more variations to the original Dogs of Dow. Try them out with different combinations.

1. Include the stocks in the S&P 500 and NASDAQ, so there are more stocks to choose from than just from the DOW.

2. Adjust the time between Dec. 1 and Dec. 15 (a little earlier is fine) instead of the start of the year to avoid the herd who follows the same strategy and performs the same task at the beginning of the year.

3. For retirement accounts or offsetting the short-term losers, buy on Nov.1 and sell on May 1 to take advantage of this statistically favorable period.

4. Sort the selected top 10 with positive earnings by P/E in ascending order and buy the top 5. A value play. I prefer to skip P/E less than 4 as there could be something really wrong with too low of a P/E. Skip stocks with high Debt/Equity ratio unless the sector requires high debts.

5. Avoid stocks in the following sectors: lenders, drug companies, miners and insurers. Avoid emerging countries.

6. Skip the companies that have serious lawsuits against them. Minor lawsuits are fine.

7. Avoid stocks that are being shorted in the range of 10% to 20%. The short % is defined by: No. of shares being shorted/Total floating shares. Stocks with short percent over 30% could trigger a short squeeze that could have good appreciation potential.

8. Do not buy on the first year after the market plunge.

It is a lazy man's stock picking and market timing. I bet it performs better than the original strategy.

Afterthoughts

*

When you test out the above strategy, try different parameters. If possible, use the most recent data (such as the last ten years) to check out whether your strategy still works. If you are less risk tolerant, select the screened stocks with P/E between 4 and 12 only.

The following are some of the variance and can be combined into this strategy for testing out the performances.

- Holding periods. Try 6 months, 11 months and 12 months.
- Buy contra ETFs during the unfavorable stock period such as May 1 to Nov. 1. It is not recommended in a secular bull market.
- Automate your test as much as possible, so you can add other parameter such as different holding periods.
- Avoid data fitting to obtain better results.
- Test for each stage of the market cycle.

*

Annualize the return if it is not 12 months to make it easier to compare. Do not get too excited on great returns. When you implement your strategy with real money, expect less performance than the performance from your test.

Review your test procedures when the return is excessive such as 60%. However, when you find one strategy yielding 60% and another one yielding 20% with the same testing conditions, stick with the winner for real money.

4 A turnaround strategy for value stocks

Many value stocks tend to stay in this phase for a long time. When the turnaround starts, it could be very profitable.

Market Timing

Do not buy any stock when the market is risky as described elsewhere in the book. Actually you should sell most of the stocks when the market is risky.

Buy Metrics

Metric	Value	Conservative	Aggressive
General			
Market Cap	>300 M	>1,000 M	>100 M
Price	> 2	>10	>1
Avg. Volume	>20,000	>50,000	>10,000
USA	Only	Only	Foreign but listed in USA
Fundamental			
Forward P/E	<15	<10	<25
Earning Gr Q-Q	>5%	>8%	>3%
ROE	>10	>15	>5
P / FCF	<10	<8	<15
Debt / Equity	<.5	<.25	<1
Technical			
SMA-50%	>10	>15	>5
Misc.			
Blue Chip Growth	A or B	A	A or B
Fidelity	>6	>8	>5
IBD	>60	>90	>50
Vector Vest	>=1	>=0.8	>=12
Value Line Proj. 3-5% return	>5%	>10%	>5%
Zacks	>=4	5	>=4
ASSS	>=2	>=5	>=2

The assignment values for the metrics are not fixed; feel free to change it according to your own risk level. I do have suggestions for conservative investors and aggressive investors.

Some of the metrics are not readily available in Finviz.com and the following describes how to modify them.

Explanation

- Market Cap- The free version of Finviz.com does not allow you to specify the range. Use 'Any' and then select the stocks according to the specified values. Average Volume has a similar restriction.

- The conservative values for Market Cap, Price and Average Volume try to select larger companies. The aggressive values try to select smaller companies, which historically are more risky but perform better.

- I prefer 'USA' for Country. Stay away from small companies from developing countries unless you can trust their financial statements.

- Forward P/E measures the value of the stock. Ensure "E" (Earnings) is positive. I prefer it over P/E (from the last twelve months).

- Earnings Growth Quarter to last Quarter is preferred to be positive unless it is during a recession.

- ROE measures how well the company has been managed.

- P/FCF. "Price / Free Cash Flow" cannot be manipulated easily. Together with low "Debt / Equity", it measures whether the company would go bankrupt.

- SMA-50%- Some stocks tend to stay in a value stage for a long while (termed value trap). We like to select stocks that start being d

- Misc.- Many sites have evaluated the stocks for us. Some only let their customers access such information, some are available for a free trial, or are available from the library.

- ASSS is my scoring system. Try it out and check the performance.

With the above, I ha 35 stocks on 10/28/16. If you need 10 stocks for further evaluation, try to sort Forward P/E in descending order and select the top 10. If you cannot find any or substantially less than normal, it thfew stocks you selected are poor, take a break too as the market conditions do not favor the value metrics we specified.

Qualitative analysis

Double click on the stock and read as many articles described on the stock as possible. If it meets all the criteria, buy the stock. I recommend that you use market orders for large companies in a non-volatile market (when the average daily fluctuation is less than 0.5%). If the selected stock is the one you just sold for a loss, make sure you only buy it back after 31 days to avoid the Wash Sale penalty.

Keeping informed

Check the company updates/news on the stock you owned every month. One easy way is to enter the stocks in a model portfolio in SeekingAlpha.com and they would inform you on any articles/news on your owned stocks.

Sell the stock
Re-evaluate your stocks every 6 months.

If it does not meet the criteria or the market is risky, sell it. If it is only a few days (currently it is 365) away from a long-term capital gain, sell the losers right away or hold on to the winners for a few more days.

Re-balance the portfolio after a stock has been sold. Ensure it has been diversified enough into market cap and sectors.

Top-down Investing
It is similar to the above. Find the sectors that performed the best last month. Under Finviz.com, select the best sector under 'sector' one at a time. Several sites such as Fidelity compare a stock to the averages of stocks in the same sector.

Section III: Riskier, short-term strategies

"Nothing risked, nothing gained."

1   Trading by headlines

On 6/29/2019, Trump and Xi seemed to settle trade war in the G20. The market would likely rise on the coming Monday. Luckily I had closed a short position. Many chip stocks would rise as they can sell their products to Huawei. I have several of these stocks expecting the trade war would be settled. The farmers and their supporting industry would breathe easier.

I bet the shipping companies would be more profitable from the news. Without doing further research, I checked out this shipping sector and found the following stocks had been up more than 4%: DHT, NM, SBLK, STNG, TNK and ASC. It was during the weekend, so your trade account should be able to trade after hours and you need to act right after the news.

I exchanged comments with Andrew McElroy, a sector rotation expert. He does not have the rules set up as in this book but he makes great trades by 'seeing' the market and using technical analysis. The following is from his article.

"The idea is fairly simple. There is more potential for profit (and loss) in individual sectors, especially when the index is trading sideways. I try to buy strong sectors which have pulled back onto support and avoid overbought sectors at resistance. I also use Elliott Wave to identify cycles of buying and selling and stages in trends."

I would like to include headlines such as Trump's election, interest rates hikes and new regulations.

When it rains in Brazil, buy coffee futures

Recently it rained too much in SE Asia, so buy rice futures. I did not trade futures, so I missed out on the opportunity and unfortunately there is no equivalent ETF for rice. In the beginning of 2012, we should know the farming crops especially corn will not be good due to the flooding and drought in different parts of the world. Act accordingly for the profit potentials.

When a war is starting in the Middle East, most likely the oil price will rise. Buy the oil ETF and sell it when the chance of the war is reduced. Many tiny drops of profit could turn into a river of profit.

Trading by headlines is profitable, but it is hard to master and is very time-consuming. Test this strategy on paper for years before you commit real money as in most strategies. Most couch potatoes read the newspaper and watch TV all day long without making a penny. He could be couch potato millionaire if he read this article, paper traded/refined the strategy and acted on it!

However, the media tend to exaggerate headlines in order to sell their ads. Ignore all the recommendations on stocks. Most likely they are outdated information and some may be used to manipulate others. Do your own research as your mother taught you that there is no free lunch.

Rules of the game

1. Do not be too emotional; ignore your past wins and losses except when using them as lessons if they are valid (i.e. educated guesses).

2. Do not trade the entire farm. Consider option, ETFs and/or small trade on stocks, which have too many other factors to be considered.

3. Trade it fast – today's headlines will not be headlines tomorrow. There are very few exceptions.

4. Where there is a winner, there is always a loser. For example, Apple was a winner with the iPhone and BlackBerry was a loser. Same for Best Buy and Circuit City.

5. Ensure you can trade after hours from your broker.

6. Do not forget when to exit for either a small profit or a small loss.

7. Quick evaluation. The headline will be gone if you do not act fast. Skip companies with poor metrics such as high debt and low earnings yield. Prefer to buy an ETF related to the headline.

8. Most likely someone has used the information before you get it. However, some info can be deducted before it occurs. Insider purchases is a good guide.

9. I recommended crude oil at $30 per barrel in Jan. 15, 2016 as the price was at rock bottom. For value sectors, you may have to wait for a long time for the market to realize its value.

10. Sometimes you ignore stock evaluations as the headline news is more important. Learn my 5-minute evaluation process of a stock (a quick way but not recommended if you have time to do thorough research):
    - From Finviz.com, enter the stock or ETF symbol. Look at how many greens in metrics over reds.
    - Check out Forward P/E (E>0 and P/E < 20), Debut / Equity (< 50%) and P/FCF (not in red color).
    - SMA20 (or SMA50 for longer holding period). If SMA20 is > 10%, it is trending up.
    - Scroll down for Insider Trade. It usually is a good buy if insiders are buying recently and heavily with market prices.
    - Be cautious on foreign and low-volume stocks.
    - If most of the above are positive, it is likely a buy. As in life, nothing is 100% certain.

If you have a hard time following the above, most likely this strategy is not for you and it is better to return to your couch. No offense.

Volatile market and headlines

As of 7/2012 (2015 too and historically a positive market in a year right before the election), the market went sideways and was influenced by headlines. 2013 had been volatile with dips and surges influenced by daily news. The trend was up though. The Federal debt problem, EU crisis... had not been resolved. Every time we had good news, the market rose, and vice versa. In this market, buy on dips (3% down from last temporary peak) and sell on temporary surges

(3% up from last temporary bottom). Some use 5% instead of 3% depending on one's risk tolerance.

Trend and calendar timing

Usually following the trend is better than ignoring it.

- Many retail investors want to get rid of the losers for year-end tax planning. Buy them at year-end and sell them early next year. In the year end of 2012, it acted the opposite as folks were selling their winners expecting a larger tax bite next year but that turned out to be false.

  This could be the reason for a sell-off of Apple in year-end of 2012 and it gave us a good entry point. To me, Apple's fundamentals were sound though the media said otherwise. In a few months, Apple became a value stock from a growth stock according to the press.

- Investors are not rational and follow the market blindly. The strategy 'Buy low and sell high' works.

- We have so much good news and bad news in the same year. Ensure the bad news will not extend to worse news. Timing is everything. Buy on bad news and sell on good news; it does not work when the market plunges.

- The media influences the market. Analyze their arguments. If they exaggerate them, do the opposite.

- Over-reaction to earnings missed or gained. When the company missed the earnings by 5%, there is a very good chance the stock will be down in a year, and vice versa. However, when it missed by 1% and the stock lost by 10%, it could be a buying opportunity, particularly when it was a temporary condition and the company is fundamentally sound.

- Buy the stock at dip when a solvable problem surfaces. Sell after the problem has been resolved. Ceiling debt is such a solvable problem and it is caused by politics. In the beginning of 2013, I mentioned that the debt problem had not been resolved and we would have this ceiling debt problem periodically until it will be eventually resolved.

Scheduled events

Some events are scheduled such as earnings announcements, unemployment reports, etc. Most likely educated guesses of the outcomes have already been circulated in the web.

The last five events on the Federal debt handling (using fancy names such as sequester and debt ceiling) were scheduled such as the government shutdown. They drove the market down by about an average of 5% each time. Sell before the event and buy back afterward. The Congress has cancelled these debt deadlines as of 1/2014.

Many sectors are impacted by events such as Trump's success in election, hikes of interest rates and trade wars.

Follow the institutional investors
They drive the market. When they see the sector is over-valued or the peak has been reached, they rotate sectors.

Use deduction
In 2014, China has a great harvest on wheat, corn and rice. China's population is #1 in the world and its middle class is growing. The farmers in the US will be hurt as they cannot export these products to their number one customer. Use the same logic to deduct that there will be problems in the companies that supply products and services to the farmers. They are combines, fertilizer companies and seed companies. It further translates into Deere, Potash, Monsanto and AGCO.

Due to increasing wealth in 2017, Chinese demanded more meat. It takes a lot of corn to produce one pound of meat and in turn corn needed fertilizers. Hence, you can expect the companies producing fertilizers will increase their profits.

Geopolitical crisis
Many times no action is the best action. It applies here. I had my experience in selling too many stocks via stops in 911. The market returned in a few days and I did not buy them back.

An analysis from Ned David Research covers 51 events from 1900 to 2014. My interpretation for actions: Trade the affected sector (via sector ETF) in the first few days and reverse the trade 2 months after. Many times it means the oil price and gold price would rise.

I bought SH (a contra ETF to SPY) in August, 2017 as August and September are statistically the worst months in addition to the high risk in the current market. It is expected to be sold on Nov. 1. The North Korea crisis did not do much to the market on the first day but the market (the S&P 500) lost 1.45% and the risky NASDAQ lost 2.13% (see my blog on FAANG) on the second day.

Caveat. Need to understand the crisis. If it would lead to World War 3, most sectors will not recover for a long while. Again, there is no sure thing in investing otherwise there would be no poor folks. However, educated guesses should materialize more often than not.

My experiences
- When the interest rates is expected to rise, plan on investments that are favorable to it and vice versa.
- On the same week, CROX lost almost 40% in one day. I bought some and made about 10% profit in a week. CROX's fundamentals were no good and it did have a history of a roller coaster ride in its stock price. After a year, I found out that I sold it too early as the stock price doubled. Better to buy a stock on its way up than down unless we identify that the bottom has been reached.
- I was on vacation while the second incident of the Boeing Max happened. Should have shorted the stock. In addition, Boeing's suppliers would suffer too similar to Apple's suppliers on Apple.

  https://www.barrons.com/articles/boeing-737-max-jet-production-cut-suppliers-stocks-51554499957?siteid=yhoof2&yptr=yahoo

- I missed applying the same trick to the rise of Apple when Apple announced its new iPod. I should at least buy the stocks of its part suppliers. I hope learn from this lesson and take advantage of future similar circumstances.

2   Earnings season overreactions

AAII has some screens for stocks with pleasant earnings surprises and bad earnings surprises (Jan., April, July and Oct.). The pleasant surprise screen always beats the other screens from the last time I checked.

Zacks ranks stocks with positive earnings revisions. Their stocks have ranked #1 has an amazing average annual return of 26% according to them. In 2019, the performance of recent tests did not hold up that well.

As with all vendors, we should check their recent performance (say, the last 5 years). If the strategy is proven to be effective, more investors will follow and usually make it less effective.

It usually starts on the first two weeks after the ending of quarters (Dec., March, June and September) as indicated in the following link. http://www.investopedia.com/ask/answers/08/earnings-season.asp

My experience
Contrary to the conventional wisdom, I enjoy the negative surprises more. If the company has a reason to come back or its problem is only temporary, I buy the stock. Sometimes it takes a few months and sometimes even a year for the stock to come back. The strategy of 'Buying low and selling high' works more often than it does not. However, avoid the stocks that start their long-term plunge.

Missing expected earnings by 1% and causing the stock to drop by 10% is a buy to me. Heading to bankruptcy is a different story though.

My momentum strategy buys stocks with positive earnings revisions. I usually do not keep these stocks for over a month.

As of today (4/6/2016), the quarter earnings season is starting. This year I have worry about the earnings due to the strong USD. It would impact the earnings as about 40% (my rough estimate) of the incomes of global companies are from foreign countries. If we feel there will be more disappointments, we should short the stocks that are expected to have poor earnings.

My lesson

Take advantage of the irrational human reactions. Retail investors and institutional investors are both human beings. Fund managers have more pressure to sell a loser to keep their jobs. Retail investors usually sell after the big institutional investors. Try to find out whether it is just a sentimental reaction or the stock is going to fall further.

How to hedge your stocks from earning surprises

Stocks might have a wide swing after the earnings announcements. Hedge the unfavorable announcements by the following three methods:

1. Stop loss.
    Usually the swing is steeper than your stop price. When the price reaches or go below a specific price, it will be turned into a market sell order. Institutional investors usually unload the stocks faster than the retail investors, opposite of buying. However, their positions are huge. We can tell they are unloading (or loading) from the unusual high trading volumes of the stocks. Ensure that your trades are allowed after hours.

2. Option.
    It is like buying an insurance to protect your loss. Protect yourself from large losses as insurance is not cheap and smaller losses could be due to volatility.

3. Earnings prediction.
    They are also known as whispers or educated guesses. Zacks has a grading system.

    Also insiders know the earnings before their announcements. However, it is illegal to use this information before its announcement.

Earnings revisions will be available before the announcement and they would provide better guesses to the announcement. With today's dividend chasers, the announcement of dividends or its increase would boost the stock price.

Personally I do not do a lot to protect my stocks from earnings announcements. I have too many stocks. However, when we have evaluated the stocks correctly and monitor them regularly, we should have more pleasant surprises.

Profit from earnings surprises

The stock price usually rises on positive earnings surprises and falls otherwise. Sometimes they are not rational such as 1% miss in earnings that causes 10% loss in the stock price. In some rare cases, the positive earnings causes the stock to plunge as the investors expected better earnings even better than consensus. Here is the example of looking for finding stocks with positive earnings (you can profit by buying puts or shorting the stocks for stocks with negative earnings).

- Find stocks that have earnings announcements next week or month. Sources are Finviz.com's screener and SeekingAlpha.
- The screened stocks should fit some basic criteria. My criteria are: Market Cap > 200M, stock price > $2, average volume > 10,000 shares...
- If you subscribe to Zacks, check out the earnings grade. Stocks with Grade 1 and Grade 2 deserve our time for further research.
- If there are meaningful insiders' purchases, the chance of positive earnings are high.
- A positive short-term trend (SMA-20% from Finviz.com) is a plus.
- A positive short-term trend for the sector that stock belongs to is a plus. The sector can be represented by an ETF for that sector and use SMA-20%.
- Read articles on the stock for a qualitative analysis. Find these articles from many sources including SeekingAlpha. Today they have fewer articles for free.

Be warned that we do not expect all wins. When we achieve more than 50% wins, we should fare very well financially. When the market is falling or the earnings are expected to be poor, do not buy stocks except those that are fundamentally sound.

Take advantage of others' orders

1. Ensure your account can trade after hours.
2. Use Finviz.com to look for stocks announcing earnings this week. Prefer fundamentally sound stocks with a market cap great than 500 (100 for smaller stocks).
3. Check out earningswhispers.com. They have two estimates: the consensus and the one from this web site. Write down the exact time too.
4. If you subscribe Zacks.com, use its rating too as a reference.
5. Be at least 15 minutes earlier than the announcement date and time.
6. Google the stock and EPS from Google News. Refresh the search every 2 minutes. Check related articles.
7. If it beats the estimates, buy it at least one penny less than the last trade price and sell it within a day or two. The logic is to take advantage of all those orders that have not considered earnings in a timely fashion. It does not always work.
8. To improve performance, include Revenue with EPS.

3   Strategies on earnings

Here are two strategies on earnings. It is supposed to make millions for my children but they are not interested in investing. You either hate or love what your old man does.

1. Buy the stocks with earnings announcement soon with Zacks rating 1 (the best) and short those with Zacks rating 5 (the worst). BTW, Zacks rating is free so far for individual stocks.

2. After the earnings announcement, Google the company every second or so. If the earnings are good, buy it fast with market order. If it is bad, short it.

Do not be greedy and set a limit on loss. Do not call me if the trade is good or bad. In addition, check insider transactions and SMA-20%. I use Finviz.com.

I have tried #1 once a long while ago. I have not tried #2 as I have a life too. In the long haul, these strategies should make you some money.

4　Year-end strategies

I have two: 1. Buy the current year winners (YEW) and 2. Buy the current year losers (YEL).

The first strategy is riding the institutional investors' window dressing to include the winners in their funds to make them look better. It did not work well in 2018, so I skip it in 2019.

The second strategy takes advantage of selling losers for tax purposes. We need to find value stocks, but not stocks that are heading into bankruptcy. I had amazing returns in 2018 and will continue this strategy in 2019.

The following describes how to create your own testing if you have a historical database. It would be a frame for testing other strategies.

- Define the starting date. For the first strategy, I would use 9/1, 10/1 and 11/1 for two sets of test data. For the second strategy, I would use 12/1 and 12/15. Check to see which starting date is better for the specific strategy.
- Define the durations, the number of months before you sell the purchased stocks. I use 1 months, 2 months, 3 months and 6 months for my designated durations.
- Define the number of tests. I would start from the year 2000, one or two years older if your historical database allows for that. Actually I started in last 3 years or so to save time. However, do not use dates older than 1995 as the market was quite different then.
- Compare your results to SPY (or the S&P 500 index).
- Ignore dividends for simplicity.
- Use annualized rates for a better comparison.
- If the date has no data such as during holidays and weekends, use the date after it for consistency.

- Take out stocks that would not be the stocks you usually would buy, such as penny stocks (that likely boost the performance due to survivorship bias), small foreign companies and/or stocks giving huge dividends or giving a return of capital.
- Use different metrics to sort, such as Expected Earning Yield (E/P) or a composite grade. Use the top 5 (or 2) stocks to calculate performances.
- Include the maximum drawdown (the maximum loss from recent height) from many selected time frames (i.e. durations described). My maximum loss is -52% from 12/1/2007 to one year later in my Year-End Loss strategy, but followed by 256% gain in the next year.
- Negative percent numbers could give you wrong calculations when comparing to an index. Check them out manually if your formula has not taken care of the negative numbers.
- A year-end winner strategy should include large companies (traded by fund managers) and stocks that have increased in values year-to-date.
- From my limited testing, my small-cap stocks better than other stocks and they have to be profitable.
- Here are my best results for the two strategies. Again, my results will not be the same as yours due to different selection criteria. Past performance may not have anything to do with future performances.

The year-end loser strategy in 2015 does not work that well as I screened many stocks that were scored very low. I found out many screened stocks were from foreign countries. Many emerging countries have had problems and I do not trust most of their financial info. Besides that, many were energy companies which I already had too many of.

Many have Expected Earning Yields over 35%. However, most have very high debts such as Debt/Equity is over 1 (i.e. 100%). If I bought them, I would unload them within 3 months fearing a market crash in 2016 [Update. As of 2019, we do not have one]. Historically, it is profitable, but I may skip most YEL stocks this year as most were deserved losers. The lesson is: Adjust to the current market conditions.

Strategy	Starting Date	Duration	Avg. Annual. %	Max. Drawn Down
YE Winners	10/1	4 months	40%	-36%
YE Losers	12/1	6 months	42%	-28%

My experience

When trying to make good money, you need to find a strategy that matches the current market. Here are my recent strategies I actually tried with real money in 2018.

* You usually see window dressing from institutional investors from Nov. 1 to Dec. 1 (some use dates earlier than Nov. 1). Buy the current winners and sell the current losers of stocks with a large market cap.

The market was risky so I did not buy winners but shorted some losers.

* Buy year-end losers from Nov. 1 to Dec. 31 (some use dates earlier than Nov.1). The companies have to be profitable (>15%), big losers (most having over 50% yearly loss) and small companies (preferred).

Incorporate the strategy with today's volatile market (i.e. buy when they plunge and sell when they rise). You need to determine what is a "plunge" and a "rise". For me, it is short-term and the percent is 5% from a recent high or low.

There is a selling part of these strategies I have not included here. Most of my strategies are based on exhaustive tests from historical data with a lot of work.

Every market is different. We need to make a lot of adjustments. From my experiences, the best research may not make you money all the time. In the long run, the more educated you become, the better chance for you to make money.

Year-End 2018

This was one of my best monthly returns. The average purchase date is 12/27/2018 and the current prices were based on 1/28/2019. The return is 53% or 648% annualized. Most likely the performance will not be repeated. However, it serves as a procedure for coming years.

I change the quantity Q to 1. Several stocks have been purchased more than once. I sold 3 stocks already indicated by the Status = 'Sold'.

Account	Screen	Year-end loser		Start	12/21/19	End	1/8/2019	Today	1/28/19			
Stock	Q	Buy	Sell	Buy $	Sell $	Buy Date	Sell Date	# Days	Profit $	Profit %	Ann %	Status
401KC												
CHK	1	2.13	2.99	2	3	01/03/19	01/18/19	15	1	40%	982%	Sold
MNK	1	16.41	21.45	16	21	01/03/19	01/25/19	22	5	31%	510%	Sold
MNK	1	16.43	21.45	16	21	01/03/19	01/25/19	22	5	31%	507%	Sold
NNBR	1	5.68	8.58	6	9	12/26/18	01/18/19	33	3	51%	565%	
NNBR	1	5.72	8.58	6	9	12/26/18	01/28/19	33	3	66%	727%	
ESTE	1	4.35	6.45	4	6	12/26/18	01/18/19	23	2	48%	766%	Sold
JT												
LCI	1	4.61	8.29	5	8	12/21/18	01/28/19	38	4	80%	767%	
MDR	1	8.01	9.13	8	9	01/08/19	01/28/19	20	1	14%	255%	
YRCW	1	3.29	5.78	3	6	12/21/18	01/28/19	38	2	76%	727%	
YRCW	1	3.26	5.78	3	6	12/21/18	01/28/19	38	3	77%	742%	
401K												
ASRT	1	3.56	4.18	4	4	12/26/18	01/28/19	33	1	17%	193%	
UTCC	1	7.13	11.00	7	11	12/26/18	01/28/19	33	4	54%	600%	
YRCW	1	2.92	5.78	3	6	12/26/18	01/28/19	33	3	98%	1083%	
Tot/avg				84	119	12/27/18		29	36	53%	648%	

I sold my YRCW (not shown above) on the earnings date that can be found in Finviz.com. When the earnings are positive, it will be sold for my asking price plus a little more but less than the surge. If it is negative, it will not be sold. I recommend to cancel any trade order before the earnings date.

As of 09/07/2019, LCI is up by 185% and YRCW is down by 27% (I sold one position in my retirement account for about 100% gain).

How long should we hold these screened stocks?

Except those in my taxable account, I sold all of them in the first two months. The following is the annualized returns for holding 1 month, 2 months, 3 months and 5 months (as of 6/22/2019). From my previous testing, I should have held the stocks for 6 months. However, I have made my objective already and I want to take advantage of this volatile market.

I could not find UTCC in my historical database. I sold it with an annualized return of 572%. It could be acquired or merged. For simplicity, I used 12/27/2018 as the purchase date for all stocks. I consider one position for each stock and hence 3 purchases of YRCW is considered as one purchase here. Again, I do not include dividends, the bid spread and commissions.

	1 Month	2 Months	3 Months	5 Months
Ann. Return	497%	366%	178%	17%
SPY	72%	74%	52%	31%

From the above, I did well in selling most of them. If I held all of them for 5 months, they would not beat the SPY, the market comparison many use.

Filler

- First bought or sold by insiders and their relatives, then followed by programmed computers, institutional investors, technicians and then retail investors.

- Missed a short of PG&E and VALE when their bad news broke. There is more in life than playing the markets.

5   Short Squeeze

When there is a short squeeze (i.e. over shorted), the stock may appreciate due to the shorters unable to find more stocks to short. The candidates can be found in Finviz.com. I use 35%. However, there may be valid reasons for the shorts such as a lawsuit pending, losing sales... Select the stocks with sound fundamentals.

The following are tests (not real trades) and many tests will be added. As of 09/04/15, the returns are:

Stock	Buy Date	Return	Annualized	SPY return
CALM	07/16/15	-3%	-33%	-1%
GME	07/16/15	-1%	-7%	-1%

The following are real trades as of 09/04/15.

Stock	Buy Date	Return	Sold date
CALM	03/11/15	47%	N/A
GME	04/06/15	8%	N/A

CALM, a candidate

Cal-Maine Foods Inc. (CALM) had fallen from over $60 to $46 recently and it was my heavy bet. The opening price on 12/15/2015 was $46.76. Readers might wonder why I still recommended accumulating a falling stock. Simply put, the race is not over and this horse has a lot of potential (i.e. fundamentally sound). The payout would be huge as it has been ignored (the short float is over 55%).

Let me show you my evaluation process, so that you may use it to enhance your strategy if you have one.

Currently, this stock was screened by my Short screen that spots fundamentally-sound companies with short floats over 35%. Most of the screened stocks deserve to be shorted, but I cannot find any justification for this stock.

Technically speaking

First, this stock has been hated as described by the following table with the exception of Finviz's "Recom". Most of the data in this article were derived from the free Finviz.com on Dec. 15, 2015. The 'Conditions' are my personal preferences.

	Condition	Indicate	12/15/2015
Short Float	>35%	Short squeeze	55%
RSI(14)	<30%	Oversold	31%
SMA-20	<0	Short-term down	-13%
SMA-50	<0	Mid-term down	-17%
SMA-200	<0	Long-term down	-9%
Recom.	1 - Buy & 5 – Sell	3 – Neutral	2

Fundamentally speaking

Did this stock deserve this hatred? From the following table, it is a big NO.

	Condition	Indicate	12/15/2015
Forward P/E	>0 and < 20	Favorable	7
ROE	>20%	Favorable	40%
Profit Margin	>8%	Favorable	15%
EPS Q/Q	>15%	Favorable	418%
Sales Q/Q	>10%	Favorable	71%
P/FCF	<15	Favorable	12
Debt / Equity	<.5 (industry related)	Favorable	.05

One or two favorable metrics do not mean a 'Buy' or great fundamentals. However, all these metrics all yell 'Buy'. They are my major fundamental metrics that have recently proven my predictability.

I combined all these metrics and scored CALM in 3 scoring systems plus PEY described below. As of this writing, CALM passed all my scoring systems with flying colors. Actually when stocks exceed the passing score by that much, I have a little concern; I cannot find any problem with this stock.

	Passing Score	Score
P-Score	3	6
Short-term score	15	40
Long-term score	15	24
PEY	5%	23%

Explanation

- P-Score, Pow's Score. It uses the metrics available in the free Finviz.com with the exception of using Fidelity's Analyst Opinion instead of Finviz's "Recom". This score system is described in my book "Scoring Stocks".
- The other two systems use additional metrics and/or scores I subscribe to. I monitor these two scoring systems periodically and adjust the scores accordingly. My Short-Term Score is used for holding stocks for less than 6 months.
- PEY, Pow's Earnings Yield. It is similar to EV/EBIT (5 from GuruFocus or 1/5 = 20% for Earning Yield). Both consider debt and cash. The advantage of PEY is all the metrics are readily available for calculation if using Cash/Share instead of Short-term Liability. PEY also uses expected earnings.

Intangibles

From Seeking Alpha, enter CALM and you should find many articles. I have not found any alarms on CALM. Some farms that are affected by the bird flu will return if not already to production and eat into CALM's market. It is always a possibility that CALM will be infected by bird flu. However, with most chickens staying inside the farm and the extra precautions, the chance is slim. Let me share three scenarios below.

Say if there is another bird flu (not in CALM) that happens, the egg prices would rocket up and also is the profit of CALM.

Let's say if that happens to CALM, it will affect onto the location involved. As I stated, the management (they had been great) should have taken precautions to minimize the chance of a bird flu.

Then what if it happens in Hong Kong or another Chinese city, they would ban chicken from local farms and bring the frozen chickens from the unaffected countries such as the US. It would bring profits to CALM.

The egg price is returning to its normal price. Hence, the EPS will be lowered. With a Forward P/E less than 7 and PEY greater than 23%, the stock price would have to fall a lot to cause any great alarm.

Bonus metrics

From GuruFocus.com (a paid subscription), F-Score was 7 and Z-Score was 8; both are favorable.

From Blue Chip Growth (no longer free), all three grades were "B". That was good but not the best. Not too long ago, most were "A". I do not know the reason for the downgrade as today's stock price is now lower and there is no change in the fundamentals.

Summary

This stock is technically unsound but fundamentally sound. It may still trend downward, but when it shoots back up, it would be like fireworks on display. Most value stocks are swimming against the tide, so we have to be patient for the market to realize its real real value.

No one can identify the bottom precisely and consistently. I expect a short squeeze is coming when the shorters cannot find more shares to short. The interest rate hike could trigger some covering of the shorts. The shorters are paying about an 8% dividends; I do not recommend to short high-dividend stocks. With this price, the risk is low and the potential appreciation is high. When one or two institutional investors move in, the price will surge. I bought it on 3/11/15 and sold it on 10/28/15 making a profit of 48% or an annualized return of 77%.

6   Multi baggers

It is very rewarding to find the next Apple making many times of profits over the original investment. It is possible, but it is not every one's cup of tea. For every winner found, there would be ten losers.

How to find them

I developed a screen to find potential multi baggers. Basically these stocks double in sales and profits (prefer to compare quarter of prior year to avoid seasonal fluctuations). Initially most are penny stocks with small market cap and are not listed in the three major exchanges. When they move up to a major exchange, it is a good sign. Usually they do not pay dividends as most of the profits have to be plowed back to research and development in the initial years.

Most likely, the screen would find them at least one year after their IPOs as we need the financial data. It is a good starting point to take out the companies that do not survive in the first year, and there are many.

Many of these stocks are traded in the $2 to $10 range. Most stocks below $5 are not 'marginable', which is important to boost its rising. These stocks usually trade within a low price range for a while before they breakout (i.e. surge in price).

When the breakout is supported with high volume, the price will tend to rocket even higher. I do not want to hold a triple bagger unless there is a good reason to do so. Need to calculate the reward / risk ratio. If it is the same chance to double as losing half of the value, I would hold or sell half of it. No one goes broke for taking profit.

When these stocks take off, most are overbought with RSI(14) above 65 for a few years to come.

IPO

There are two kinds of IPOs: from established products such as Facebook and from companies without established products. The former is less risky. Roughly, about 60% lose money in the first year while 40% make up the loss. IPOs are the best way to fund research and/or marketing of new products/services. Investors have to analyze whether the new product(s) is/are innovative enough and profitable to pay back their investments.

There are many investors specialized in new companies. Most IPOs make money on the first day with the recent exception of Facebook. Buy in the morning and sell at the end of the day. Most retail investors cannot participate in IPOs without connection with some brokers. However, there are successful investors spotting Microsoft, Wal-Mart, Tesla and companies involved in 3D printing in its early stage after IPO.

As of this writing, I do not find too many potential profitable companies with the exception of 3D printers. Zynga is a typical example. It seems it is repeating the usual sad chronology of a hot IPO:

1. Founders and the initial investors make a fortune on a good idea or a product.
2. Most initial investors make money.
3. The stock skyrockets. The insiders cash in after the restricted period that they cannot sell after the IPO. Usually most retail investors do not sell.
4. The stock purges. Most losers are retail investors.

You're buying for the company's new vision and/or the innovative products. However, many of these new companies do not make it as expected. You have to evaluate their product potential and review the progress of the company periodically. Innovative products that everyone wants may not be able to bring to the market due to regulations and the opposition from its potential competitors.

The first year will be a honeymoon period that most investors ignore the fundamental metrics. The second year on, evaluate the company again with fundamental metrics. For example, if the P/E is over 50,

most likely the company's stock will be in danger or the investors have been moving the price too fast and too high. Check out Debt/Equity. If the company cannot pay back the loan, it may go bankrupt.

Cisco was one of top-valued companies. It went down and then in the first half of 2013 it recovered. Again, fundamental metrics (such as P/E) and technical analysis guide us better as to when to trade Cisco. The long-term outlook of Cisco is good envisioning more devices connected to the routers. However, we need to examine its future offerings and its competitors.

The second phase

The initial investors before the IPO are not allowed to sell the stock. When it expires, the stock price may fall. When the stock price keeps on climbing, evaluate the appreciation potential. When they reach the peaks, sell. When the expected P/E is still reasonable (such as less than 35), check the PEG (P/E growth). If they are reasonable, hold on to the stock, but I would use a stop loss to protect profit. From my limited statistics, successful companies are usually less successful in the stock price after the first 10 years. It could be their peaks may have come.

It is a balancing act, sit on a winning horse on its way up and sell the winning horse at its peak. No one can find the peak consistently. Use technical analysis's SMA (Simple Moving Average) to determine the enter/exit points. If you're not too sure, sell half of your holding.

Company turnaround

When a stock loses most of its value, it could go to zero or it could turn around. Check the possibilities in both scenarios. Sometimes the chart together with insider purchases could indicate a turnaround.

The staircase pattern described next is a good sign. The stock stays in the current value for a while before it moves up to the next peak. It then stays there for a while and moves up to the next peak again.

More losers than winners

I suspect many small companies fail for each of the multi baggers found. The losers may not show up in the database as they're taken away from the database when the stock price goes to 0 (termed as survival bias) or the stock is delisted from the exchange. If your test database does not take care of survival bias, your test result will appear far better than your strategy really is.

You need to have cash that you do not need for a long while, a lot of patience and the mental power to experience many losses.

Apple, Microsoft and Oracle all have the right products in this generation. Judging from the recent IPOs including Zynga and Groupon, I do not think that we have too many potential multi baggers from the current offerings, but I could be wrong. No stocks can justify a forward P/E over 40 unless they have very high potential like a promising new drug.

Many big winners can shoot up 200% in 6 months. It needs one or more catalysts to boost this kind of performance. It could be a new product that could change the world, a potential acquirer (very seldom the acquirer pays more than 50% of the current price). Fundamental analysis seldom finds these stocks, but technical analysis can.

2015 IPOs

2015 is a loser year for IPOs especially compared to the better years in 2013 and 2014. The tiny Hong Kong was number one in IPOs in term of the total market value for IPOs and most of them are Chinese companies. NYC took a back seat for the first time in what I can remember.

Shenzhen Exchange was even crazier than Hong Kong with its volatility and huge price fluctuations. It supports financially the growing high-tech companies in South China. If you have a new high tech gadget such as a drone, it is the best place to build it. Most of your component suppliers are close by.

The average NYSE stock price lost about 15% at the close of the first day in 2015. Is it a trend? Only time can tell.

Tax considerations

You may want to sell a loser when it does not show any future promise to offset any gain from other stocks. When you find a big winner and you're not young, you can keep it until you die so the cost basis will be stepped up and your heirs do not pay the tax on the capital gain according to the tax law of 2016. Alternatively, give it to a charity for an extra deduction. Tax law changes and I'm not a tax professional, so ask your lawyer for advice.

My personal experience

I sell most stocks when they double. Very seldom do I keep a stock long enough to be a triple bagger. Most of my double (and once in a blue moon triple) baggers were acquired by larger companies, or I need to hold them longer to be eligible for long-term capital gain. One's opinion. However, I recommend to keep rising stocks and protect the profits by adjusting stops.

Finding the next wave

You can make more than 10 times of your investment when you invest early in the companies that can change the world. Some are started via IPOs. Many others are initially invested by venture capitalists, then they are listed in small exchanges and eventually are moved to one of the three major exchanges. By the time these companies are noticed by the market, they usually are already fully valued.

I saw many in the last 30 years, and unfortunately I did not act on many of them or did not buy them early enough. It is primarily due to my conservative nature. The examples are:

- Apple in its early stage and so are many high tech companies such as Microsoft, Google and Cisco. When I see my stock prices doubled, I am tempted to sell them and would miss the opportunity of its doubling again.

  Use technical analysis and fundamental analysis to determine the exit and reentry points. To protect the profit, use stop orders and adjust the stop price when the stock appreciates by more than 10% (more frequently if you have time).

- Drug companies discovering new drugs. I had some successes via a subscribed newsletter and followed insider trading from public information.

- Change of the retail business by Wal-Mart via importing products from China especially after Sam Walton who estimated wrongly the difference between the Chinese and American prices on similar products. It is similar to Amazon creating a new channel for retailing.

- Change of policy such as one allowing GPS for public use or banning importing of Chinese solar panels. GPS devices are eventually obsoleted by smart phones that provide the same function. Solar panels are still not ready economically even without the cheap Chinese import. The recent legalizing of a drug is a good example. I knew about it and I did not act on it due to my ethical reasons. Fidelity has a social score.

Currently we had some new drugs, cloud computing (too cloudy for my taste as I cannot figure how they can make money as of today), 3D printing... Amazon revolutionizes digital publishing and internet retailing. Amazon's stock skyrockets even the fundamentals look bad. Amazon invests its money for the future.

There are many small companies that would offer products that would change the world. However, most of them will be acquired by larger corporations as it is too expensive to launch these new products / services unless their IPOs provide a lot of cash.

In ten years or so, China would have more of these innovative companies for the following reasons. However, I do not trust the financial data of most developing countries especially small companies.

1. There are many educated scientists and engineers. Contrary to popular belief, they do have genius schools that will produce more geniuses such as Gates and Jobs.

2. The government encourages science and technology and has long-term objectives. However, they need to set up regulations to protect intelligence properties.

3. Chinese engineers' wages are only a fraction of ours. A typical Chinese engineer works far more hours than our engineers. When a Chinese engineer works 10 hours a day while the US

engineer works 8 hours, it is more than the 2 hour difference in productivity.

4. They have a large internal market.

Profit from IPOs

If your broker does not have the connection, most likely you cannot buy them on the first day of the IPOs. Skip trading the stock for the first few days. When it makes a new high, consider buying it. Unless the fundamentals/outlooks are good, sell it before the insiders are allowed to sell (6 to 12 months after the IPO depending on the company).

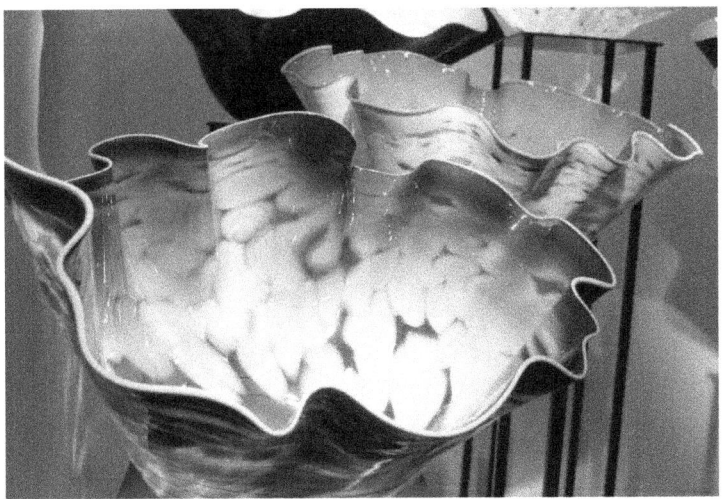

7   An aggressive strategy

I use a similar strategy that includes metrics and composite grades from vendors that I subscribe to their services. The following is a brief description. As in life, there is no guarantee.

The basic major steps are:

* Use market timing to determine when to buy and sell.
* How to screen stocks.
* How to modify the screen to fit the current market conditions.
* Score the stock fundamentally.
* Intangible analysis.
* Qualitative analysis.
* Optionally, technical analysis.

Market Timing

Refer to the chapters on this topic described in this book.

Screen stocks

Most small cap stocks are not followed by analysts, so we can find some gems. The common screening criteria will be mentioned briefly here.

* Skip the following sectors and countries: financial companies (banks, loaners), miners, drug (generic OK), insurance, emerging countries including China, India and Mexico.

* Ensure the company is not heading into bankruptcy. "Price / Free Cash Flow" cannot be manipulated easily. Profit growth and sales growth compared to the last quarter are good indicators too. Massive insider dumping is another one.

* Common filter criteria:

    1. Listed in one of the three major exchanges, or specific exchange(s) for your country.

2. Market cap > 200 million and < 800 million.

3. Price > 2 and less than 20.

4. Average daily volume > 8,000 (some use 10,000) shares.

5. Short % less than 15% (some use 10%).

6. Expected earning yield (E/P, reversal of P/E) > 5% and < 30%.

7. Ensure the SMA%-200 (simple moving average for the last 200 trade sessions) is positive. In other words, the stock price is above the SMA-200 line. You can obtain this value from Finviz.com.

The above information can be easily obtained from Finviz.com. Try any extras criteria your broker offers. Use the Equity Summary Score from Fidelity and ignore stocks with ranks less than 6.

The next useful comparisons are the averages of its industry or sector. The common parameters are: Price / Cash Flow, Debt percent, P/E (also its own 5 year average), Price / Sales, etc.

Sorting the screened stocks

If you have too few stocks from your screen, the market may be risky. If not, ease up on your filter criteria.

If you have too many stocks, sort them in descending order by the expected earnings yield. Select the top stocks for further evaluation.

What the current market favors

If the market favors growth, sort them in descending order of the SMA % (use 50 or 200 depending on how long you expect to keep the stock) from Finviz.com, or any growth metric such as earning quarter-to-quarter growth rate. The higher the SMA % indicates the higher chance the stock is moving up, but it should not be excessive as that could indicate a peak. Also determine whether the stock is over-bought indicated by the RSI(14) indicator.

If the market favors value, sort the screened stocks in descending order of the expected E/P.

Qualitative analysis
Most of the above information or criteria belongs to quantitative analysis. Check out the tangibles and qualitative analysis.

Use screens to select a handful of stocks for your further evaluation as it saves time.

Screen sites

There are many sites to screen stocks and many have built-in screens for immediate use. Your stock broker may provide you with screens. There are many good ones that are free including Finviz.com, Fidelity.com and Yahoo!Finance.com. AAII provides screened stocks from the basic subscription and provides screens that you can modify for an extra fee.

Some vendors provide a historical database and/or better tools at an extra cost: AAII, Stock 123, Zacks, Vector Vest... It would be useful to test screens with past data. Some sites provide back testing features for technical analysis. Validea (http://www.validea.com/home/home.asp) has some promising screens at a cost, and so is GuruFocus.com.

Interesting screens

- There are screens that simulate what the gurus such as what Buffett would buy. They may beat the market but not by a wide margin. It could be too many followers using these screens.

- Include stocks that were not in any major exchanges one year ago. It includes the companies that started in the basements, moved to a local exchange, and now have moved to a major exchange. Most major companies such as Apple and Microsoft belonged to this group at one time. Some may skip the local exchange as Facebook did.

- Sort PEG and select the stocks with the best PEGs such as lower than 1. It is a growth strategy.

- Select stocks that have been increasing in prices in the last 3 months. It is a momentum strategy.

- Stocks with better metrics compared to companies in the same industry sector. Compare Apples to Apples.

- Combine growth metrics and value metrics. It is the Growth with a Value strategy. It is also known as "Growth with a realistic price".

- Candidates for being acquired.
  Usually they are small companies in specific markets and / or having specific technologies. 2009 was a good year for acquisitions, especially when there was a lot of corporate cash and the interest rates were low.

- Candidates to be listed in the three major exchanges.
  Usually they are gaining in profits, market shares and/or market capitalizations. When they are listed, some ETFs are required to buy them.

- Sell last year's big gainers and buy last year's big losers. It is contrarian's strategy. Need to ensure they can turn around and are fundamentally sound.

- Select the best stocks from the top 5 sectors (I prefer industries) when the market in rising. It is a top-down approach.

- Stocks with favorable earnings revisions. This strategy works better before the earnings announcements.

- Stocks with high insiders' purchases.

- Dividend growth stocks.
  They perform very well in the last few years as of 1-2014. Income seekers flock to dividend stocks when CDs and bonds cannot give them equivalent incomes.

- Besides from your broker's site on screening tools, Kapitall has a lot of ideas on building screens and the stock recommendations. Check his articles in Seeking Alpha or their website (http://seekingalpha.com/author/kapitall).
- Garbage in and garbage out. I do not trust the financial statements from most emerging countries. If your screening tools do not provide this filter, check the company's profile and skip these companies that you may not trust.
- Fidelity's Predefined screens.
http://research2.fidelity.com/fidelity/screeners/commonstock/strategies.asp?

- Many sites provide guru screens to simulate what gurus would buy. GuruFocus.com is one of them.

Back testing

If your screening service does not provide a historical database, you may have limited testing capability. However, you can still compare the screened stocks six months later. To simplify, use a virtual portfolio for each strategy.

Find out why your screen does not work when you invest with real money:

1. Survivorship bias. The historical database you use may have taken out all the stocks that have been delisted and they're usually bad. Stocks with less than $1 have a higher chance of survivorship bias.

   Most of them bankrupted, so your performance of a screen looks better as you have avoided these stocks unknowingly. A small percent of the 'disappeared' stocks are merged, acquired, or spin-offs and usually they're doing well. However, there are far more bankrupt companies than the above.
2. Humans are not rational. We usually buy high and sell low. Sticking with a strategy will take out this aspect.
3. Use the wrong screen for the current market conditions. A value screen should not be used when the market is trending up.
4. Market conditions change. Many years ago, selecting low P/E and foreign companies listed in the US exchanges provided above-average returns. However, it was not true in 2011 to 2014.

8   Four basic **strategies for momentum**

We have 3 strategies according to the different holding periods and the screening is a little different from each other. The screen parameters (i.e. selection criteria) are briefly described here. Adjust them to fit your risk tolerance and requirements. Monitor them from time to time as the market always changes.

Metric	Strategy #1	Strategy #2	Strategy #3
Avg. holding period	< 30 days	60 days	90 days
General			
Market Cap	300 M – 2 B	300 M – 2B	2B – 10B
Avg. volume	>100K	>200K	> 300 K
Analyst Rec	Buy or better	Buy or better	Buy or better
Country	USA	USA	USA
Price	>$5	>$10	>$10
Fundamental			
P/E	>0	>0	>0
Forward P/E	>0	>0	>0
Return on Equity		>10%	>10%
EPS Growth next year		>15%	>10%
Technical			
Performance	Week up	Week up	Week up
SMA-20%	> 10%		
SMA-50%		>0%	
SMA-200%	>0%	>0%	>0%

In addition, they should be in one of the 3 major exchanges: NYSEX, NASDQA and AMEX (Finviz.com allows you to select one exchange at a time).

In general, Strategy #1 does not care about fundamental. Strategy #2 is a typical sector rotation candidate. Strategy #3 cares more about fundamentals.

I recommend to paper trade your strategy using different selection criteria. When you are comfortable, commit a small sum and increase your portfolio size gradually. My own screens incorporate timing grades from various vendors.

Vendors

Most charge a fee for using their services. Most have a score (or rank) for timing. Usually they are based on the momentum of the price. If the price jumps very fast and high, this score is high. Use mental stops to protect your profits and reduce your losses. When the price is below a set price (such as 10% from your bought price), use market order to sell it. This would reduce the potential loss of a flash crash. When the timing score is the highest, be very, very cautious as it cannot go higher.

Example

Here is an example on how to find the momentum stocks.

Bring up finviz.com. Select Screener. Select 20-Day Simple Moving Average above 20%. Sort the screened stocks with this parameter. Today I have about 100 stocks.

Limit your selection to fit your requirements and preferences. Here are some sample criteria: U.S. companies only, capital cap over 100 M, price over $2, relative volume over 1 and no leveraged ETFs.

Check whether the screened stocks are peaking (say have appreciated over 200%). Check the reason for recent surges and evaluate whether the momentum would continue or not. Check out any insides' purchases at prices close to market prices.

Strategy #4

This is a variation of the described three strategies. I explain it with a step-by-step approach in implementing it using Finviz.com. Bring it up by typing Finviz.com in your browser.

1. Only buy momentum stocks when the market is not risky. When the tide is up, all ships flow up. Check out my market timing technique. In the simplest way, enter SPY (or any ETF that simulates the market) in Finviz.com. If SMA-20%, SMA-50% and SMA-200% are all positive, most likely the market is not risky.

2. Select Screen. The following are my preferred metrics and you can change them to suite your requirements and risk tolerance.

3. From Descriptive tab, Select Small (300M to 2B) for Market Cap, Over 100K for Average Volume, Over 2 for Relative Volume, USA for Country and Over $5 for Price. Repeat it for other ranges such as 100M to 4B in Market Cap and over $1 for Price.

4. From Fundamental tab, select Positive in Insider Transaction.

5. From Technical tab, select 10% above SMA-50 in SMA-20 (Simple Moving Average for the last 20 days) and 20% above 200-SMA in SMA-50. Change the selection if they are not desirable for you and/or the current market conditions. As of 11/07/2016, I have the following 4 stocks: AAOI, BOOT, LC and NILE. They already have good price increases. Will report the performances in the future edition of this book or in my blog (http://tonyp4idea.blogspot.com/).

6. Click on the selected stocks one by one such as AAOI. From most other metrics, it is not a value stock. The Forward P/E is 16. Hence, it has some value despite the high P/E of 80. All SMA%s are positive to indicate it is trending up.

7. Qualitative Analysis. After you bought the stock, use stop loss to limit any loss especially in this risky market. Conservative investors should stay away from risky market. I would set a 15% stop loss (i.e. sell it via a market order when it loses 15%).

8. Most likely you cannot buy it via discount prices on a stock trending up.

9. Save the screen with a name such as Momentum, so you do not have to reenter the metrics again.

10. This free site does not provide historical database. You can run the test every week (or month) and write down the results. Only invest in real money when you're comfortable with your tests. Enter the position with money you can afford to lose. Making 55% profitable trades could be very profitable.

11. There are many variations to this strategy. Some are described here. Select Overbought (20) in RSI(14), Double Bottom in Pattern and New High in 52-Week High/Low.

12. If it is moving up, review it every month (preferable every week) and set up a trailing stop. To illustrate, when it is up by 20%, set the stop at the current price (not the price you paid for the stock).

9   Sector rotation in a nutshell

How to start

I have been rotating sectors in my annuity for quite a long time and this strategy has increased about four times over the years. My employer had a lot of restrictions for me to trade stocks, so switching sector funds in my annuity was the best investment for me. When your account grows to a large amount, it is better to use a subscription service to determine the rankings of sectors.

For starter, I recommend to paper trade your strategy. Use Finviz.com to select the best performing sector and/or use my quick analysis of ETFs. Switch it every month (or two) to the ETF corresponding to the best sector. Again, switch to cash when the market is risky.

After the basic, this book provides many features to further refine your strategy. Use Technical Analysis. Start with the technical indicators such as SMA-50% and RSI(14) and a handful of sector ETFs to rotate (suggested sectors are technology, bank, health care, housing, consumer and material).

In addition, some sectors are more profitable in different phases of a market cycle. We examine several industry sectors and country sectors in more detail. The rise of China is affecting the global economy. When the interest rates is low, it would affect bonds and stocks yielding high dividends. Many books ignore market timing. It turns out to be the most important as the last market plunges have an average loss of 45%!

The key to profitable sector rotation

Sector rotation could be very profitable and less risky than most of us expect. There are two ways to profit:

1. Buy when the sector is trending up and sell when the sector is trending down. It is the common approach to sector rotation.

2. Buy at the bottom of a sector and sell at the peak. It is hard to detect the bottom/peak. It will be briefly described next.

The following is the very basic way to rotate sectors. Many investment subscriptions and free sites such as finviz.com select favorable sectors every month. We assume the best-performed sector last month will perform better in the coming month. It does not always happen such as the tech sector in April, 2000 and the reversed direction of drug sector in 2015. To protect your investment, use mental stops to avoid flash crashes.

Alternatively, we can select them via simple charts as described in this book. Beginners should start with Single Moving Average. Using more than one technical indicator without understanding them completely could cost you money.

Detecting the bottom of a sector

It is not easy and no one can detect the bottom or the peak of a sector consistently. The SMA-350 (Single Moving Average with 350 sessions) detects the market quite accurately for the last two market plunges. I have tested out the "days" with different numbers and 350 is the best fit for the last two market plunges.

Besides technical indicators, there are hints that indicate a sector is close to the bottom. Use the ETF for the sector and check out the fundamental metrics similar to evaluating a stock. To illustrate, enter XLE in Yahoo!Finance or finviz.com to get the current price and other info about this sector.

Calculate the percentage of its current price from the bottom in the last 350 trade sessions. We assume the last bottom should be close to the next bottom in a sideway market. The intangibles should be considered too.

Detecting the trend

Detecting the trend is easier than detecting the bottom/peak. To illustrate, bring up finviz.com from your browser and enter XLE. For most sectors, I use the SMA-50 (50-day single moving average), which is readily available as one of the metrics. When the stock price is 3% above SMA, buy. When it is 3% below the SMA, sell. It is simple, but it has been proven many times.

You can adjust the 50-day and the 3% (some use 1%) to how long your average holding period of an ETF or a stock and how often you want to trade. If your holding period is longer, use higher number such as 90 days. If you want to trade more often use 1% instead of 3%.

Personally I use 60 days if I use charts (from Yahoo!Finance among one of the many free sites that provide charts). One of my accounts requires 60 days for minimum holding period without incurring a fee.

To detect market crashes and when to reenter the market or a sector ETF or a mutual fund after the crash, I use 350 days (some use 300 days). The 'days' is actually trade sessions.

RSI(14) indicates whether the sector is overbought or oversold. RSI oscillates between zero and 100. Traditionally, and according to Wilder, RSI is considered overbought with a value above 70 and oversold with a value below 30 as described in the article. This indicator is available from Finviz.com.

   (http://stockcharts.com/school/doku.php?id=chart_school:tec hnical_indicators:relative_strength_index_rsi)

   A simple way is to buy last month's winner(s). Ensure the ETFs are not leveraged if you are conservative. Include contra ETFs when the market is risky for aggressive investors. Here are the links to the web sites that keep track of top performers varying 1 to 3 months.

Seeking Alpha's ETF Hub.
http://seekingalpha.com/insight/etf-hub/asset_class_performance/key_markets
Morning Star. Select the period (1 month for example).
http://news.morningstar.com/etf/Lists/ETFReturns.htm

What to buy

I prefer ETFs for specific sectors and sector funds (check out the holding period to exit without penalties) are another choice. Sector funds are better than ETFs in specific sectors such as banking, drug companies and mining.

ETFs charge less for maintaining and they have all the advantages of a stock. However, mutual funds select the stocks within a sector selectively. Fidelity offers the most complete sector mutual funds. Compare the 3 or 5 year performance between the ETF and the sector fund in this same sector.

The third option is top-down approach. First, when the market is not plunging, select the favorable sector and then the stocks within the sector. Many free sites provide a filter for favorable sectors.

Here is a list of sector ETFs.
(http://www.bloomberg.com/markets/etfs/)

Here is a list of commission-free ETFs from Fidelity.
(https://www.fidelity.com/etfs/ishares)

Some sector funds automatically switch sectors for you. My experience did not prove to me to be profitable. Check out their past performance.

Favorable sectors according to the market cycle

Refer the chapter on Market Timing and Spotting Market Plunge for specific strategies. I remind myself to close most positions when the market is plunging.

Favorable sectors according to the interest rate

It is similar to the above. Retailing, auto and housing are usually hurt by high interest rates. However, the improving economy would take out this disadvantage as more employed folks can afford big-ticket items.

Favorable sectors according to geography

It is not an easy task. China and India had their best performing years. Japan had one of the best years in 2013 during the two decades. For foreign countries, currency fluctuation should be considered. Most emerging countries have their ups and downs. Most ETFs or sector funds buy larger companies that are more trustworthy in the financial statements.

Global economies have never been that tightly connected. When the US economy is down, China is affected and so are the resource-rich countries.

Favorable and unfavorable events

The EU crisis has been taken more than three years as of 4/2016 and the EU stocks are still close to the bottom. I prefer to buy an ETF specialized in EU or a mutual fund when the trend is up.

When the Treasury says the interest will be lower, the market and the long term bond funds will move up, and vice versa. To me, the interest rates will move up slowly from the 1/2014 bottom. Most likely the new Fed chairwoman will not raise the interest rates until the economy totally recovers.

Recent favorable and unfavorable sectors
There are many sources to check what sectors perform recently. Finviz.com is one of them. From the top menu bar, select Group, and the best and worst sectors will be displayed. Skip one day or one week unless you have special interest on these short durations. Select the duration depending on your purpose. Personally I would use one month (or two) for my monthly rotation strategy betting the momentum would pass to the next month.

Technical analysis would spot the trend. Select Simple Moving Average with n-day. It is similar to the TA used in the chapter spotting market crash. Instead of using SPY or another ETF market index, use an ETF that represents the sector.

Sector rotation by fund managers

We cannot beat these institutional investors. We need to follow them or one step ahead of them. They rotate sectors when they find another sector has better appreciation potential or the current favorable sector has reached its peak.

When to rotate

Rotate for the following reasons:

1. When the market is plunging, rotate the sector ETFs and/or mutual funds to cash. Aggressive investors would rotate their equities to contra ETFs. The average loss of the last two market plunges is about 45%. This chart will not determine the peak as it depends on the falling data. However, it will tell you when to exit to prevent further loss and tell you when to reenter the market.
2. When the fundamentals of the current sector bought are turning bad.
3. When there is another sector that has better appreciation potential. Finviz.com tells you the rankings of the sectors.
4. When the sector is overbought or peaking, and / or has met our objective.

Do not forget market timing

Do NOT buy any stocks except the contra ETFs when the market is plunging. Playing defense usually wins the game more often than playing offense. You can make good money without sector rotation by following market timing. When the market is peaking, protect your profits by placing stop loss orders.

Positions and how often to switch
It depends on the size of your portfolio and how much time you can afford to monitor your portfolio. To me, it varies from 2 to 6 positions and 20 to 90 days to monitor the switches.

Statistics show that a portfolio with 5 positions rotating in 20 days give you slightly better performance and less drawback (maximum loss for the period). I recommend 4 (2 for a portfolio of less than $20,000) and 30 days (and 60 days for Fidelity sector funds).

Conclusion

Sector rotation is described in very basic terms here. The links in Afterthoughts provide additional information.

As a reminder, roughly half of a stock's price movement can be attributed to the sector it is in.

Afterthoughts
- There are many articles in this topic. They are:

Sector rotation strategies ETF investors must know. There are many useful links.
http://www.bloomberg.com/markets/etfs/

Sector rotation based on performance.
http://stockcharts.com/school/doku.php?id=chart_school:tradi ng_strategies:sector_rotation_roc
Fidelity on Sectors.
https://www.fidelity.com/sector-investing/overview
Video instruction.
http://www.YouTube.com/watch?v=j5yYoOoATRM

- No one can consistently predict the bottom or the peak of any sector. Sometimes we move in too early and lose another 25% or so, or we leave the sector too early to lose another 25% or so potential gain. It is quite normal. Learn it why we move in the wrong time, and a lot of times it is just bad luck or events beyond our control.
- A free (as of this writing) service on sector rotation.
http://www.gosector.com/

The flowing are related topics.

Specialize in a sector
When you work in a sector or you're interested in a specific sector, you may want to specialize in that sector for investing. High tech is a popular sector. You need to specialize in a growing sector unless you short stocks.

With aging population, health care is a good one. With growing population, commodities and agribusiness (including water) are good sectors.

Major sectors
Consumer Discretionary, Consumer Staple, Energy, Financial (banks, insurances, brokers), Heath Care (including drugs), Industrial, Material, Technology and Utilities. They are sub divided into many subsectors (a.k.a. industries).

For more information on a sector, google it. This link is an example describing all industries within the health care sector.

10   The contrarian

<u>Contrarians invest</u> in the manner opposite of the crowd. Look for extremes in the market sentiment and investing activities and do the opposite.

However, timing is everything. You want to follow the herd and switch gears when the market or the asset is overpriced.

When an asset or a strategy is overbought, it will return to the normal price. There are one or two exceptions. Gold is one but it is not due to gold alone, but the depreciating USD and the long term depreciating of gold after inflation.

Blindly taking contrarian actions could cost you. You need to analyze and determine whether the herd is wrong.

To illustrate, do you want to move to equities when their prices have been down as of 7/2012? It really depends on the following factors.

- If the long-term trend is down (i.e. moving to a W-shaped recession), we want to wait longer before we move back in.

- If we're heading to the same path as Japan's lost decades, we may want to wait even longer.

- If we're heading to a secular bull market (not today), then waiting too long will be bad.

- The counter argument is the excessive printing of money that could lead to a rising market.

Do we want to buy bank stocks after 2008 or tech stocks after 2001?

- With the rear mirror now, the answer is 'No' even some of these stocks had lost half of their value. As long as the root problems have not been fixed, they might fall further and some companies may even go bankrupt. Do not invest in equities one year after a market plunge and two years in the sector that caused the bubble in general. They are quite correct in the last two bottoms (2000 and 2007). It has more chance to be right than wrong in the future, but as in life nothing is 100% sure.

Individual analysis

Ignore what the media says. A lot of time the 'news' is obsolete by the time it reaches us. It is the group thinking. Sometimes they magnify the news in order to sell their ads. The worst is that the smart money manipulates the news which tells us to trade while they're doing the exact opposite.

Buffett told us to ignore airline stocks. However, many airline stocks made over 4 times their stock prices in the last few years. Popular books are no different. One predicts the Dow at 40,000 and one predicts a market plunge in 2009. As of 2016, they're all wrong. When they are right, they will tell the world.

Links

Contrarian
(http://en.wikipedia.org/wiki/Contrarian_investing

#Filler: Tips

- When you have a lot of money to invest and you're not using a financial adviser and/or not subscribing to any investment service, it could be a big financial mistake.

- LTCM, with two Nobel-prize winners, best supporting team and best technologies then, ran their hedge funds into the ground.

- The so-called modern portfolio theory is most likely based on the wrong and/or insufficient testing parameters / assumptions.

Summary

This book is lengthy with a lot of information on strategies. I have used some of them based on the current market conditions and my own requirements. I include some I believe they have values to some investors. For just a moment, forget everything you've learned here and elsewhere on strategies and use your common sense to see whether the following makes sense to you.

- Evaluate your requirements and select the strategy or strategies you want. Test them thoroughly on paper before committing real money.

- Need to check recent performance of your screens. There are no evergreen strategies that I know of. This is why many gurus have failed in 2015 (and so far in the first part of 2016) as the market changed.

- Some strategies perform better in up markets and vice versa.

- Stick with my three-step process: Market Timing, Screen Stocks and Evaluate Stocks.

  When the market is risky, do not buy stocks. "Strategy" is the first part of Screening Stocks and the second part is when and why to sell stocks. You need to provide exit strategy such as stop orders to reduce further losses.

  Some strategies perform better for holding stocks short term (3 months or less), while some (most based on value) perform better in the longer term (12 months or more).

Some strategies perform better in a specific stage of a market cycle. Select several strategies for paper trading. Use the one that performs best in the last month or two. It could continue the performance in the coming month. In any case, use stops to protect your investments.

Fillers:

On Shooting and any violence. "Forgive" is the most powerful word in any language in any culture. "Pray for the victims" do not do any

good, but take actions to prevent similar shootings from happening. PLEASE.

Why fillers? A blank page space is too much to waste. Most if not all of the fillers are created by me.

Consumption vs. Investing. We consume more than we produce (causing deficits) and investing much less (causing our downfall).

Teach the able welfare recipients how to fish instead of giving them fish for the rest of their lives. They will not work if you take out their welfare benefits for working.

*** Book 6: Trading stocks

This section will answer some of the questions with regard to trading stocks. They are but not limited to:

The fair price of your trade.
- Protect your profits.
- Make extra money with covered calls.
- Diversify your portfolio.
- Bonds.
- Taxes.
- Trading plan.
- Brokers.

The following link from Charles Schwab offers a lot of insightful articles on this topic.
http://seekingalpha.com/author/charles-schwab/articles#regular_articles

1   Chronology of a trade

This is a summary in the life of a trade as described throughout this book. In a sentence, do your due diligence (same as do your homework). It is a general summary. Modify the plan to fit your personal requirements and risk tolerance.

- Is the market favorable to buy stocks?
    - Market timing. Early Recovery, a phase of the market cycle defined by me, is the best time to invest.
    - Even in a bear market, there are valued stocks to buy but the chance is slim for appreciation.

- ETFs - If you trade ETFs only, skip the next step.
    - Know the sectors to avoid unless you are knowledgeable in the specific sectors.
    - Sector/Industry[1] risk:
        - Rank sector (many subscription services have a current rank for the sector/industry). Alternatively, check out the recent performance of the ETF for that sector.
        - Sector metrics (e.g., average for debt/equity, average P/E...).

- ▪ Sector outlook.
- Screen stocks to buy
  - ○ Use screens and strategies that were successful recently.
- Analyze Stocks.
  - ○ Scoring a stock.
  - ○ Intangible analysis.
  - ○ Qualitative analysis.
  - ○ Technical analysis.
- Buy a stock.
- Sell most stocks when the market is going to plunge.
- Sell a stock when the fundamentals deteriorate or objectives are met.

[1] Companies are categorized into sectors and sectors are further sub divided into industries. For example, bank is a sector and regional bank is an industry.

Filler: Consumer or stock holder
The more you bash the airlines, the more profit the airlines make.

How? The less service they give, the more profits they get and so are their stock prices. However, do not go to the extreme. Do you want to be a consumer or an investor?

2   Order prices

Market orders
It is simply trading the stock at the prevailing market price. Place market orders only when it is necessary as stocks price can easily be manipulated especially on stocks with low trading volumes. To avoid manipulations, do not place market orders after hours.

However, in a rising market, many fast rising stocks can only be bought via market orders. Many winners never take a breather on their way up. In this case, you can only buy the stock via market orders.

Consider bid and ask. A 'bid' is the price a potential buyer would like to buy while the 'ask' is a potential seller would like to sell. Your market price is usually the worst price in either case, but it is a guarantee that you would trade the stock. A large spread would mean that it would take a longer time to use a limit order and/or the trade volume of the stock is small.

In my momentum portfolio on 11/2013, I placed a sell price for GERN far higher than the market price. Surprisingly I sold it for this price making an annualized return of 1,176% for holding it for 21 days. When there are few or no other sellers for the stock, the market price would be the price you set. If I cannot sell it in the next 9 days (30 days is my holding period for momentum stocks), I would set it lower. Update: One year later, GERN lost 29%.

Sensible discounts
I prefer to buy the stock at the price closest to the last trade price (to most it is the market price) via a limit order. I seldom lose buying these orders. Sometimes I use the day's lowest price to buy (or the highest to sell) plus a penny (or minus a penny for sell prices to sell).

My other purchase strategy is using 0.15% or 0.25% less than the current prices for stocks I really want. For some promising stocks, I buy them at almost the market price and then place another order on the same stock at 0.5% less than the last traded price (and sometimes 2% depending on the current market trend).

We all want to buy less and sell at higher prices. However, if the trade price is too far away from the current market price (such as

5% from the market price), these trades may never be executed. I have had a long list of buy orders that were not executed and turned out to be big gainers. Learn from my bad experiences.

Use a good discount (such as 10% from the market price) if you believe the market, the sector or the stock will dip by 10%. After you bought the stock, you place a sell order 10% more than the price you paid for it hoping the stock will return to the original price and you pocket 10%. Wishful thinking! However, it has happened to me several times primarily due to temporary market dips.

It works when there is a correction and/or the stock is very volatile. It is usually within the 5% range to take advantage of these situations, not the 10% as described. For a 10% plunge, it usually is due to some serious problem of the company surfacing. One common reason is not meeting its earnings expectation and in this case it usually continues its downward trend.

Larger discounts on a falling market

During a falling market (or a mild correction), 3% less than the current prices for buy orders may be fine for some stocks (use 5% for volatile stocks). To illustrate, I placed about 10 of these orders over the last two months during a market dip. Most of the orders were filled. When the market is plunging, do not buy any stock.

Caterpillar and Cisco were some of my buys at these discounts. They were in my watch list to buy. Initially these shares often fall even lower as the trend was downward. As of 12/18/12, CAT earned me from 3% and 14% (bought in 6/12 and 7/12) and CSCO bought in 7/14/12 returned about 34%. My original objective: Buy deeply-valued stocks, wait and sell them when the economy returns.

When you predict the market will dip by 5%, set your buy orders accordingly. Again, predictions are just educated guesses. From my experience, they work most of the time but not all of the time.

On the day of the earnings announcement, the fluctuation of the stock is usually high. Check any change in the earnings estimate before the announcement and act accordingly. Zacks is supposed to be a useful tool to predict earnings estimates. Do not leave orders during the earnings announcement dates, which can be found in Finviz. When the earning turns out to be good, the stock price surges and your order will not be executed. When the earnings are bad, the stock price will plunge usually and you most likely over-payed.

Option _expiration_ dates usually cause more volatility. Retail investors do not have to be concerned except you may use wider stops. In theory, dividend days have little effect on the stock price as it will be lowered by the dividend amount.

High volume of a stock could mean opportunity

High volume usually increases the stock price volatility. If the volatility of a stock increases substantially (such as doubling its average daily volume), there could be important news on the company, recommendation changes from a major analyst or trading by the institutional investors. It usually takes the institutional investors a week to trade a stock with their sizable positions.

Many times it is started by the insiders who know about the breaking news of a stock before it is publicized. Some investment services / sites specialize in identifying the increasing volumes on these stocks.

Because day traders do not want to leave any open positions overnight, higher volatility occurs at the end of the day. It is the same on the day (usually on Friday) when the options are expiring.

Monitor your trade prices
You cannot tell whether you are paying a fair price without keeping a record. To illustrate, you're paying 1% less than the market prices in buying stocks. You may have missed buying some winners. If the 1% you saved is smaller than the appreciation of the stocks you would have bought at market prices, then you should adjust the buy prices to 0.5% less than the market price and monitor again.

Market trend makes a difference too. When the market is trending up, buying any stock would most likely be profitable and usually the purchase orders with higher discounts will not be executed.

Follow the same logic on sell orders. Need to have at least 25 stock purchases (and potential purchases) to make the conclusion meaningful. If you do not trade a lot, you will not have enough data to verify. As described, I prefer not to place an order during the earnings announcement dates which can be found in Finviz.com. If you cannot buy the stock, consider to use market order the next day. With most brokers offer no commission trades, the "All or none" option is not valid.

Good prospects

When you find gems especially those stocks that are followed by analysts, buy them at market prices and consider doubling the bet if you are really sure you have a winner. From my super stock screens, I spotted NHTC. I placed several bets and one market order. All of them were NOT executed except with the market order. At the end of the day NHTC is up 18% and my executed order is up 14%. I did not have the best buy but made a good profit. NHTC was on its way to a huge appreciation and I sold it too early. I have earned not to sell a winner and protect the profit with a stop.

Lower the buy for risky stocks (if the beta from Finviz is greater than 1 for example) even if they have good fundamentals.

Quality over quantity

If your time is limited, spend all the time on researching one stock one at a time. However, you need to own at least 3 stocks (more stocks for a large portfolio) for your diversification purposes.

Double your normal purchase position on stocks that look great after the research. For risky stocks that look good, you may want to halve your normal purchase position to cut down on the risk. If you are less risk tolerant, do not buy risky stocks at all. My results are not conclusive on risky stocks but I do get a good sleep.

A recent example

Recently I sold EA with $1 more than my order price but $2 less than the current price of the day, which was the earnings announcement day. I do recommend not placing orders right before the earnings announcement day for the stock. If the earnings are good, you do not get all the profit as in this real example; my broker did get me $1 more. If the earnings are bad, you will not sell it any way. It is the same for buying stocks.

Afterthoughts

- Besides luck, the smart investor never sells at the peak but usually within 10% of the peak. No one can predict the peaks consistently.

- I made mistakes like most of you. One time my buy price was higher than the last price executed. Luckily my broker adjusted it to the right price but I may not be that lucky next time. Several times I switched the buy price and sell price by mistake. One time it was due to my boss coming by that forced me to enter my order hastily. Try to avoid the first hour of a trade session.
- Some experts do not suggest their clients to buy stocks on the way down. With respect, I offer opposing arguments.

  - It is fine to buy them on the way down, if you have the conviction that the company or the economy will recover.
  - No one knows where the bottom is, but averaging down could be beneficial if the company or the economy can recover. Check why its stock price is falling and whether the company can fix its problems. Some major problems are only temporary or easy to fix.
  - Most of my big profits are made by buying close to the bottom prices on stocks that have a good potential to recover.
  - Many value stocks are on sale when the market dips. The most favorable time is in the Early Recovery, a phase in the market cycle defined by me.
  - Most experts agree that: The best time to buy is when there is blood in the street. It is demonstrated by the year 2003 and 2009.
  - Contrarians never follow the herd, but you need to have a good reason to be contrary. I recommended Apple in 2013 when every institutional investor was dumping Apple.
  - Stocks are manipulated via selling shorts. When the shares of a stock to short (like over 30% of shorts) are running out, there is a good chance for a short squeeze. Ensure the company being shorted heavily is not heading into bankruptcy.

- Make good money when you are right only 45% of the time by: 1. Limit your losses via stops and 2. Place higher stakes on stocks with higher appreciation potential.
- Some make money on earnings announcement (found in Finviz.com). Earnings would amplify the stock price by at least 5%. Once in a while, there are exceptions. In the last quarter of 2015, Disney posted great results, but the stock dropped. It could be that the market even expected better results or the market is not rational. I believe the later in this case.

Links
Selling short:
http://en.wikipedia.org/wiki/Short_%28finance%29
Short squeeze:
http://en.wikipedia.org/wiki/Short_squeeze
Fidelity Video: Stop Loss.
https://www.fidelity.com/learning-center/trading/trailing-stops-video

3   Stop loss & flash crash

You can limit your stock loss with stops. There are some incidents where you do not always want to use a stop loss.

- <u>Flash crash</u> (May 6, 2010 and August 2015).
  It would turn your stops into market orders that could be substantially lower than your stop prices. Some brokers offer stop limits, but they do not guarantee the orders will be executed.

  The better way is a "mental stop" (my term). You do not place a stop order but place a market order to sell when your stock falls below a pre-defined price. During flash crashes, you do not want to place the market orders to sell but place orders to buy from your watch list.

  I bought some stocks at more than 10% discount during the flash crash (actually I could buy them even at better discounts) and within a week most had returned to the prices as before the flash crash.

  Placing buy orders with huge discounts to the market prices works better for volatile stocks. You should cancel the unexecuted trades before the weekends / holidays and reenter them afterwards to avoid unexpected events that may affect the stock prices.

  Avoid trading drug and bio tech companies with huge differences to the market prices. High tech is a good sector for this purpose and fluctuating 10% in this sector is more of a norm than an exception. Buying an ETF at 5% discount is a better bet than buying specific stocks from my experience.

- My experience with 911.
  I sold many stocks due to stop orders during 911. The market came back in the next three days and I missed the recovery from the stocks that were sold and did not buy back them in time.

- If your stocks are rising, you need to adjust the stop loss prices accordingly. To illustrate- in maintaining a 10% stop loss, your stop is at 90 when the current price is 100. When the stock price rises to 200, it should be adjusted to $180 (10% less than the current price). It is also called a trailing stop. Need to review these rising stocks, and change the stop price periodically (one week to one month depending on how volatile is the stock)).

Most brokers allow you to enter most trades "Good till Cancelled". Even for that there is an expiration date such as 6 months for Fidelity. Fidelity's trades for Short Sell expire by the end of the trade session. Check your broker's current policy.

- Risky markets.
  When the market is risky, you may want to use a stop loss. To prevent another flash crash, you may want to use a 'mental' market order. It is not perfect, as it requires constant watching of the market.

  There are many investing services and sites that give you the 'right' prices for a stop loss. Basically it depends on how volatile are the specific stocks. The chartists will tell you under normal conditions stocks are trading between the resistance line and the support line. Use the stop loss just below the resistance line to avoid the stop order from being executed due to the volatility of the stock.

  For simplicity as I have too many stocks in my portfolio, I use a percent. In the old days, it was recommended 8% or so below the prices you paid. In today's volatile market, I recommend 12%.

- Risky stocks.
  A stop loss is the only way that you can limit your loss for big drop (such as 25%). Affimax lost 85% of its stock value in one day with the news that three of its patients died.

- Low-volume stocks.
  The market order could drive the prices right down as there are few buyers in low-volume stocks. If there is only one buyer, he will buy with the best price for him (or the worst price to the seller).

Unless I have good reasons, I would skip the low-volume stocks. I define low-volume: If my buy amount is higher than 1% of the average daily amount (= average daily volume * stock price).

- Beta.
  Stocks may be more volatile than the market. Beta is used to measure its volatility. The market can be measured by the S&P500 index. If the beta of a stock is 1, its volatility is the same as the market. If it is 1.2, it is 20% more volatile.

  Set a lower stop loss for volatile stocks to prevent stocks from selling due to regular fluctuations.

Afterthoughts

Let me show you my bitter experience. The following are 5 stocks I wanted to buy and the average return was quite good.

Stocks	Return
URI	63%
GMCR	572%
MTW	186%
PII	-74%
TSCO	-127%
Avg.	124%

I placed buy orders at 5% less than the market prices as most 'bargain' investors do. I bought both of the two losers but no winners. The winners never took a breather on its way up, but the losers went down. I did buy GMCR via a market order in my momentum strategy in a separate account.

4   Selling short

This article describes the advantages, disadvantages and how to avoid the pitfalls in selling short. Next we describe the procedures.

Advantages

You consider short selling (same as shorting) when you believe the stock and / or the market is going down. It is easier to make money via selling short than buying stocks especially in a plunging market. Many mutual funds cannot short stocks, and consequently they spend less time in searching for poor companies. The other factor is psychology: Most retail investors do not want to sell losers.

You should start paper trading. Commit a small amount of money gradually when you have proved to yourself your strategy (i.e. what and when to short sell, and exit) is profitable. Consult your financial advisor first and read my Disclaimer under Introduction.

Beginners should try to short the sectors by buying contra ETFs. The major advantages are: 1. Less volatile, 2. Can trade in retirement accounts (some brokers have some restrictions), 3. Do not lose more than your initial trade position, and 4. Fees and dividends are handled for you. Short selling stocks is risker but more profitable than a group stocks in ETFs.

Disadvantages and some suggestions

- Short stocks when the market is plunging and limit your shorting positions when the market is rising. The market rises more than falls, and hence be careful. However, when the market plunges, it is fast and steep.

- Could lose more than 100% of the investment.
  Actually, in theory, there is no limit. If the price of the shorted stock rises by 10 times, the loss is well over 10 times the money of the short position. The 2015 example was Weight Watchers. The price boosted up by more than 170% when Oprah took out a position on them. Fundamentally this stock was not sound and it should be shorted. No stock pickers without insider information (that is illegal) can predict that. Use stops to protect

your trade (i.e. cover your short when you lose a percent specified by you).

- Need to pay dividends and interest for the shorted stock.
  The higher the dividend rate for the stock, the more you have to pay. Investors should avoid high-dividend stocks when shorting unless the expected shorting period is only brief.

  In addition, you need to pay interest for 'borrowing' the stocks to sell. Brokers charge interest rates differently and it could be huge savings to shop around if you short stocks a lot.

- Need both fundamental and technical analyses.
  From my experience, technical analysis is more important than fundamentals in shorting especially for short holding periods.

- If shorting a stock is successful and closed within a year, the gain is usually subjected to the short-term capital gains taxes which are typically higher than the long-term capital gains taxes. Check the current tax laws and consult your tax lawyer.

- Not all of the stocks can be shorted. Your broker may not have the stock you want to short. It is also possible that your broker can close out your short positions for various reasons; they need to protect their 'loans' to you. Check the margin status with your broker.

- Selling short is not allowed in retirement accounts as of 2020. However, you can buy contra ETFs for a group of stocks to bet against the market or a specific sector, but not on a specific stock in retirement accounts.

- The following sectors are riskier: the drug, mine, bank (unless you know the quality of their mortgages) and insurance sectors. An approval of a drug could drive the stock price up by more than 25% in one day. The same for earnings announcements. It could drive the stock more than 10% in either direction.

- Your screens may find many stocks in bio tech companies. These companies especially with a market cap of less than 1B may have the worst fundamentals. However, when they have a new discovery, the stock prices could rocket. Do not short them when insiders are buying (Insider Transaction in Finviz.com) and high SMA-20% or SMA-50% (from Finviz.com).

- There is no perfect timing. Some stocks fluctuate a lot with no rational reasons, or the prices are driven by institutional investors. Some stocks could be manipulated. The shorted stocks could move up for a long time until they finally crash. Hence, do not short against a rising stock, a sector or a market. When the market is rising, shorting a rising stock in a rising sector is dangerous, and the opposite could be profitable for shorting.

- The best time to short is when the market is plunging. At that time, the best sectors to short are those sectors that are plunging. Hence, find the worst stocks in a worst sector in a plunging market.

- A bad company could be acquired by another company due to a good buy; it could boost its stock price. It is same when the major problem of a company has been fixed.

- Use mental stops (i.e. set a price you can afford to lose and when it reaches the specific price, place a market trade to exit the shorted shares. You do not want to make 5% several times and lose 50% in one trade.

- You may not want to short companies that are fundamentally unsound but with a good momentum (i.e. trending up). They may have good prospects such as improved profit, being turned around, settling a lawsuit and/ or new products are being legalized and/or approved. If you do, then use mental stops to protect your trades.

- Never short sell the stocks that are rising even they are not fundamentally sound such as FAANG in 2015 to 2020. Tesla has gained many times and you have to pay the gains, not limited to your short position.

- I have turned some short selling candidates into buying due to the high insiders' buying and/or high short squeeze potential.

- Watch out for short squeezes when the short percentage approaches over 25%. In a nut shell, the stock is running out of shares to be shorted. As a result, it would rise in price especially on any good news. As of 8/2015, I expect short squeeze for PPC and SAFM (CALM in 12/2015) for the following reasons:

  1. The shorting has no bases. It is most likely from one or two hedge funds.
  2. Fundamentally sound.
  3. Beef will be replaced by a lot of healthier and cheaper chicken if not already, esp. during the drought in California.
  4. In Hong Kong for example, they do not allow live chickens imported from China during the bird flu breakout, but they did allow frozen chicken from the USA if there was no political game going on.

What to buy & how

Refer to the chapter on screening short candidates. If Fidelity's Equity Summary Score for the stock is below 4, it is a short candidate.

The following are my suggestions on shorting stocks that have the potential to go down. Basically these stocks are both fundamentally unsound and technically unsound. Many sites (some require paid subscriptions) provide a composite grade for fundamentals and technical. Finviz.com. a free financial site, does provide most of these metrics and many of them are discussed here. If you do not hold the shorts for a long period, technical (the trend) parameters are more important. Parameters for short candidates are:

- Fundamentals

  - The price is more than four times the book value.
  - EY (= $1 / (P/E)$ is negative. Negative PEG is another consideration.
  - High debts (Debt/Equity > .5) except for industries that require high debts such as utilities.
  - Insiders are unloading their company's stocks. They do this for many reasons. But, when they are buying, do not short the stock as they may know some positive events that we do not know.

- Bad intangibles such as losing market share and/or a major lawsuit(s) is pending.
  Read articles on the company from Finviz, Fidelity, Seeking Alpha, etc.
- Do not short stocks that are on their uptrend. It includes the current marijuana stocks that most have no fundamental values and/or historical data.
- Do not short small stocks with a small market cap or float. I usually short stocks with a market cap or float > 200M (100M for riskier investors). Use higher values for conservative investors.

  The stocks with small floats may be controlled by the owners; if they do not sell, the stocks available to trade will be limited. Another indicator is the Avg. Daily Vol. Personally it should be 100 times higher than my bet.

- Technical metrics:

  - Be careful on stocks that have plunged more than 15% recently (Finviz's last quarter performance gives us some hint). It could mean the bottom has been reached.
  - Overbought (RSI(14) > 65). There may be a reason, so it is only a secondary consideration. Most stocks to be shorted may have RSI(14) less than 30.
  - The momentum metrics such as SMA-20 and SMA-50 are important too. SMA-20% and SMA-50% from Finviz.com should be negative (i.e. trending downwards).
  - Some sites especially the paid sites may give you a momentum grade. Select the stocks with a bad momentum grade (a.k.a. timing grade). However, if it is the lowest grade, be careful, as it has nowhere to go but up.

Trading considerations

- Do not trade in the first hour (first half hour for me) as there may have new developments overnight.
- I use subscription services. I do not trade on Monday or the day after a holiday, as the data is at least one day late.
- Your broker may limit your short trade (limited order) to be valid for the day; check this with your broker.
- Your broker may need to approve whether you can short stocks based on your experiences.

- When you sell short and are using limit orders, enter a sell price higher than the last trade price just like selling a stock.
- Close the short position when your trade loses a pre-defined percentage which depends on your personal tolerance.
- Put Option is similar to shorting a company. It is not for beginners.

Margin

Margin should not be used extensively. It is expensive and most brokers try every trick they can to squeeze profits from all transactions to subsidize their low-commission incomes. Usually you can borrow up to 40% of your current position and the rules and the margin rates vary among brokers.

Many investors had losses during the last two market plunges. However, many including myself had made a killing in 2003 and 2009 using margin. I use it for the following reasons.

- For convenience in placing buy orders that exceed my cash position in my taxable accounts.
- I can pay back my outstanding margin loans from my home equity loan (check the current tax laws) as it is far, far lower than my broker's margin interest rates. However, I do not recommend this for conservative investors.

Links & Articles

Introduction
https://www.youtube.com/watch?v=oMnmTV5HF5Y&list=WL&index=3&t=605s

Tilson
Put Options.http://en.wikipedia.org/wiki/Put_option
Fidelity Video: Options.https://www.fidelity.com/learning-center/options/finding-options-strategies/options-analysis-tool-video
Fidelity Video: Selling short.https://www.fidelity.com/learning-center/trading/selling-short-video

5   Experience in selling short

It is easier to make money on the right side of the market. From March, 2009 to today (August, 2018), the market has been rising. Hence it is easy to make money in the stock market by buying an ETF such as SPY.

Today, the market may be peaking and it may seem to be over-priced. The market is fundamentally (P/E example) unsound but technically sound (moving averages example).

Let me examine how the SPY performs and how my short strategies (about 30) performed in recent months in 2018. As in this book, most performances are annualized without including dividends. All figures are for illustration purposes.

Perform.	May	June	July	Aug.	Sep.	Avg.
SPY	38%	-7%	40%	34%	8%	23%
Strategies	-88%	-52%	42%	-74%	66%	-21%

The averages of my short strategies are not doing well. It loses 21% while SPY gains 23% for the last 5 months. The market may be changing for shorters. If I use the top strategies, I could have achieved positive returns even in this market. It shows several promising hints for shorting the market. Use paper trading.

- The market may be declining from July in the above test dates.
- The strategies are better now with 2 months being positive out of the last 3.
- I further look at big winners and big losers. I identify timely metrics (a.k.a. momentum by some vendors) as the only one that matters.
- Several strategies use 52-week highs. They did not perform well as I expected.
- I will exclude risky stocks such as low average volume and low cap.
- Drug companies appear to be risky but some have great returns for shorting. Use stops particularly for drug companies.
- My small tests do not show any differences in holding the stocks for 4 weeks or 6 weeks. Momentum could change in short durations.
- If you subscribe to a database that is refreshed by the end of the day, skip Monday or the day after a holiday. If not, pay attention to moving averages, RSI(14) and other technical metrics from Finviz.com.

- Some brokers may not have the stocks you want to short and/or expire your orders by the end of the day. This is an introduction guideline on how to short stocks.
- I did not short for a while as the market had been rising. In September, 2020, I started to short again as I expected the long-term rise of the market would come to an end. My broker charges about 8.5% while another one offers 2.5% interest. It took some time to switch shorting and funding to this broker and had to be familiarized with their way to trade.
- On 9/2/2020, I bought AXDX instead of shorting it due to the high insider purchases (139% from Finvix) and high shorting percent (46% that could lead to a short squeeze).
- My broker #1 has more restrictions than broker #2 such as not extending the trade to next day.
- A Youtube video on shorting: https://www.youtube.com/watch?v=oMnmTV5HF5Y&list=WL&index =50

Filler: How to win the PowerBall
1. Go to the local lottery office and ask to buy all combinations with a check dated today when it is over 500 M. It worked yesterday. If you have more than one PowerBall winner (or someone using the same trick described here), you may have to skip town.

2. Borrow my time machine which is being repaired or the car from "Back to the Future".

#Filler: Vaccines
Chinese announced to give the formula of the vaccine(s) to the world free of charge. I do not know the impact to these drug companies. 90% of the active ingredients for drugs are from China and hence China is a factor.

The vaccines are being rushed to Nov. 3 to coincide to the election. Usually the vaccine takes about 3 years to be proved effective with few side effects.

6   Covered calls

For basic descriptions on a covered call from Wikipedia, click here or enter (http://en.wikipedia.org/wiki/Covered_call) in your browser.

It is like collecting rent from the apartment you bought. The difference is that the renter has an option to buy the apartment at a preset time and price.

The rent is quite substantial if you do good planning. To start with, you want to buy stocks that have a market to sell. Usually they are large companies with high trading volumes.

Since one contract is for 100 shares of a stock, you cannot sell a covered call on 50 shares of a stock. On the other hand, when you have 1,000 stocks, the commission of 10 contracts would be more than the cost of 1 contract depending on your broker's schedule.

It is time consuming to keep track of the covered calls but it is well worth your time and effort. If the stock price exceeds the strike price of your covered call, you may want to buy the same shares back, so you would not miss any further appreciation of this stock.

However, if it is in a taxable account and you have a loss in a forced sell, do not buy it back otherwise the tax loss is not allowed (i.e. a wash sale) for the year as of 2016. When the contract expires, you may want to start another contract on the same stock if the stock has   not   been   sold.

Covered calls do have their disadvantages such as higher commission rates and sometimes forcing you to sell at a higher tax rate for short-term capital gains in taxable accounts. It is avoidable by using covered calls on stocks that are qualified for long-term capital gains. In addition, you need to buy them back when they increase in price beyond your strike price or lose its potential to appreciate further. Using another put could keep you from not losing any gains beyond the strike price. However, I prefer to use my time in more productive ways and this insurance is not cheap. One's opinion.

One company advertises their techniques using covered calls which could give their users 3 to 6% monthly returns. If you believe in this fantasy, you do not need this book. There is no free lunch.

My recent experience

I sold Netflix covered calls with the strike price about 2% higher and a 3% premium (from my memory) but the price shot up 12% higher in one day, so I was potentially losing 7% profit. However, it turned out to be a good experience as Netflix went downhill later (8/2012).

Normally I prefer to sell covered options for stocks with a quantity from 100 to 600 shares (i.e. 1 to 6 contracts) for the longest time (about 2-3 months). Some non-volatile and small stocks are not candidates to write covered calls on. Some stocks are not optionable. Typically high-tech stocks have a higher premium to be collected as their stock prices fluctuate more. The right stocks can generate 10% or even more a year in addition to the fluctuations of the stock prices.

In general, if I feel the market will be down for the period, I use covered calls especially for stocks holding over one year (unless I have short-term loss to offset any short-term gains) in taxable accounts. Watch out for any tax change that may affect your total return.

Recently I attended a sales pitch on a 3-day training course on a strategy for making 24% per year and it is quite possible especially with the S&P 500 returns about the same. I wish it were available to me 15 years ago. It seems to be too good to be true.

How to sell covered calls

First you need to open an account with your broker and apply to trade options including covered calls.

Check how your broker charges commissions. Ask how much they charge for one contract and 10 contracts of a stock.

The covered call is an agreement to sell the rights to the buyer of the stock at the strike price for a specific date range (a.k.a. expiration date). Typically options expire on Fridays.

You need to write covered calls on the stocks you already own. One contract is 100 shares of stocks. Check out the option chain to select the price, expiration period and the strike price. Normally, the strike price should be higher than the current market price. You may want to have an expiration date 2 weeks or longer. When the contract is expiring in a few days, the contract has little value and most likely the small 'rent' is not worth the risk and the commission.

When the covered call is sold, you receive the 'rent' immediately and any dividend during the 'rental' period.

When the option is 'called' due to a price rise above the strike price, your stock will be sold and you will have to pay the regular commission.

At this point, evaluate the stock to check whether you want to buy it back. If the stock surges, you may have to pay a higher price – thus losing the extra appreciation. In addition, you may have to pay a higher capital gains tax if it is held less than the required period for long-term capital gains in a taxable account.

Note. Notice that some stocks are not optionable and/or not practical to write options on. Most brokers charge a flat rate for the first contract (such as $7) and an incremental fee for each additional contract. Shop around as the fees vary if you write a lot of covered calls.

The best stocks for covered calls are large US companies with a large average volume. The option (a.k.a. the 'rent') pays better for volatile companies such as high-tech companies. From my rough estimates for illustration purposes, the annualized return on covered calls for AAPL is 25% and C is 12% after commission.

#Filler: Double standard
We set up our standard in everything and the entire world has to follow our standard. Shooting citizens at each other, separating children from the illegals, and police brutality are fine according to our standard.

7   Diversification

LTCM, a hedge fund which was run by smart people, and Isaac Newton both made one serious mistake in investing. They bet all their money in one investing vehicle and lost it all in one bet. They were the smartest folks on earth but they violated one basic principle in investing: diversification.

Another example was the potato famine. Irish people made a good living with their primary crop: potato. When a virus came, they lost all the potatoes and caused the potato famine.

Diversification improves a portfolio's performance in the long run and it reduces risk. Diversification includes other asset classes besides stocks such as oil, gold, cash (yes even cash as a safety net to grasp better opportunities ahead), real estate, etc. However, stocks historically produce the best return. In addition, most stocks are quite liquid as it takes a minute to sell them compared to selling a house for example. You can buy other assets such as gold (GLD), money market funds and real estate (via REITs) via their low-cost ETFs.

When an asset is over-valued, it will return to the average historical value with one or two exceptions. Gold is one exception, but it is partly due to the depreciation of the USD and the previous prolonged downfall of gold adjusted for inflation.

Simply put, owning 10 to 15 good stocks with less than three stocks in the same sector (which have to be good sectors to start with) achieves a diversification goal for most people. When one sector crashes, you still have two more good sectors.

Every one's situation is different:

- Depends on your wealth and your age.
  For younger folks with limited wealth (less than $50,000 to invest), a portfolio of 3 stocks (preferably most in ETFs) in different sectors or one diversified ETF could be enough. Your objective in investing is saving money for a down payment for a house, paying your loans including college loans and/or improving your earning power by taking classes.

Retirees may want to maintain a larger percentage of your holdings in cash and/or invested in bonds (long-term bonds could be very risky when the interest rates is going up). Those wealthy enough can fully invest in stocks as losing 50% of their portfolio may not alter their lifestyle. Most business owners should invest in stocks and other vehicles instead of plowing back into their businesses in order to diversify their investments.

Portfolios with more than a billion dollars such as in most large mutual funds could own 10 stocks with 100 million each, but that is just too risky for me. In this case, I prefer they own 20 stocks with 50 million each.

Holding cash is safe but it loses its value due to inflation. To illustrate this point, consider these three scenarios in 1950:

1. An apartment bought in for $10,000 in NYC or in your home town.

2. An investment in the Dow Jones 30 Industrials for $10,000.

3. A 3.5% certificate of deposit or one of the U.S. Treasuries for your $10,000.

By now, all real estate investments should have appreciated many, many times over and most stock shares value would have multiplied also. The $10,000 CD gain has lost real value due to inflation. Our capitalist system punishes us for not taking risk. In the long term, risk is smoothed out over time.

- The excessive frequency in re-balancing your portfolio for diversification takes up time from evaluating other stocks. It may cost you in transaction fees but they are low in today's self-directed brokerage accounts. In addition, it may have some tax consequences in taxable accounts.

The advantage of churning the portfolio (but not excessively) can improve the quality of your portfolio with most updated information about the companies you invest in.

Many brokers display your current diversification in your monthly statement summaries. If not, use a simple spreadsheet to classify the sectors and the asset classes in your portfolio.

- Diversification can easily be achieved by buying indexed funds and/or ETFs. They are less volatile. I recommend it to all folks with less than $50,000 to invest.
- Diversification does not mean to pick simply a stock in other sector that has the opposite correlation of the stock you own. The stock quality comes first.
- Diversification takes a back seat to spotting market plunges. When most stocks plunge such as during 2007-2008, diversification does not save your portfolio, but spotting and reacting to market plunges will.

- Some of our stocks will lose values. If they were due to our mistakes, write them down and learn from them. If they were frauds (not avoidable in many cases), diversification would limit our losses.

- Over diversified is not good either. It takes out our resources to 2monitor the stocks we own. I usually have a lot of candidates of stocks to buy in a rising market. To compromise, stay focus on stocks that I have heavy bets. Focus investing could be very profitable.

My suggestions on diversification

Portfolio up to	Strategy	For stock pickers
$ 50,000	ETF that simulates the market	5 stocks
$100,000	80% in ETF and 20% in a sector ETF(s)	10 stocks
$500,000	10 stocks with less than 3 in same sector.	15 stocks with less than 3 in same sector.
$1 Million	15 stocks + at least 20% in ETFs.	20 or more stocks depending on your time available and less than 4 in same sector.

8   Tax avoidance

Tax avoidance is a good way to save some money legally. Tax laws change all the time. Check Wikipedia on current investment taxes. Consult your tax lawyer as my knowledge in taxes is limited, and the tax laws are always changing.

In general for Federal returns on your taxable accounts (as opposed to IRA, Roth IRA, IRA-Rollover and 401K), you have to pay taxes on dividends either at the ordinary income rate or at a qualified rate which is usually lower. If the stock that was held longer than a year, you pay long-term capital tax (max. 20%). The short-term capital tax rate at the ordinary income rate up to 37%. In addition, you may have to pay state and local taxes. Currently, you can offset $3,000 or up to your total losses from your regular income.

Do not implement what I did as tax laws change frequently and every one's situation is different. Here is what I did and I hope it will be applicable to you.

- Sold most profitable stocks that I held more than a year in taxable accounts in 2011 to qualify for long-term capital gains. Usually they have more favorable tax treatments than the short-term capital gains, which are treated as ordinary income. I bought some back. I maintained a 15% tax bracket, so the tax bill from Uncle Sam is virtually 0 (not exactly due to more tax on social security and Medicare as a result of the trades). I still had to pay state tax. As a retiree, I can control my income.

- Converted part of my Rollover IRA to Roth in 2012 and 2013. I paid taxes today. However, the Roth conversion gives me tax-free appreciation for the future trades in this account and it will lower taxes and my minimum withdrawal requirement in the future. Check whether it is still available.

- The taxes from dividends in the retirement accounts are deferred but eventually they will be treated as regular income when they are withdrawn. Very few people have higher income during their retirement. If you are the lucky few due to the successful investing in your retirement accounts, you may end up with a higher tax bracket during your retirement, particularly when you are forced to withdraw at age 70 ½.

- Gifted some appreciated stocks to my children. The current price of the gifted stock is used in calculating the total cost allowed, not the price you paid for them. I prefer the value stocks that have potential for long-term appreciation. It is good for them and not good for Uncle Sam. You can gift up to $15,000 (in 2019) for each spouse to each child without paying any Federal tax. For a family of four, you and your spouse can gift up to $60,000 (= 15,000 * 4) a year.

  The link: https://www.irs.gov/businesses/small-businesses-self-employed/frequently-asked-questions-on-gift-taxes

The cost basis of the transferred stock is quite complicated. Check out the current tax law. The cost basis of the appreciated stocks are carried to the receiver, so it would lower your capital taxes as most of us are in higher tax brackets than our children.

From my experience, the cost basis of the depreciated stocks after the transfer is the market price on the transfer day as of 2016. I do not understand it enough to comment but just to tell you what I have experienced. I tried to offset my son's unexpected short-term capital gain by transferring a losing stock and that does not work.

- My lawyer set up trusts for me including my house. They will avoid probate hopefully. From the current tax law (as of 2016), the cost basis of your stocks will be stepped up or down to the stock prices on that day you pass away. Ask your heirs to keep a business paper for the stock prices or tell your brokers to adjust the cost basis on the day you pass away. Of course, you have to tell your heirs now to take care of these tasks. Again, ask your tax lawyer for details.

Make sure you specify the beneficiaries in your and your spouse's accounts to avoid probate. Check your local state laws. Some states take more than a year to finish the probate process for a house. As of 2014, my state (Mass.) has an exemption of 1 million, not portable to your spouse, and they calculate the entire estate when it exceeds the exemption. There is no estate tax if my estate is a million dollar. I have to pay a rate on

1,000,001 if it just exceeds it by one dollar. That's why we should move 30 miles north to New Hampshire.

I estimate that it takes about three years for the average estate to be distributed. You want to cut down the duration by having a will to start with, so you do not want to pay extra for your lawyer.

- At age 70 ½ (as of 2016), you are required to withdraw them in a schedule and it could put you in higher tax bracket. Roth withdrawal is not counted in the mandatory withdrawal for a person's lifetime as of 2016.

- Roth IRA if qualified could be the best deal for most. However, you have to use after-tax money to fund your Roth IRA.

- I simulate my next year via my tax preparation software and adjust my income accordingly.

- Most oil partnerships and many MLPs require you to file special tax forms for non-retirement accounts in 2017. I avoided most of them as my time is limited. Some ETFs require you to file the complicated K-1 (vs 1099) in your tax return. You can find this requirement in ETFdb.com. You can avoid them by not buying these ETFs; I prefer to buy them in my non-taxable accounts (i.e. retirement accounts). Usually the taxes on these dividends are lowered as they are treated the return of investment after depreciation.

- Avoid wash sales in your taxable accounts
  http://en.wikipedia.org/wiki/Wash_sale

You cannot claim the loss for the year if you buy back the stock within 30 days. Before I buy, I check whether I sold this loser in the last 30 days. Before I sell a loser, I check whether I bought it in the last 30 days.

I placed one order to sell a loser at a higher price and another one to buy it back at a lower price. When there is a big swing in price for that stock, both orders were executed within 30 days. I cannot claim the loss of the sold stock for that year. However, the loss can be adjusted to the cost basis of the newly-acquired stock as of 2013.

There are many ways to avoid it. Try not to buy it back within 30 days (check the current regulation) and this is the best way. IRS has more restrictions and it is better not to push it to the limit. Buy a similar stock in the same sector. Buy it in your children's account. Again, check the current tax laws.

Afterthoughts

- Tax audit signs.
  http://money.cnn.com/gallery/pf/taxes/2014/03/14/tax-audit/index.html?iid=HP_LN
  Your business would be treated as a hobby if you do not have a profit in three out of the last five years. Day traders and businesses can deduct all the trading expenses. Some form an investing company in some Caribbean island to avoid paying taxes. Again check the current tax laws.
- As of 2013, the dividend tax is at 20% max. Do not believe it is no tax in tax-deferred accounts. When you withdraw, it will be treated as a regular income and it can be as high as almost 40% (as of 2013). Your dividend tax rate depends on your income.
- When you trade 5 times or more a week, investigate whether you're eligible to trade as a business by the current tax rule. A business allows its owner to deduct business expenses.
- Fidelity: Investment tax.
  https://www.fidelity.com/learning-center/mutual-funds/tax-implications-bond-funds

  ETF Taxes on Foreign Stocks:
  http://seekingalpha.com/article/2491465-foreign-withholding-taxes-in-international-equity-etfs

Links

Tax Avoidance:
http://en.wikipedia.org/wiki/Tax_avoidance
Tax Law:
http://en.wikipedia.org/wiki/Income_tax_%28U.S.%29
Without paying (gift tax):
http://en.wikipedia.org/wiki/Gift_tax_in_the_United_States#Gift_tax_exemptions

9   Trading plan

You should have a trading plan and it should include the following basics:

1. Your overall objective.
2. When to buy, what stocks and how many.
3. When and what stocks to sell.
4. When and how to monitor your trading strategies.

The follow are my suggestions. Adjust them according to your personal requirements.

Be disciplined

Being disciplined will provide better results in the long run and save you time. Following the trading plan will not allow your emotions to take over.

To illustrate, you have a specific day (Monday or the first day of the month) to check the value of your portfolio. By checking it several times a day, it becomes a waste of time and energy. It could cause harm to your emotions.

Set your objective(s)

Set up your objective and requirements first. Your objective could be seeking the highest profit, profit at the least risk, protecting principal, generating income or a combination. Beating the market should not be your primary objective.

For example, a better objective is making more than 5% per year in the next 10 years with the least risk. Why 5%? I estimate that we have a 3% inflation rate and 2% taxes. The higher risk you can take, the higher the return it would be.

You can be conservative and aggressive at the same time by setting up two accounts, one for each objective. In addition, you may want to define the maximum investment amount for each account.

I have three objectives and they usually fall into different accounts and different holding periods.

- Non-taxable account. Profit at the least risk. Buy value stocks. Review purchased stocks every 6 months.
- Roth account. Buy momentum stocks seeking for the maximum short-term (1 month) profits.
- Conservative investing in all accounts. Define a larger safety net. Conserve my cash. Move all to stocks only when the market is the most favorable.

Contrary to the above, most investors' or traders' tend to have an objective in beating the market by a specific percent. It is fine also to measure how you perform against the market. For ultra conservative investors, not losing money may be your primary objective. In any case, consider safety.

If you made 10% and the market was up by 20%, you under-performed the market. However, do not blame yourself if your primary objective is conserving wealth. Most likely you may have had a high percent of your portfolio in cash and/or safer investments which do not appreciate a lot but they conserve your wealth.

Be flexible
Every one's trading plan is different. You should start with a simple one and add features that would be useful for you. Keep it simple as you will not likely follow a complicated one.

Other features are: how to screen stocks, your average holding period, tax consequences, performance monitoring, etc. This chapter shows you the very basics of a trading plan and you should start one if you do not have one.

You can refer to any chapter of this book in your trading plan. To illustrate, refer to the chapters when to sell a stock and spotting market plunges.

You can change your objective. When the market is risky, you may want to be more conservative for example.

Disciplined but adaptive
Stick with your plan consistently unless you have a good reason. When your previous strategy that has worked but it does not work now, you should still stick to it. It is a common mistake for traders

switching different technical indicator when the current one does not work. It explains why most of the beginner traders lose money.

It should be adaptive. When the current market favors growth, stick with a growth strategy.

A sample trading plan
You can review what stocks to buy and sell once a week or once a month depending on how active you are in the market. List the criteria you buy stocks. Define your average holding period for a specific objective. Also define when and why you want to sell a stock.

Personally I prefer to have two sections: Common Tasks and Specific Tasks. Common Tasks include 4 categories: **Weekly Tasks, Monthly Tasks, Quarterly Tasks and Yearly Tasks**. Evaluate stocks to buy on Tuesday on every week for example. Update the portfolio and check out the chart on marketing timing on the first week of every month. Review the performance of your portfolio quarterly (or half a year). Perform year-end tasks.

Specific Tasks include tasks we have to do on specific dates such as filling tax return, transferring stocks to my children and renewing investing subscriptions.

Weekly Tasks:

Mon	Covered calls
	IBD-50 review.
Tue	Finding momentum stocks.
Wed	Sell Momentum stocks held over 2 weeks.

Monthly Tasks:

Mon	House keep all stock transactions.
	Review market timing and any corrections.
Tue	Find stocks using selected strategies.
	Find stocks using screens.
Wed	Evaluate stocks
Thur.	Buy stocks
	Review sector rotation.
Fri	Evaluate any stocks to sell.
Any	Monitor momentum performance.

Quarterly Tasks:

1	Monthly tasks.
2	Monitor performance.

Year-end Tasks:

1	Tax adjustments for taxable accounts including selling losers in non-retirement accounts.
2	EOY purchases.
3	Fully invested on Dec. 15-Jan. 15 esp. on 2nd year of the presidential cycle.
4	Monitor performance of screens.
5	Review Dogs of the DOW.
6	Optional. Gift appreciated stocks to your heirs.

Review your performance and your trading plan

If you do not know what you did, how will you know where you're going? Review every trade transaction and monitor their performances.

Learn from your losses. Did you stick to the trading plan? If you lose too many times and/or take too much risk (evidenced by many losses and/or big losses), you may have to modify your trading plan. However, the trading plan may not be good in the current market (for example trading growth stocks in the bottom of the market cycle).

If you have to let the winners get away too often, review what went wrong. Sometimes, a lesson is not a lesson but just bad luck.

Learn about yourself

Learn about your risk tolerance, how mentally prepared are you for big losses and big wins. If you have more money than you can use for the rest of your life, conserving wealth should be your primary objective.

To illustrate with a portfolio of one million dollars, your average stock position is $100,000 if you only have time to follow 10 stocks.

To many, a portfolio with 10 stocks is quite risky. You may consider having 10 stocks of $50,000 each and invest the rest ($500,000) in

ETFs, mutual funds and/or bonds. Ensure that no more than three stocks (some prefer 2) are in the same sector.

Prepare for some losses. Reduce the average loss to only small amounts. I prefer to use 25% maximum loss for volatile stocks and 20% for other stocks. Some prefer using stop loss orders of 10% to 15% loss. Today's market is too volatile to stop losses less than 15%. My opinion. You should have some big winners but you may let some get away by selling them too early. One way is to use stop orders (10% less than the market price) and adjust the stops periodically (say a month) for the appreciating stocks.

Summary
Write down your objective and what tasks you do every week, month and year in the inside back cover of this book (hard copy only). If you don't do it now, you never will.

Trade journal
Keep a journal of your trades along with your ideas. Review it from time to time and look at why you bought a specific stock. It is far better than trying to recall the experiences from memory.

Your journal should be part of a trading plan. You use it to monitor the performance of your trade and how the current market conditions affect your performance. When you use a screen that is for short term, you want to exit the trade accordingly. When the screen does not perform, it may mean the market is not favorable to this screen and you should skip using it with actual money. Here is a screen shot of mine. I group the trades under different screens.

			Prce		$					Date			Return		Status
Stock	QTY	Account	B.P.	S.P.	Buy $	Sell $	Profit	Curr P.	% better	Buy Date	Sell Date	Days		Ann. Ret	
LAKE	2,000	401K	10.93	13.99	21,860	27,975	6,115	9.45	48%	07/15/15	11/24/15	132	28%	77%	S
ABTL	1,500	ROTH	16.60	18.50	24,900	27,750	2,850			07/16/15	09/10/16	422	11%	10%	B
ELMD	5,000	401K	4.01	4.22	20,054	21,095	1,041	4.81	-12%	03/17/16	04/07/16	21	5%	90%	S

When using an excel spreadsheet, the formulae is:

B.P. (Buy Price) =IF(B3="","",IF(D3="","",D3*B3))
% better =IF(I3="","",(E3-I3)/I3)
Days =IF(K3="","",L3-K3)
Return =IF(D3="","",(E3-D3)/D3)
Ann. Ret =IF(N3="","",N3*365/M3)
Add any columns you want such as Account.

10   Fidelity

On 10/2019, Fidelity announced there was no commission for most trades.

I have been satisfied with the trades so far. It is more important to me than commissions. One broker offered free trades for keeping a balance. However, there are many times the orders that should be executed have not been executed. More than 2 times, the completed orders have been reversed. I have not had this with Fidelity so far and actually some orders have been executed with better prices. Fidelity passes the best price to you while some brokers keep the difference for themselves.

As with most major brokers, Turbo Tax can load all my stock transactions for the year in filing my tax returns. It saves me a lot of time. Fidelity used to have more sophisticated order options such as "Execute based on certain conditions". Most investors do not need this feature.

They require you to apply for trading options, after-hour trading, using margin and trading penny stocks. Gift appreciated stocks to your children who have a tax bracket lower than yours up to $15,000 of the current market value for each receiver ($30,000 per couple) in 2019. Gifting depreciated stocks is not recommended. Consult your tax lawyer or CPA.

Ensure all accounts have primary beneficiaries and secondary beneficiaries. I have a simple trust for my taxable account for myself and my spouse. Consult your lawyer for estate planning.

Fidelity offers CD ladders so they mature in different time frames. I prefer Fidelity rather than local banks as it saves me trips to the bank (to purchase and renew) by doing my purchasing CDs on-line. However, my state offers some tax deductions for the interests from local banks. The other advantage is the bank CDs can start right away.

Save some interest in the cash account. If you have the CASH account (FCASH), change it to Government Money Market fund FDRXX by clicking on the core account. Today I have to buy SPRXX that pays better dividends than FDRXX. Automatically SPRXX will be used when the core account is exhausted. Check the current information and dividends. SPRXX should be part of the choices.

My annuity has gained 4 times during decades. I do not recommend the use of an annuity, most of which have high commissions for the sales persons. My tax rate today is higher than during my work life. Compared to many other offers, Fidelity's annuity is better than the average.

The only negative I have found is their margin interest rates are quite high. If you use margin a lot, open a second account that has a low interest rate such as from Interactive Broker.

I transferred my appreciated stocks to my son's account as he is in lower tax bracket. The performance of my account was less while my son's increased. It may be correct, but it is not I want.

I use their two-factor log in for better security that I recommend you to use for all financial accounts if available.

Traders should use Fidelity's Active Trader Pro. Their low-cost ETFs are attractive.

My major credit card is with Fidelity that gives me 2% cash back. I have no relationship with Fidelity except being a retiree of Fidelity.

Link

Fidelity vs Vanguard. I believe Vanguard will improve to be competitive.
https://www.youtube.com/watch?v=tskh-QCCH-o

#Filler: Simple measures to reduce net security.

Do not click any links from unknown sources. Some seems to be ok but not.

"MalwareBytes", for checking viruses, is free for download (they do not pay me).

Personally I use a Chromebook for my financial transactions and a two-factor logon for my stock trading.

Epilogue

Some Chinese words have no straight-forward English translations or equivalents and here is one. We have the mutual privileges to connect to each other via this book. We call it 'Yuen' in Chinese or 'fate' in very, very rough translation.

English is not my native language and investing is not my career which is IT. I have never taken any class in economics, accounting, business and investing except those required in my Industrial Engineering degrees. Hence, writing a book on investing is quite remote.

After my early retirement, I have been spending most of my time in investing, running thousands of simulation and reading over one hundred books in investing. Starting from 2000, I have been doing extraordinary good. I comment in financial blogs and save the good ones in my own blog, so I can refer them later on. After several years, I have enough information to write a book.

At first, I want to write a book for one reader only: Me. My children have better things to do than investing. I do not need to keep my 'secrets' for them. That's why I publish this book. It also serves as my small 'legacy'. It has been very rewarding, when my readers tell me how much they enjoy and benefit from this book.

Shamelessly I use many public web sites to promote my book. My mission is different. I use it to help my fellow investors to be a better investor. The income from this book and the articles provides me less than 1% of my income so far.

It is far more financially rewarding working on my investment including finding new strategies. Writing books and articles takes time away from my investing and it actually costs me more money. However, it has been fun to write this book and to interact with my readers. Money cannot buy everything and the satisfaction of holding a printed book with my 'ugly' picture on the book cover.

I do not believe that this book or any book is the Holy Grail in investing. However, it has a lot of fresh ideas and good pointers that have brought me financial success (at least so far). I ask my readers to challenge my pointers and ensure they are applicable in today's market and meet their objectives and requirements.

A good pointer can make you thousands of dollars, and a bad or misinterpreted one can do the opposite. Always do paper trading on any strategy and / or idea before you commit real money on it. Start your strategy with cash in small increments until you have more confidence.

Hopefully, this book's primary objective enabling you to be a better investor is met. Actually, you should be a better investor than I am if you can integrate your knowledge you already have with mine – I called it adding wings to a roaring tiger.

This book should be read repeatedly to remind us (I am a reader too) of any error(s) we repeated. Some chapters are not easy to read as this book is not intended to be so. You need to practice what it suggests such as learning how to detect market plunge. In any case, try out any strategy with paper trading before committing real money gradually and slowly.

If you order the printed of this book from Amazon.com, check whether you are eligible for a free or at low cost for the Kindle version that has all the clickable links.

Appendix 1 – All my books

- Complete the Art of Investing (highly recommended combining most of my books on investing). The Kindle version has over 850 pages (6*9).

- Sector Rotation: 21 Strategies (highly recommended for short-term investors) has more specific chapters on the topic and shares many articles with "Complete the art of investing".

- Best stocks for 2021. Not a promise: Another "Best stocks" books available on July, 2021 and Dec. 15, 2021.

- China: "Apocalypse or Co-prosperity (highly recommended). Trade War (most popular here) with China. Trade War & Pandemic. Rising China. Fall of an Empire: U.S.A. A Nation of No Losers. Can China Say No. Global Economies. Pandemic.

- Books for today's market: Profit from Coming Market Crash.

- The following books are in a series: Finding Profitable Stocks, Market Timing and Scoring Stocks. Alternate book Using Fidelity.com.

- Books on strategies: Shorting, "Profit from bull, bear and sideways markets" (Rotation + Momentum + ETF Rotation + trend following), Trading System (similar to printed version of Complete), Swing (Rotation + Momentum), ETF Rotation for Couch Potatoes, Momentum, SuperStocks, Dividend, Penny & Micro Stock, and Retiree.

- Books for advance beginners: Be an expert (highly recommended), Introduce . Billionaire (perfect gift for recent college graduates and they will thank you when they become millionaires), Investing for Beginners, Beat Fund Managers, Profit via ETFs, Buffett, Ideas, Conservative and Top-Down.
- Miscellaneous: Lessons in Investing. Investing Strategies. Buy Low and Sell High. Buy High and sell Higher. Buffettology. Technical Analysis. Trading Stocks.
- Concise Editions and Introduction Editions are available at very low prices and are competitive with books of similar sizes (50 pages) and prices ($3 range).

Most books have paperbacks. Links and offers are subject to change without notice.

Filler: The most powerful word

I was deeply moved by the family members of the church victims forgiving the shooter. I wrote a brief post: "Forgive" is the most powerful word in every language and in every culture. I forgot it until I received a response from Jim.

"Tony, Without even knowing it, you made the greatest comment I have seen on here--and it had nothing to do with investing. You mentioned somewhere that "Forgive" is the most powerful word in every language. Wow."

Appendix 2 – Complete the Art of Investing

Instead of buying 16 books, why not buy one book (Complete the Art of Investing) consisting of 16 books? Besides saving money and your digital shelve space, it gives you quick reference and concentration on the topic you're currently interested in. It covers most investing topics in investing excluding speculative investing such as currency trading and day trading.

The Kindle version has about 850 pages (6*9), about the size of three books of average size. With the cost of $10 and at least 850 investing ideas, it is about one cent per idea. Most other books have only a few ideas in the entire book

The 16 books

This book "Complete Art of Investing" is divided into 16 books as follows. Click for the link to the book described in Amazon.com. I squeezed more than 3,000 pages into 850 pages by eliminating duplicated information such as evaluating stocks.

Book No.	Amazon.com
1	Beginner & Billionaire
2	Finding Stocks
3	Evaluating Stocks
4	Scoring Stocks
5	Trading Stocks
6	Market Timing
7	Strategies
8	Sector Rotation
9	Insider Trading
10	Penny Stocks & Micro Cap
11	Momentum Investing
12	Dividend Investing
13	Technical Analysis
14	Investing Ideas
15	The Economy
16	Buffettology

The book links are subject to change without notice.

"How to be a billionaire" is for beginners and couch potatoes, who can use the advanced features of this book in the simplest and less time-consuming techniques. Most advance users can skip this section unless they want to use some of the short cuts described.

We start with the basic books Finding Stocks, Evaluate Stocks, Trading Stocks and Market Timing. You can select and start with one of the many styles and strategies in investing such as swing trading and top-down strategy. Many tools are described in other books such as ETFs, technical analysis, covered calls and trading plan.

Many books start with "Why" to lure you to read more and are followed by "How" and then the theory behind the book.
If the book you're reading is beneficial to you, imagine how it would with 850 pages.

#

Most readers' comments are on "Debunk the Myths in Investing", which this book is originally based on.

"I skipped ahead to his chapter book 14 (of "Complete the Art of Investing"), Investment Advice just to get a feel of his writing style. His research is phenomenal and doesn't overwhelm with big words or catchy "sales-like"   tactics.

I truly believe this ordinary man, Mr. Tony Pow, has a gift of explaining his experience as an investor without the bull crap of trying to make you buy his stuff. He seemingly just wants to share his knowledge, tips, and clarity of definitions for the kind of folks like me who want to understand something FIRST before jumping in with emotions of trying to make a boat load of money. I like the technical analysis side he brings.

Mr. Tony Pow talks about hidden gems in his book; well....quite frankly, he is a hidden gem. Thank you and I will also post my comments about this author to my Facebook page!" – JB on this book.

"Excellent book, recommend to all investors... great knowledge. It has fine-tuned my investing strategies... Your book is hard to set aside, as I read it all the time learning good techniques and analysis of stocks, ETF... Since I purchased your book in March, I have underlined, highlighted and placed tabs on top of pages for quick reference." – Aileron on this book.

"Tony, I just finished reading your 2nd edition. It's my pleasure to report that I found it most interesting. You're welcome to use this blurb if you like:

Debunk the Myths in Investing is an all-encompassing look at not only the most salient factors influencing markets and investors, but also a from-the-trenches look at many of the misconceptions and mistakes too many investors make. Reading this book may save not only time and aggravation but money as well!"

Joseph Shaefer, CEO, Stanford Wealth Management LLC.

"Tony, Great work!" from James and Chris, who are portfolio managers.

"'Debunk the Myths in Investing' is a comprehensive book on investing that deals with many aspects of this tense profession in which with a lot of knowledge and a bit of luck (or vice versa) one can greatly benefit...

Therefore 'Debunk the Myths in Investing' is an interesting book that on its 500 pages offer a lot of knowledge related to investing world and many practical advice, so I can recommend its reading if you're interested in this topic."
- Denis Vukosav, Top 500 Reviewers at Amazon.com.

"490 pages (Debunk) of a genius's ranting and hypothesis with various theories throughout, written light-heartedly with ample doses of humor...Yes, the myth of not being able to profitably time the market is BUSTED...

One might ask... Why is he giving away the results of his hard-earned research for only $20? He states that his children are not interested in investing and wants to share his efforts with the world." - Abe Agoda.

"Excellent book, recommend to all investors... great knowledge. It has fine-tuned my investing strategies... Your book is hard to set aside, as I read it all the time learning good techniques and analysis of stocks, ETF... Since I purchased your book in March, I have underlined, highlighted and placed tabs on top of pages for quick reference." - Aileron on this book.

"Great stuff, Tony. It's great to meet experienced traders such as yourself. I had a browse through the book and think your method is a little more refined than mine."
"Your strategy is very rules based and solid. I sometimes envy people who have developed something like this."

Making 50% in one month

I claim to have the best one-month performance ever for recommending 8 or more stocks without using options and leverage. My following return is 57% in a month or 621% annualized. They are slightly different as I calculated the average from the averages of three different accounts. The average buy date is 12/26/18 and the "current date" is 01/28/19.

The performance may not be repeated. I will use the same screen for the coming years and even the expected 10% (or 120% annualized) is very good.

I used the same screen for searching stock candidates. I spent a total of about 20 hours from Dec. 15, 2018 to Jan. 5, 2019.

Stock	Buy Price	Sold or Current Price	Buy date	Sold or Current date	Profit %	Profit % Ann.	Status
CHK	2.13	2.99	01/03/09	01/18/19	40%	982%	Sold
MNK	16.41	21.45	01/03/19	01/25/19	31%	510%	Sold
MNK	16.43	21.45	01/03/19	01/25/19	31%	507%	Sold
NNBR	5.68	8.58	12/26/18	01/28/19	51%	565%	
NNBR	5.72	8.58	12/26/18	01/28/19	66%	727%	
ESTE	4.35	6.45	12/26/18	01/18/19	48%	766%	Sold
LCI	4.61	8.29	12/21/18	01/28/19	80%	767%	
MDR	8.01	9.13	01/08/19	01/28/19	14%	255%	
YRCW	3.29	5.78	12/21/18	01/28/19	76%	727%	
YRCW	3.26	5.78	12/21/18	01/28/19	77%	742%	
ASRT	3.56	4.18	12/26/18	01/28/19	17%	193%	
UTCC	7.13	11.00	12/26/18	01/28/19	54%	600%	
YRCW	2.92	5.78	12/26/18	01/28/19	98%	1083%	

Best one-year return

I claim to have the best-performed article in Seeking Alpha history, an investing site, for recommending 15 or more stocks in one year after the publish date without using options and leverage.

Your choice

"Complete the art of investing" should be your first choice. "Sector Rotation: 21 Strategies" and "Sell Short Stocks /ETFs" are your better choice depending on how often you rotate sectors or selling short. All three books share most articles. "Best Stocks" select the stocks for the period. "Be a stock expert in 5 minutes" and "Beat the fund managers" are books for beginner investors. "China and U.S." is my book on politics.

Sector Rotation: 21 Strategies

- On 5/26/2020, I searched for "Sector Rotation" under Amazon's Book. They are listed in the same order except my book Sector Rotation: 21 Strategies.

Book	Date	Size[1]	Kindle $[1]	Hard $
Sector Rotation: 21 Strategies	**05/2020**	**425**	**$9.95**	$24.95
Super Sectors	09/2010	289	$26.39	$49.95
Dual Momentum Investing	11/2014	240	$40.40	$42.20
Sector Investing	05/1996	260		$29.94
Sector Trading Strategies	08/2007	164	$26.39	$16.66
The Sector Strategist	03/2012	225	$26.39	$44.96
ETF Rotation	10/2012	125	**$9.95**	**$14.99**
Optimal... Sector Rotation	07/2015	80		$44.07

[1] From Amazon on size and prices as of 5/25/2020.

My book won in all categories except the price for hard copy in one. However, my book won as the lowest cost per page by a wide margin. In addition, as of 5/2020 I bet that no author besides me made over 4 times using sector rotation starting the amount more than his yearly salary then.

- I have **21** strategies in sector rotation while most books have only one. It ranges from simple rotation of a stock ETF and cash for beginners to many advanced strategies for experts. Most other books have one or two strategies.

- Andrew, a contributor on Sector Rotation article at Seeking Alpha, said, "Great stuff, Tony. It's great to meet experienced traders such as yourself. I had a browse through the book and think your method is a little more refined than mine."

- "You have written the book in a way that makes good and logical sense." Bill.

- Do not be fooled by past performances. Just check the recent performance of the top 50 stocks selected by IBD in the last five years. The mediocre result (hopefully it will change) could be due to too many followers and/or there is no evergreen strategy. I seldom heard the fantastic results from the followers of O'Neil, our greatest chartist. The adaptive strategy of this book shows you how to select the most profitable strategy for the current market.

- I switched most (if not all) my sector funds in April, 2000 from technology sectors to traditional sectors (better to money market fund). We can reduce losses by spotting market plunges and the sector trend.

My motivation to write this book is sharing my experiences, both bad and good. I provide simple-to-follow techniques using the free (or low-cost) resources available to us. I have been successful in investing for decades. I am enjoying a comfortable financial life. I do not hold back my 'secrets' as my children are not interested in investing. If you are looking how to make 100% return overnight, there are many other books claiming to do so and this book is not for you. This book describes how to be a 'turtle' investor making fortune gradually and surely. Be warned that many books written by authors who have never make money in the stock market.

Best stocks to buy for 2021

We care about performance only. The last book beats the market (SPY simulating S&P500 index) by 29%. Click here for the book or type the following for more info on the book.
https://www.amazon.com/dp/B08Q8R6SXQ

This is the performance of my last book "Best Stocks to buy from August, 2020". Past performances do NOT guarantee future performances.

The performance is the returns from 07/28/2020 to 12/07/2020. The average of the 14 recommended stocks beats SPY (an ETF simulating S&P500 stocks) by 29%. There are 13 winners and 1 loser.

Dividends have not been included. CMCSA and FDX are big winners profiting from the pandemic.

Symbol	Name	Sector	True EY[1]	Return[2]	Ann. Return[2]
ABBV	AbbVie	Drug	7%	10%	27%
ABT	Abbott	Drug	3%	8%	21%
CHE	Chemed	Diversified	4%	4%	12%
CMCSA	Comcast	Media	11%	19%	52%
FDX	FedEx	Transport	8%	76%	211%
GTS	Triple-S	Health	N/A	26%	72%
JNJ	Jonson & J	Drug	6%	2%	4%
MCK	McKesson	Drug	8%	16%	45%
MSFT	Microsoft	Software	4%	6%	18%
SCHN	Schnitzer	Metal	10%	46%	127%
SMCI	Super Micro	Computer	11%	9%	24%
UFPI	Universal	Building	10%	-6%	-17%
UNH	United Health	Health	9%	15%	43%
ZBRA	Zebra Tech	Computer	5%	39%	107%
Avg.				19%	53%
		SPY		15%	41%
	Beat SPY by				29%

[1] True EY is the reciprocal of "EV/EBITDA". [2] Rounded up for easy reading, but not in the calculation in "Beat SPY by".

It is not a promise: I may have a similar book after 7/1 and 12/1 every year. Check my blog. https://tonyp4idea.blogspot.com/

Sell Short Stocks / ETFs

Book	Date	Size	Kindle $	Hard $
This book (Sell Short Stocks /ETFs)	**10/2020**[1]	**700**[2]	**$9.95**	**$26.95**
Short selling with the O'Neil Disciples	04/2015	336	$31.99	$43.22
The New sell & sell short	03/2011	368	$20.79	$31.57
Sell Short	03/2009	240	$18.39	$26.88
Sell and sell short	05/2008	250	N/A	$43.21

China and U.S: Apocalypse or Co-Prosperity

On 11/2020, I searched for "Trade War China" under Amazon's Book. They are listed in the same order except my book. This represents and summarizes most of my books on politics.

Book	Date	Size[1]	Kindle $[1]	Paper $
This book	**12/2020**	428	**$4.95**	**$14.95**
The U.S. – China Trade War: Conflict	**10/2020**	302	$9.95	**$14.99**
Us Vs China: From trade war…	09/2019	346	$11.59	$28.00
The China-US. Trade war and future economic relations	12/2018	222	$39.00	$39.00
Stealth War	10/2019	255	$7.95	$18.29

You have been brainwashed by our government and the media on China that has been demonized every day. I can say the same to the Chinese in China. My book is a summary of all my books on politics and hopefully represents the unbiased views from many overseas Chinese. That is why we have conflicts between the two countries.

Appendix 3 - Our window to the investing world

The paperback version of this chapter can be found in the following link.
http://ebmyth.blogspot.com/2013/11/web-sites.html

- **General**
  Wikipedia / Investopedia /Yahoo!Finance / MarketWatch /
  Cnnfn / Morningstar /CNBC / Bloomberg / WSJ / Barron's /
  Motley Fool / TheStreet
- **Evaluate stocks**
  Finviz / SeekingAlpha / MSN Money / Zacks / Daily Finance /
  ADR / Fidelity / BlueChipGrowth / Earnings Impact /
  OpenInsider / NYSE / NASDAQ / SEC / SEC for 10K and 10Q
  (quarterly) reports required to file for listed stocks in major
  exchanges.
- **Charts**
  BigCharts / FreeStockCharts / StockCharts /
- **Screens**
  Yahoo!Finance / Finviz / CNBC / Morningstar /
- **Besides stocks**
  123Jump / Hoover's Online / FINRA Bond Market Data / REIT /
  Commodity Futures / Option Industry
- **Vendors**
  AAII / Zacks / IBD / GuruFocus / Vector Vest /
  Fidelity / Interactive Brokers / Merrill Lynch /
- **Economy.**
  Econday / EcoconStats / Federal Reserve / Economist /
- **Misc.**
  Dow Jones Indices / Russell / Wilshire /
  IRS / Wikinvest / ETF Database / ETF Trends /
  Nolo (estate planning) / AARP /

Appendix 4 - ETFs / Mutual Funds

What is an ETF

ETFs have basic differences from mutual funds: 1. Lower management expenses, 2. Trade ETFs same as stocks, and 3. Usually more diversified but not selective than the related mutual funds such as NOBL vs FRDPX.

The major classifications of ETFs are 1. Simulating an index such as SPY, QQQ and DIA, 2. Simulating a sector such as XLE and SOXX, 3. Simulating an asset class such as GLD and SLV, 4. Simulating a country or a group of countries such as EWC and FXI, 5. Managed by a manager(s) such as ARKK, 6. Betting a market or sector to go down such as SH and PSQ, and 7. Leveraged (not recommended for beginners).

Fidelity: Index ETFs (https://www.fidelity.com/etfs/overview).

Wikipedia on ETF (http://en.wikipedia.org/wiki/Exchange-traded_fund).

List of ETFs

ETF Bloomberg
http://www.bloomberg.com/markets/etfs/
ETF data base
http://etfdb.com/
ETF Trends
http://www.etftrends.com/
A list of ETFs. Seeking Alpha.
(http://etf.stock-encyclopedia.com/category/)

Fidelity's commission-free ETFs. Check current offerings and whether they are still commission-free.
(https://www.fidelity.com/etfs/ishares)

Fidelity Annuity funds with performance data.

http://fundresearch.fidelity.com/annuities/category-performance-annual-total-returns-quarterly/FPRAI?refann=005

A list of contra ETFs (or bear ETFs)
http://www.tradermike.net/inverse-short-etfs-bearish-etf-funds/

Misc.: ETFGuide, ETFReplay (highly recommended).

Other resources
Your broker should have a lot of information on ETFs and many offer commission-free ETFs.

Most subscription services offer research on ETFs. IBD has a strategy dedicated to ETFs and so does AAII to name a couple. Seeking Alpha has extensive resources for ETF including an ETF screener and investing ideas.

Not all ETFs are created equal
Check their performances and their expenses.

Small but well-performing ETFs
Here is a list.
http://finance.yahoo.com/news/small-etfs-pack-big-punch-195430875.html

Guggenheim Spin-Off ETF (CSD) looks interesting. The ETF tracks corporate spinoffs. It has beaten SPY for a long time; check the current performance. Not a recommendation.

When not to use ETFs
I prefer sector mutual funds in some industries but you need to do extensive research. They are drug industry, banks, miners and insurers.

Half ETF
Taking out half of the stocks that score below the average in an index ETF could beat the same full ETF itself. I call it HETF (half the ETF). You heard it here first.

To illustrate, sort the expected P/E (not including stocks with negative earnings) in ascending order and only include the stocks on the first half. Add more fundamental metrics. It will take a few minutes.

Disadvantages of ETFs
- When you have two stocks in a sector ETF one good one and one bad one, the ETF treats them the same. Stock pickers would buy the one that has a better appreciation potential.
- The return is better than the actual return due to stock rotation. To illustrate this, on August 29, 2012, SHLD was replaced by LYB in a sector fund. SHLD was down by 4% and LYB was up by 4% primarily due to the switch. Unless you sell and buy at the right time (which is impossible), your return would not match the ETF's returns due to the replacement.
- Ensure the performance matches the corresponding index, but will most likely not include dividends.

Advantages of ETFs
- We have demonstrated that you can beat the market by using market timing. Between 2000 and Nov., 2013, you only exit and reenter the market 3 times and the result is astonishing.
- It is easy to rotate a sector vs. buying/selling all of the stocks in this sector. It makes sector rotation the same as trading a stock.
- The risk is spread out and your portfolio is diversified especially for a market ETF or buying three or more ETFs in different sectors.
- Eliminate the time in researching stocks.

Leveraged ETFs
I do not recommend them. Some are 2x, 3x and even higher. They're too risky. However, when you are very sure or your tested strategy has very low drawdown, you may want to use them to improve performance. I recommend skipping all leveraged ETFs.

My basic ETF tables
I use a list of selected ETFs and commission-free (check the details) ETFs from Fidelity for my purpose. I include some mutual funds in Fidelity's annuity. Some of these may be interesting to you. I use ETFs for sector rotation and parking my cash when the market is favorable and I do not have stocks that I want to buy.

ETFs and funds come and go. Some ideas and classifications are my own interpretation.

Table by market cap:

Category	ETF	Fidelity ETF	Mutual Funds	Fidelity's Annuity	Contra ETF
Size:					
Large Cap	DIA		See Blend		DOG
	SPY				SH
	QQQ	ONEQ			PSQ
	RYH				
Blend	IWD	IVV	BEQGX		
Growth	SPYG	IVW	FBGRX		
Value	SPYV		DOGGX		
Dividend	NOBL	DVY	FRDPX		
	VYM				
Mid Cap				FNBSC	MYY
Blend	MDY	JJH	VSEQX		
Growth		IJK	STDIX		
			BPTRX		
Value		IJJ	FSMVX		
Small Cap				FPRGC	SBB
Blend	IWM	IJR	HDPSX		
Growth		IJT	PRDSX		
Value		IJS	SKSEX		
Micro	IWC				
Multi					
Blend			VDEOX		
Growth			VHCOX		
Value			TCLCX		
Bond					
Long Term (20)	VLV		BTTTX		TBF
Mid Term (7 – 10)	VCIT		FSTGX		
Short Term (1 – 3 yrs.)	VCSH		THOPX		
Total	BOND		PONDX		
Corp Invest Grade	VCIT		NTHEX		
High Yield (junk)	PHB		SPHIX		
Muni	MUB		Check state		

Special situation				
Buy back	PKW			

Table by sectors:

Sector	ETF	Fidelity ETF	Mutual Funds	Fidelity's Annuity
Banking[1]			FSRBK	
Regional	IAT			
Bio Tech	IBB		FBIOX	
	XBI		Large	
Consumer Dis.	XLY	FDIS	FSCPX	FVHAC
Consumer Staple	XLP	FSTA	FDFAX	FCSAC
Finance	KIE	FNCL	FIDSX	FONNC
	IYF			
Energy	XLE	FENY	FSENX	FJLLC
Energy Service			FSESX	
Gold	GLD		FSAGX	
Gold Miner	GDX		VGPMX	
Health Care	IYH	FHLC	FSPHX	FPDRC
	VHT		VGHCX	
House Builder	ITB		FSHOX	
	ITB		Perform	
Industrial	IYJ	FIDU	FCYIX	FBALC
Material	VAW	FMAT	FSDPX	
	IYM			
Oil	USO			
Oil Service	OIH		FSESX	
Oil Exploration	XOP			
Real Estate	VNQ		FRIFX	FFWLC
REIT	VNQ			
Retail	RTH		FSRPX	
	XRT			
Regional bank	KRE		FSRBX	
Semi Conduct	SMH			
Software	XSW		FSCSX	

	IGV			
Technology	XLK	FTEC	FSPTX	FYENC
	FDN		FBSOX	
			ROGSX	
Telecomm.	VOX	FCOM	FSTCX	FVTAC
Transport	XTN			
	IYT			
Utilities	XLU	FUTY	FSUTX	FKMSC
Wireless			FWRLX	

Footnote. [1] Also check Finance.

Table by countries outside the USA:

Country	ETF	Fidelity ETF	Mutual Funds	Fidelity's Annuity
Australia	EWA			
Brazil	EWZ			
Canada	EWC		FICDX	
China	FXI		FHKCX	
EAFE	EFA			
Emerging	VWO		FEMEX	FEMAC
Europe	VGK		FIEUX	
Global	KXI		PGVFX	
Greece	GREK			
India	INDY		MINDX	
Indonesia	EIDO			
Latin America	ILF		FLATX	
Nordic			FNORX	
Hong Kong	EWH			
Japan	EWJ		FJPNX	
S. Africa	EZA			
S. Korea	EWY		MAKOX	
Singapore	EWS			
Taiwan	EWT			
	TUR			
United Kingdom	EWU			
Foreign:				
Combination	1	2	3	4
Intern. Div.	IDV	DWX		
Small Cap	SCZ	GWX		
Value	EFV			
Europe	VGK			

Quick analysis of ETFs

Evaluate an ETF
ETFs are a basket of stocks according to the market, a specific sector, country or a specific theme.

Yahoo!Finance used to give the P/E of an ETF. Try to get it from ETFdb.com. Enter the symbol of the ETF such as XLU, and then select Valuation. If it is below 15 and above zero, it could be a value ETF. Also, if the current price is lower than its NAV, it is sold at a discount (or premium vice versa). Compare its YTD Return to SPY's.

Alternatively, get similar info from http://www.multpl.com/. In addition, this web site provides the following metrics: Shiller P/E, Price/Sales, and Price/Book.

From Finviz.com, enter the ETF symbol. If SMA-20%, SMA-50% and SMA-200% are all positive, most likely the ETF is in an uptrend. To illustrate, SMA-200 is Simple Moving Average for the last 200 trading sessions (no trading on weekends and specific holidays). The percent is how much the stock price of the ETF is above the SMA. If the percent is negative, it means the stock price is below the SMA.

If your average holding period of your stocks is about 50 days, SMA-50% is more appropriate to you.

If RSI(14) > 65, it is probably over-sold; if it is < 30, it is probably under-sold (indicating value).

In addition, ensure the ETF's average volume is high (I suggest more than 10,000 shares), the market cap is more than 300 M, and it has low fees. Most popular ETFs have these characteristics. Beginners should avoid leveraged ETFs.

How to determine if the sector has been recovered
It is easier to profit by following the uptrend of an ETF using the above info. It is hard to detect when the bottom of an ETF has been reached. If SMA-20%, SMA-50% and SMA-200% are all positive, most likely the ETF is in an uptrend or it has recovered. It does not always happen as predicted, so use stops to protect your investment.

An example

First, determine whether the market is risky. Most beginners should not invest in a risky market. Advanced investors can bet against the market or a specific sector by buying contra ETFs or puts.

Next, you want to limit the number of sector ETFs by selecting those that are either in an uptrend or hitting bottom (bottom is hard to predict). Personally I prefer sectors with long-term uptrends (indicated by articles found in many web sites including cnnfn.com and Seeking Alpha.

For illustration purposes only for deteriorating market conditions, I would select the following ETFs: SPY (simulating the market based on large companies) and XLP (consumer staples). XLP should perform better than XLY (consumer discretionary) during a recession as those products are the necessities.

Technical indicators such as SMA-50 (Simple Moving Average for the last 50 sessions), SMA-200 and RSI(14) are obtained from Finviz.com and the rest are obtained from Yahoo!Finance.com. After you buy the ETF, use a stop loss to protect your investment. For example, bio tech sector moved up for many months until it crashed in 2015. Change the stop loss value every month to protect your gains in this case.

As of 2/5/2016	SPY	XLP (staples)	XLY (discret.)
Price	190	50	71
NAV	192	50	73
• Technical			
SMA-50	-4%	0%	-7%
SMA-200	-6%	2%	-7%
RSI(14)	44	50	36
Other	Double bottom at $186		
• Fundamental			
P/E	17	20	19
Yield	2.1%	2.5%	1.5%
YTD return	-5%	0.5%	-5%
Net asset	174 B	9 B	10 B

Explanation

- The figures may not be identical among web sites due to the dates they are using.

- XLY has best discount among the 3 ETFs as most investors believe a recession is coming.
- XLP has less down trend among the 3 ETFs as expected.
- XLY is more undersold among the three as expected.
- Double bottom is a technical pattern that indicates the stock would surge upward.
- SPY has a better value according to its P/E.
- XLY's dividend is the least among the three as they have more tech companies in the ETF. They have to plow back the profits to research and development.
- XLP has the best YTD return among the three.
- As long as the asset is above 500 M (200 M for specialized ETFs), it is fine and all three pass this mark.

There are many metrics such as Debt/Equity not readily available from most web sites. Many sites list the top holdings of a specific ETF. Just average the metrics of the top ten or so of its stock holdings.

An example

This example evaluates RING, a gold miner, using ETFdb and Finviz that are free from the web. The data is from July, 6, 2020.

Bring up ETFdb and enter RING in the search. There are basic info that are important to me: Sector (gold miners), Asset Size (Large-Cap), Issuer (iShares), Inception (Jan. 31, 2012), Expense Ratio (0.39%) and Tax Form (1099).

They fit all my requirements. The expense ratio is higher than most ETFs that simulating an index such as SPY. I try to trade ETFs using Tax Form 1099 in my taxable accounts. The large cap created about 8 years ago by a reputable company are good.

Select "Dividend and Valuation". P/E of 17.39 is fine in a rank of 11 in 27 in similar group of ETFs. As in my books, I stated it is hard to evaluate miners. I buy this ETF primarily to fight the possibility of inflation and the potential depreciation of USD. The dividend rate of 0.52% (0.70% from Finviz) is in the low range of the scale; it is fine for me as dividend is not my concern.

There are more info from this web site. For simplicity, bring up Finviz:

- The short-term trend is up (SMA-20% = 8% and SMA-50% = 7%).
- The long-term trend is up (SMA-200% = 26%).
- It is close to overbought (RSI(14) = 64%; 65% to me is overbought).
- It is -4% from 52-w High. It has performed well from the YTD, Last Year, Last Quarter, Last Month and Last Week.
- It almost doubles in price from mid March this year.
- Avg. Vol. is fine.

From ETFdb, check the Holding. It has 39 stocks, so it is quite diversified for this industry. The two top holdings are NEM (19%) and ABX (18%), which is listed as GOLD in NYSX. I also consider to buy these two stocks in addition to RING. You can estimate the other metrics that are not available by averaging these two stocks. Here is my summary:

STOCK	NEM	GOLD
Forward P/E	20	25
Debt / Share	0.31	0.24
ROE	17%	22%
Sales Q/Q	43%	30%
EPS Q/Q	389%	254%
SMA50	2%	4%
RSI(14)	59%	60%
Insider Trans	-13%	N/A
Fidelity's Equity Summary Score	6.1	6.8

#Filler: Honey, my book can play music.

https://www.youtube.com/watch?v=HxGT5z6d-GA&list=PLMZa6mP7jZ2b1otqG4tfbgZpLEdh6YiNF

It may cut down commercials by casting it to TV.